Luminos is the Open Access monograph publishing program from UC Press. Luminos provides a framework for preserving and reinvigorating monograph publishing for the future and increases the reach and visibility of important scholarly work. Titles published in the UC Press Luminos model are published with the same high standards for selection, peer review, production, and marketing as those in our traditional program. www.luminosoa.org

High-Tech Trash

High-Tech Trash

Glitch, Noise, and Aesthetic Failure

Carolyn L. Kane

UNIVERSITY OF CALIFORNIA PRESS

University of California Press
Oakland, California

Suggested citation: Kane, C. L. *High-Tech Trash: Glitch, Noise, and Aesthetic Failure*. Oakland: University of California Press, 2019. DOI: https://doi.org/10.1525/luminos.83

Library of Congress Cataloging-in-Publication Data
Names: Kane, Carolyn L., author.
Title: High-tech trash : glitch, noise, and aesthetic failure / Carolyn L. Kane.
Other titles: Rhetoric and public culture (Oakland, Calif.) ; 1.
Identifiers: LCCN 2019030106 (print) | LCCN 2019030107 (ebook) | ISBN 9780520340145 (paperback) | ISBN 9780520974494 (ebook)
Subjects: LCSH: Glitch art. | Art and technology—20th century. | Art and technology—21st century. | Failure (Psychology) in art. | Aesthetics, Modern—20th century. | Aesthetics, Modern—21st century.
Classification: LCC N7433.8 .K36 2019 (print) | LCC N7433.8 (ebook) | DDC 700.1/05—dc23
LC record available at https://lccn.loc.gov/2019030106
LC ebook record available at https://lccn.loc.gov/2019030107

28 27 26 25 24 23 22 21 20 19
10 9 8 7 6 5 4 3 2 1

For life, love, and trash on the Lower East Side

Life is what is capable of error.

—MICHEL FOUCAULT

CONTENTS

ILLUSTRATIONS

FIGURES

TABLES

ACKNOWLEDGMENTS

I wish to thank the dedicated and talented research assistants at Ryerson University who helped me with this material: Harnoor Bhangu, Myriam Couturier, Michel Ghanem, Evangeline Holtz-Schramek, Jaclyn Marcus, Rachel Rammal, and Rachel Palen. I am also grateful to the students and faculty who allowed me to share this work with them: Zeina Koreitem and John May at Harvard University's Graduate School of Design; Shane Denson and Doug Eacho at Stanford University's Digital Aesthetics workshop (2018); Dilip P. Gaonkar at Northwestern University's 2019 *Media Aesthetics* workshop; Ellie Abrons and Adam Fure at the University of Michigan's *Becoming Digital Conference* (2017); Jakub Zdebik at the University of Ottawa (2016); TIFF's Film & Media Seminar (2016); and the e-flux lecture series in New York City (2016). This book also benefited from conference participation at Yale University, New York University, and the Precarious Aesthetics conference at the University of California, Berkeley (2015).

I received generous support for this work from the Pembroke Center at Brown University, under the auspices of the Nancy L. Buc Postdoctoral Fellowship in "Aesthetics and the Question of Beauty" (2014-2015). As a faculty member at Ryerson University, I received generous support from the Faculty of Communication and Design (FCAD) and the truly exceptional Social Sciences and Humanities Research Council of Canada (SSHRC).

A draft of chapter 2 was published in 2014 in the *Journal of InVisible Culture* as "Glitch Art: Failure from the Avant-Garde to Kanye West." A version of parts of chapter 6 appeared in *Theory, Culture & Society* in 2016, and an early draft of the Postscript was commissioned by Tom Holert and e-flux for the 2015 Venice Biennale, reprinted by Verso in 2018. Portions of chapter 3 are forthcoming in the *Colour Turn.*

Introduction

"Welcome to the Failure Age"

I. THE FAILURE AGE

Western culture's simultaneous embrace and denial of failure is frustrating.[1] On the one hand, failure touches everything from environmental breakdown and unwanted computational errors to business, social life, and personal psychology. On the other hand, only a very narrow constituency acknowledges these fiascoes as anything beyond mere fashion—the vast majority of people and institutions want to rid themselves of the slightest hint of failure at the earliest possible opportunity. In Silicon Valley, for instance, entrepreneurs are encouraged to heedlessly "Fail Fast, Fail Often," regardless of risk. On "Fuck-up Night" at the annual FailCon conference, founded in San Francisco to address digital failure, entrepreneurs are invited to share their startup mistakes with a packed audience. Fuck-up Night started in Mexico City in 2012, but has since become so popular that it now convenes annually in more than seventy cities in twenty-six countries around the world (in short, it is a huge success).[2] One might also cite Elon Musk's fail-friendly autopilot software for Tesla; RAND-style zero-sum scenarios;[3] and General Electric's Six Sigma, a program aiming to measure and eliminate at least 99.99 percent of potential defects in every GE product.[4]

Once found by hackers, even undetected high-tech errors, known as "zero-day exploits" (because a company has spent "zero days" trying to resolve the yet-to-be acknowledged problem), can sell upwards of $50,000 on China's black market, a precarious "dark net" of hackers and high-tech competitors who participate in activities ranging from traditional hacking disruptions, to extracting unforeseen errors in software, to finding entry points into a product's highly secret proprietary code. With Apple's iPhone, one single line of unobserved erroneous code, if caught by hackers, can be sold on China's black market for millions, leading to lucrative profits in the production of cheaper knock-offs.[5]

Beyond high-tech vogue, failure shapes the contours of contemporary culture. In 2017, the Swedish Innovation Authority in conjunction with curator Samuel West launched the Museum of Failure in Helsingborg, Sweden, and at the A+D Architecture and Design Museum in Los Angeles. The exhibition featured a collection of "failed products and services from around the world," including the Apple Newton, Bic for Her, Google Glass, Harley-Davidson Cologne, the Sony Betamax, and Swedish Fish Oreos. The idea was inspired by West's 2016 visit to the "Museum of Broken Relationships" in Zagreb, Croatia (2003–), an exhibition dedicated to failed love relationships. Upon his return, West extended the concept to industry at large. According to West, "80 to 90 percent of innovation projects fail and you never read about them, you don't see them, people don't talk about them."[6] His claim is endorsed by market research firms like Fahrenheit 212, whose co-founder Mark Payne contends the number is actually closer to 90 percent.[7] One might thus infer the annals of technology deal with only 10 percent of the data available to them. From this perspective, it is not surprising to find our so-called innovation age steeped in failure.

On a deeper level, humankind has always been marked by failure. "Life is what is capable of error," Michel Foucault wrote in 1991, and indeed, because we *can* err, it is also in our capacity to grow and change thereafter. This insight returns us to what many philosophers have deemed the essence of life itself: failure and error, not only as circumstances of existence, but as the very conditions of possibility for its flourishing. Similarly, in *Being and Time* (1927), Martin Heidegger invokes the Latin fable from Hyginus, *Cura,* meaning care or concern. In this myth,[8] Cura is crossing a river and pauses to mold some clay. In selecting a name for her creation, she is caught in a dispute between Heaven (Jupiter) and Earth (Gaia). Saturn, god of time, decides that Heaven will have the clay's spirit in death, and Earth will have it in life. Since Cura is its creator, she will keep it in her care as long as it lives. Saturn names her creation *homo* or, "human," and thus humans, insofar as they are alive, live between two worlds, in and through care. Life is a gift in which we always owe a debt; perpetually "falling" as Heidegger puts it; or simply, failing in our alive-ness.

Clearly the denial of failure is a problem deeper and older than any high-tech trend and yet, we have permitted myths of unfettered success and advancement to shape our cultural ethos for centuries. The explosion of industrial developments offers one set of examples, as does postwar consumer culture. Together, these relatively modern movements have made it seem safe to expect an endless chain of newer and better things for oneself and one's family. However, we can no longer afford to assume that modern life is always progressing.[9] *High-Tech Trash: Glitch, Noise, and Aesthetic Failure* illustrates this by weaving a narrative of disenchantment against a backdrop of breakdown and noise. To map this archaeology of aesthetic failure, apropos of a culture ill-equipped to deal with it, the book abstracts from subjective, personal failure and disappointment to see them as meaningful symbols of a broader human struggle. Specifically, by connecting twenty-first century digital aesthetics and contemporary media art, to critical issues in the history of high-tech, the book elucidates what it means to be an error-prone, fallible human in an age of hyper technology; to fail again and again without recourse to anything else. After filling in the contours of the "Failure Age" below, I address my analytic methods in aesthetics and media studies and define the book's five key concepts—glitch, noise, error, trash, and failure. I conclude this Introduction with an overview of the chapters in the book.

In the early 1990s, pop culture theorist Joshua Gamson shed light on the patently American cultural fascination elevating a person to the status of a celebrity and then, at the height of their stardom, finding perverse pleasure in catalyzing— authoring even—their downward spiral.[10] Deluded hubris must be returned to the soiled earth plane. This is our cultural legacy, Gamson infers, and it is equally applicable to our blind faith in the omnipotence of science and technology. The accomplishments of medicine, media, and machines are certainly magnificent and should not be undervalued, but science and technology, like humans, are in no way perfect or beyond critique. Put differently, to make concrete and lasting change, we must adopt a more balanced understanding of innovation as intrinsically bound to failure. A fruitful life, or rather, life at its most fundamental level, as Heidegger suggests, is always a negotiation between falling and advancing.

How do we develop this dynamic on a practical level? First, we must address the denial of failure as a largely unresolved problem and seek out new ways to acknowledge it while still finding security, stability, and success in life. The largely superficial messages from Silicon Valley and self-help cultures—to embrace weaknesses and defect, to "accept yourself as you are" is hardly what I have in mind. Rather, I suspect we are missing one of the most valuable strategies for long-term success. By working *with* our failures and shortcomings, and facing them head-on, we can grow in new and intellectually humble ways.

Unfortunately, such thinking could not be further from actual practice. Despite failure's current fashionability, research reveals most entrepreneurs "fear any kind of failure." In Silicon Valley, the "pressure to succeed is so intense that some new businesses instead find themselves looking for shortcuts," calling on "growth hackers" to create a veneer of success.[11] Even Six Sigma's aim to measure all manufacturing defects reflects a concern less with error than with an age-old addiction to perfection. On a practical level, it is equally obvious that no one actually wants to fail, even if we try to reassure ourselves, "It's okay, you're only human." But how else can we change and become better humans if we do not find a way to fail safely and make real mistakes?

The widespread disavowal of failure is even more surprising given that the so-called innovation economy was only made possible *through* mass failures. As each new, allegedly better gadget appears, Adam Davidson explains, it becomes that much easier to replace the next worker, object, or outdated piece of software, ensuring accelerated cycles of innovation, which is also to say, the proliferation of failure.[12] As the "slow culture" of nineteenth-century agriculture transformed into a culture of mechanical production, Davidson argues, we doomed ourselves to be eternally dependent on these successions.[13] Our rapacious appetite for "new and improved" gadgets and toys hastened cycles of obsolescence. And thus, "we"—privileged "First world" citizens—find ourselves surrounded by a surplus of quick-and-cheap "made in China" objects, from shiny new things to unwanted trash and waste, some of it still accepted back at the same exploited offshore sites that manufactured it. A case in point is Apple's recent decision to purposely slow down "older" iPhone models, accelerating their obsolescence and catalyzing consumption of a negligibly newer model.[14] This is only one example of thousands that happened to bubble up in the mass media.

Even the seemingly benign plugs and portals on the majority of our digital devices are strategically engineered to become outdated within a few years, forcing one to purchase bulky adaptors in the interim, and eventually, an entirely new computer system to be compatible with the latest series of wires and plugs. Stefan Johannes Al claims that electronic products "are deliberately designed with limited backward compatibility," through a "series of careful omission of features that its future model will have, or designed with a limited lifespan. In short, these products are designed to fail."[15] We have allowed all of this to proceed unchecked, ushering in novelty objects under the auspices of the new and improved, but whom do these pseudo-improvements actually serve? The innovation economy must be reassessed and understood anew as imposing a series of great deficits on us—consumers and users—and the planet. The iPhone may be among the 10 percent of technological successes in the innovation economy that West and Payne postulate, but from this perspective, it too will all too quickly become obsolete with the next model, at which point it basically becomes trash. Let us also keep in mind that in the case of the slowed-down iPhone, the obsolescence cycle is driven not by culture or competitors, but by the company's own marketing and engineering teams.[16] We live in a time where, as Davidson points out, high-tech success has become exceedingly short-lived, characterized by a few "loosely knit" experiments in "decentralized networks" that gain recognition—by way of sales and stock indexing—for a precarious length of time. Uber, Lyft, Juno, Airbnb, Blu-ray, eBay, and their like will all fail in the end. To Davidson's point: to claim we are in an age of innovation is to acknowledge we are saturated with failure.

High-Tech Trash speaks to this paradox. The book analyzes creative strategies with glitch, noise, and error to chart the development of an aesthetic paradigm rooted in failure. I theorize the ways in which technologically influenced creative practices, primarily from the second half of the twentieth and first quarter of the twenty-first centuries, critically offset a broader culture of pervasive risk and discontent. And yet on we go, striving to do better and acquire more, despite the inevitable disappointment derived from seeking existential solutions by way of material wealth and consumption. Why? And can emergent media strategies help us to see or do things any differently?

II. FAILURE'S CRITICAL AESTHETICS

In creative spheres, failure is dealt with quite differently than it is in industry. Here, aberrant creations marginalized in the business world are welcomed back into the fold as inspiration for artmaking. Take, for instance, the American artist John Baldessari's black-and-white photograph *Wrong* (1966–68) which challenges unconscious assumptions about "correct" representation. In *Wrong*, the artist stands directly in front of a palm tree, visually aligned with the vertical axis of its trunk. As a result, the tree "appears to sprout from his head."[17] According to the norms of traditional portraiture, the overlap is "off," deemed an error relative to the standards of "good" taste. And yet, Baldessari's error is deliberate. He intends to incorrectly depict the scenario in order to bring to light the invisible norms governing the conventions of visual correctness. Baldessari's *Wrong* is one simple "error," which, Abigail Solomon-Godeau argues, when stylized in this way, ends up creating a "correct" conceptual critique of visual convention.[18] In short, it is no longer an error at all. Granted Baldessari's edifice depends on an understanding of error as relative to truth and fact, which opens up another can of worms not addressed until the next chapter, for now, we can take his point at face value. As an analog, noncomputational, conceptual "error," Baldessari's photograph is a useful starting point for this book's discussion. It forces us to think of the related phenomena of glitch, noise, and failure as metaphors: stylistic modalities that extend beyond the physical technologies they signify. Compare this with my opening scene from business fashion, where the embrace of failure *seems* welcome, but at the end of the day, is deemed shameful. As mere fashion void of critical analysis or historical contextualization, failure aesthetics are void of meaningful and systemic change.

Does digital technology herald a "new dark age" and "the end of the future," as British writer James Bridle suggests? Bridle argues "something is wrong on the Internet," but from the perspective of those who value creative innovation, the case is in fact the opposite. He outlines the ways in which algorithmically assembled children's videos found on YouTube are automatically queued with disturbing outcomes, ranging from Peppa Pig drinking bleach instead of naming vegetables, to Elsa from *Frozen* appearing in sexually compromising positions with Spider-Man, to violence and full-fledged abuse.[19] Granted the videos are disturbing and morally offensive, especially to children, from a logistic perspective, these inserts prove the system is accurately following its own protocols. The perpetual iteration of identical sequencing leaves the door wide open for a potential hacker's exploitation of

FIGURE 1. John Baldessari, *Wrong* (1966–68). The subject is placed directly in front of a palm tree so it appears to be sprouting from his head. Courtesy of John Baldessari.

the automated search algorithms. There is thus something very *right* about the ways in which ill-intentioned programmers exploit oversights in the system.[20] Unsurprisingly, following a host of parents' complaints, YouTube changed its protocols for video filtering and removed the videos in question. And yet, a recent report demonstrated YouTube's algorithm was still "encouraging pedophiles to watch videos of partially-clothed children." As Stokel-Walker explains for the *New York Times*, "creators . . . recognize the flaws in YouTube's algorithm" and exploit them accordingly. For example, "the algorithm relies on snapshots of visual content, rather than actions," so as long as it recognizes "Peppa Pig in the frame, it doesn't matter what the character does in the skit." This awareness allows creators to exploit the algorithm's logic to support "bad behavior in viewers."[21] Both examples of YouTube hackings can be construed as a low-level "zero-day exploit" where the damage was, and hopefully will continue to be, promptly amended by the governing entity, even if their solution is only temporary—until hackers find the next exploit.

III. METHODS

As new technologies play an increasingly prominent role in modern life, the need to place them at the center of the critical analyses of visual art, media, and design becomes unavoidable. Accordingly, this research draws on two general fields: visual studies (aesthetics) and media history and theory (media archaeology).

Visual Studies

Broadly speaking, the field of visual studies investigates images in history and culture. This book focuses on the visual phenomenological and material aesthetics of high-tech objects and the creative works they have been used to produce.

Classical research in aesthetics derives from studies in philosophy and theories of representation. This book draws on this tradition, focusing on aesthetic philosophy, including discussions of representation in chapter 3 (Plato, Kant); Heinrich Wölfflin's notes on style in chapter 5; Michael Fried's observations on contemporary photography in chapters 4 and 7; an analysis of Edmund Burke's and Immanuel Kant's theories of the sublime in chapters 5 through 7; Gilles Deleuze's orthogonal take on these classical concepts (chapters 5 and 6); and Sianne Ngai's contemporary critique of aesthetic categories (the end of chapter 3). I also cull from traditional and contemporary theories of color (chapter 3) and conventional histories of photography (chapters 4 and 7) to update them for a digital age of high-tech trash by positioning them alongside more recent theories of digital signal-processing (chapters 1, 4, 5) and the new aesthetic practices conditioned therein.

A long history of aesthetic philosophy has also paved the way for modern offshoots in phenomenology. Defined as an investigation of being and appearing in the world, phenomenology is committed to finding new models of human experience, perception, and freedom that resist rational and normative conventions. However, while the classic phenomenologists argue that an essentially ahistorical bracketing (Husserl) of authentic human experience (Heidegger) and a pure perception (Merleau-Ponty) is possible, I update this claim for the present to argue that human and machine perceptions are inextricably fused in what I have previously theorized as the "algorithmic lifeworld."[22] In *High-Tech Trash*, I further concede that digital electronic technologies have become integral to almost all forms of creative production (chapters 1 through 7), the mediation of experience (chapters 1, 2, and 4), and the formation of cultural knowledge writ large (chapter 1).[23]

Media Archaeology

In the equally long history of media and communications theory, many survey histories have assumed uncritical narratives of technological progress.[24] From cave painting and writing, to the printing press, telegraph, radio, cinema, television, video, and digital computing, the story until recently went: modern man has progressed; developing reason and science to overcome the challenges of the "natural" world. Strides in industry support such claims, illustrated through the production of smaller, more compact, and compressed media capable of transmitting more data in less time to more people. In recent decades, however, these one-sided histories of progress, with cliché benchmarks and grandiose heroes have come under the gun of a new generation of "media archaeologists" committed to critical revisions of media history.

As the second of my two analytic methods, media archaeology plays a subordinate role in the pages that follow. Nonetheless, it merits a brief exegesis. Defined as the archival examination of the materiality of media objects, media archaeology breaks from traditional models of epistemology and hermeneutics to argue that the frame, window, page, or specificity of a material platform through which informational content is delivered, is just as important as the content itself. The field derives from both Foucault's concept of archaeology, and his and Nietzsche's concepts of genealogy—a set of relations that run horizontally, and in opposition to, official, chronological histories. Foucault set the stage when he ironically referred to the archive as the "historical *a priori*"—placing concrete, material history and relations prior to the formation of concepts and knowledge. The actual artifact or material stuff of the world is here, reconstrued as the condition of possibility from which all knowledge in culture can emerge. The historical a priori is an a priori *in* history. The concept harks back to Nietzsche, who argued in *The Genealogy of Morals* that the relevant material of a genealogy is based on shattering disillusionments that a subject causes a presumed effect. He gave the example of a lightning flash: where the "popular mind" separates the flash from the lightning, or, the doer from the deed, and "takes the latter for an action," called "lightning," the two cannot in fact be separated, he argues, "'the doer' is merely a fiction added to the deed."[25] It is the "seduction of language," he continues, "which conceives and misconceives all effects as conditioned by something . . . by a 'subject.'"[26] Nietzsche's discursive focus dealt with language and its effects, but the underlying insight was adopted by Foucault, as noted, and together, their work helped pave the way for what has become the field of media archaeology proper.

In recent decades, the growth of media archaeology has been largely influenced by such scholars as Friedrich Kittler, Siegfried Zielinski, Wolfgang Ernst, Lisa Gitelman, Wendy Hui Kyong Chun, Erkki Huhtamo, and Bernard Stiegler. Collectively, the project aims to place the materiality of a technology in the position of what Kittler provocatively calls, the *"media a priori."* Zielinski refers to this approach as constitutive of a "deep time" of the media; a cyclical and alternative time, forcing thought in another, nonlinear direction.[27] The Brechtian method of "direct address" is an apt metaphor. The capacity to cut through theatrical pretense to call attention to the singleness of the present moment encourages "thinking as intervention," not as catharsis or self-expression. In the following pages, media archaeology unfolds through my material (and aesthetic) analysis of glitch and noise. Glitch is not theorized as a free-floating form of personal expression or agency of individual desire, but rather—from the point of view of media archaeology—as a necessary and often unconscious mode of structuring existence in a digital age which valorizes information, transparency, and speed against a political and historical background chock-full of noise, static, and breakdown. In this way, a media archaeological analysis of "perception" is not about looking at the surface of images or things in the world, or even about vision. Rather, perception is historically mediated through a set of power and knowledge relations that are often invisible, concealed, and unconscious. Together, my two core methods in visual studies (aesthetics) and media history and theory (media archaeology) allow me to demonstrate how glitch, noise, and error constitute dominant forms of technologically-mediated perception and knowledge-forming practices in the historical present.

The Myth of Transparency

In the digital age, critiques of visual transparency rise to the top of the to-do list. The history of Western representation turns on the development of perspective, defined here as the illusion of three-dimensional space represented on a two-dimensional plane. Because the following chapters discuss work that depends so heavily on undermining Western perspective's logic of false transparency, a brief exegesis is in order.

Theories of perspective date back to Renaissance designers Filippo Brunelleschi (1377–1446) and Leon Battista Alberti (1404–72). In Alberti's 1435 book *On Painting,* he identifies the importance of using "correct" line and measurement to create the illusion of depth on a two-dimensional surface. He also emphasizes the need to conceal the perspective lines used to create the illusion, because letting a line show would generate a *fractura,* or "crack," in the "transparent" viewing experience. The contradiction is clear: perspective lines are essential to structuring the "visually transparent" composition and yet, to create a successful illusion of transparent reality, they are precisely what needs to be concealed in the final viewing.[28]

Transparency has reigned supreme in Western visual culture, and it continues to play a pivotal role in everything from architecture and interior design, to interface aesthetics. In contemporary media culture, new forms of transparency are fostered through the rhetoric of invisibility. "We believe that technology is at its very best when it is invisible," Apple's 2012 iPad trailer asserted, epitomizing high-tech's uncritical adoption of transparency. Similarly, Kevin Kelly, founding editor of *Wired* magazine and former editor of the *Whole Earth Review,* argues that a technology is only successful when it is invisible. The "best technology in the future is invisible," he explains, "things that draw your attention are not good enough."[29] Presumably, to draw one's attention while using a device would allow the matter of the medium to be seen and heard and, therefore, lack the illusion of immateriality required for transparency. But identifying the matter in the medium is precisely what it means to do a *material* history of technology. Because we are so immersed in the present, in our screens, texts, and compressed channels of communication, it is difficult to see the palpable nature of the noise and grainy matter that surrounds us. In this way, the matter of new media—insofar as it is still new— is also (temporarily) transparent, precisely as Kelly desires. In this study, however, the materiality of our otherwise invisible media noise is brought into focus by way of aesthetic and archaeological critique.

In 1970s film culture, around the same time Jacques Derrida and Roland Barthes were calling out the hidden implications of structuralism, cinema scholar Peter Wollen developed a complementary strategy in his analysis of the French avant-garde.[30] Wollen demonstrated how the frame structuring the cinematic image disappears from awareness in the same way that a window's frame recedes from our conscious experience as we focus instead on what lies "behind" it. In short, as attentiveness to the technical apparatus withdraws and the "content" of an image moves to the fore, it successfully presents itself as an autonomous, unbarred image of the world. Cinematic transparency is thus achieved. Wollen considered Jean-Luc Godard's use of "foregrounding" as exemplary of the introduction of noise into this process.[31] Godard's techniques are now old hat in media culture, but at the time, they broke illusions of immediacy by using devices such as the famous "jump cut," direct address, and including a camera in the content of the image—a technique that dates back to Sergei Eisenstein's prewar radical cinema.

Prior to Wollen, French philosopher Gilbert Simondon observed a related strategy in Le Corbusier's architecture, which he termed "phanero-technics."[32] *Phanero* comes from the Greek meaning to show or reveal. The compound implies a built structure that reveals the materiality of its technical artifice (internal structure), as also the conditions of possibility for its surface appearance.[33] More recently, studies in the history of science have provided corresponding theories. In a 2012–13 seminar at the University of Chicago, Peter Galison introduced the term "building crashing thinking" to describe a nonchronological back-and-forth between subjectivity and modern technology.[34] For Cornell University professor

Steven Jackson, the twenty-first-century is characterized by "risk and uncertainty, growth and decay, fragmentation, dissolution, and breakdown." Jackson thus recommends that, instead of more "innovation" or "creative destruction," we adopt a new critical model rooted in "broken world thinking."[35]

This book builds on these theories and critiques of transparency in communications and cinema studies to argue that in the digital age, instead of looking at technology when it is working at its optimal speed and capacity, we need to use the frameworks of error, glitch, and noise, as Jackson suggests, to analyze how our ostensibly "new" and "better" media break, revealing new insights at their seams. In this way, the book also falls within a newer legacy of scholars working in a vein alternative to numerous nineteenth- and early twentieth-century models that define culture and technology through narratives of progress and unprecedented advancement, contingent on the presumption of endlessly expanding frontiers.

Even within current media archaeology studies, we encounter such naïve tendencies. Traditionally, the field has drawn from pioneering critical theorists who reflect on media at the height of its optimization: Jacques Derrida, Siegfried Kracauer, Anne Friedberg, Miriam Hansen, Mary Ann Doane, Jonathan Crary (especially his recent analysis of the incipient demands on attention in 24/7 global culture),[36] and Walter Benjamin's theorization of mechanical technology as a "complex training o[f] the human sensorium," which brings to light the ways in which *functioning* media engender shifts in perception. Marshall McLuhan's dictum, "the medium is the message," also highlights the formal importance of an optimized and standardized media platform. Derrida's *parergon*, like Wollen's notion of foregrounding, further presumes that the frame and content are always functional. While this scholarship has been crucial to the first and second generations of media archaeology, and to the understanding of the psychic, social, and cultural effects of technology at their apex of efficiency, it nonetheless fails to discuss how technology influences and structures experiences at points of failure and breakdown.[37] In response, this book proposes a refocusing of media studies away from the formal attributes of media in their ideal state, to consider instead their precarious status in a much larger system of ephemeral and dynamic failure.

IV. KEY TERMS

Glitch, error, failure, noise, and accident all imply devaluation. Like waste and trash, they are unwanted and of no obvious use. Across the board, culturally normative goals for them remain the same: maximize their negligibility. This is of course expected, if we want things to work, have a better quality of life, and live in clean, healthy environments. My objective in analyzing these terms is not to assess their efficacy in industry, but rather, to analyze their eccentric appropriation in emergent aesthetic practices. To do so, it is necessary to first examine each term's unique linguistic, cultural, and historical contingencies, after which they can be used somewhat interchangeably throughout the book.

Noise

The physical sciences treat noise and sound as homogenous vibrations through the same medium (air), but dramatic differences emerge in culture. What counts as noise in culture is largely subjective, defined by social norms, dependent on distinct phenomenological, biological, or computational contexts. Take the example of a city. Some noise may be perceived as passive, fading into the background of experience (street crowds or construction sites), while other noises protrude into consciousness, halting habit or thought patterns (exceedingly loud drilling noises, a fire engine rushing by, static storms on a cell phone). Regardless, few would disagree that noise defines the modern world. Sound scholars have dated the origins of our noise environment to the Industrial Revolution. Others, like Emily Thompson and Michel Serres, argue that we have always existed "in" noise; in Serres's words, "surrounded by an inextinguishable [noise] . . . we cannot close our door to."[38] When Serres's work emerged alongside poststructuralism and deconstruction in the 1980s, he positioned noise at the baseline of human culture; as "always already part of the signal, [a] blindness inescapably accompanying vision" from which no definitive meaning or stability could be had.[39] For Thompson, there has also always been a constant sonic background in human civilization, intensified through urbanization and industrialization.[40] Similarly, Paul Virilio argues that noise (and accident and error) are pre-programmed into any cultural object from the moment of its inception. For him, such noise predates the industrial era, but is aggravated thereafter. Even as we see and seek to experience only the clean "innovations" of new media and move to widespread "digitalization," we require ever more progressive forms of optical "correction" of images and representations. And yet, as this occurs, we only pay attention to one side of the equation. By focusing only on optimization, we not only decrease awareness of noise, but also, we increasingly lose the ability to detect its inversely proportionate growth. In the communications environment, machines become opticians, Virilio suggests, reconstructing perceptions as true versus false and correct versus incorrect, a process in which the mechanically deemed "invalid" results are deleted from the system, and consequently, from culture and human experience. "It is extraordinary to see to what extent accident was censured in the name of the cult of happiness, the cult of success," he writes; "consumer society demands optimism."[41]

Roland Barthes submits a slightly different definition of noise through his distinction between the physiological and psychological. For him, physiological noise is a sound, subconsciously heard as acoustic waves interact with the body, while psychological noise is actively listened to and consciously perceived.[42] Is his sentiment a romanticized one? Idealizing a division between mind and body implies that sound perceived through the body is unconscious and mysterious, and by the same token, that sound perceived by the mind is conscious and acute. Even common sense suggests otherwise: on any given day, chirping birds, traffic noise, or street musicians may or may not be consciously experienced.[43] Barthes reiterates the distinction in his essay "The Grain of the Voice." For him, the grain of the voice is the body as it sings, the "hand as it writes, the limb as it performs." Perceiving the grain in a piece of music occurs as the "emergence of the text in the work" itself; to see and hear grain is to connect with the materiality of the medium "performing itself."[44] The "grain" of a medium is erotic and "outside of any law," which is to say ahistorical, unabashedly romantic, and thus problematic in this book's aims to contextualize glitch and noise in history and culture.[45] Moreover, Barthes notes, in recent years, there has been a "flattening out of technique," an evisceration of grain to produce clean sonic "perfection" that leaves behind "nothing but [the] pheno-text," or simply, the cultural-linguistic meanings.[46] These claims resemble those who mourn the loss of analog to the flat digital files that began to dominate in the 1990s. Barthes's attention to grain as a kind of bodily noise is useful for thinking about glitch across media platforms, but his inability to detect noise in the present is merely a symptom of the newness of new media taking its novel effects.

For Michael Godard, Benjamin Halligan and Paul Hegarty, noise operates on the thresholds of normative social interactions, making it a powerful political tool that can be used to control populations, or unveil—"foreground" to use Wollen's terminology—power relations.[47] Jacques Attali likewise defines noise as a "means of power *and* a form of entertainment," a refuge for "residual irrationality," and a potentially discordant force in the "audition of a message," associated in many cultures with the "idea of the weapon, blasphemy, [and] plague."[48] Consider the use of noise in biological warfare or military defense systems, such as the "Long-Range Acoustic Device" (LRAD), or "sound cannon," an acoustic hailing device and sonic weapon developed by the LRAD Corporation and currently in use in the U.S. Navy. In this way, noise, as understood through culture, is always political. For Raymond Brassier, noise must perform some form of interference in cognitive processing in order for it to be considered noise at all. When noise disrupts cognitive schemas and perceptual fields, it changes our experience of the world.[49]

By the same token, noise can also be used therapeutically. In 1763, the French botanist François Boissier de Sauvages de Lacroix noted in his *Nosologia Methodica Oculorum* the likely mythic belief that some noise could help cure tarantula bites. Today we are all too familiar with the use of certain sounds to guide meditation or relaxation practices. White noise machines are commonly used to generate one "color" of noise and mask out another "unwanted" noise during work, sleep, or meditation. Intentionally generated noise can also be used aesthetically, to layer sonic communications. Avant-garde musicians from Arnold Schoenberg to noise rock bands (see chapter 2) have worked in this tradition. In this book, noise is treated as an abstract concept, applied almost exclusively to the *visual* field. To reconstrue noise from the sonic to the visual domain, it must be treated as a metaphor, akin to abstract line and color. In the city metaphor, visual noise may take the form of distracting advertisements or electronic signs, graffiti, or dust storms from a construction site. Noise is a part of the mediated environment; often ignored but always present.

In what is now referred to as "noise studies," broadly construed, definitions of noise differ significantly.[50] Peter Krapp's *Noise Channels* offers a critique of the first generation of new media art, calling attention to the precarious line between information and noise. Error, frustration, and breakdown are not only inevitable with new media, he argues, they define them. Krapp's case studies include analyses of the net art duo JODI, Max Mathews, John Cage, Brody Condon, Nick Montfort, and Cory Arcangel. *High-Tech Trash* also analyzes new media art and the precarious line between noise and information, but it focuses on new genres in glitch art, datamoshing, and eco photography. Krapp is concerned with net art of the 1990s: hypertext, hacking, game theory, and database narratives, whereas *High-Tech Trash* is concerned with the twenty-first century visual rhetoric of anti-communication that speaks more to economic, environmental, and human registers than to the formal aspects of game culture or hypertext narratives. Studies in *Error: Glitch, Noise, and Jam in New Media Cultures* (2011), edited by Mark Nunes, also address digital culture and the ways in which artists use noise to disrupt dominant cultural values, albeit focusing on glitch in music, whereas *High-Tech Trash* focuses on *visual* glitch aesthetics in art, media, and contemporary photography. Lastly, this book, also unlike its precursors, links emerging and experimental aesthetic practices to broader historical and philosophical discourses on error and failure in the environment.

Error

Etymologically, "to err" means to waver from a predetermined mark or axiom. The original Latin meaning of *error* is "wandering," implying an almost creative response to a dilemma, a far cry from the seemingly fixed judgments associated with contemporary uses (as chapter 1 accounts). The concept also retains traces of objectivity (laws, axioms, moral judgments) from which an error *can* occur. Put differently, "error," glitch, and noise have been culturally constructed as binary concepts where what determines right and wrong, noise or music, mistake or intention, is determined by history and convention. Chapter 1 analyzes the ways in which post-Enlightenment concepts of error have begotten widespread presumptions that *any* error is an unintentional deviation from a code or convention. In my metaphor of the city, we might think of error as a clogged sewer or traffic jam. Engineers and city planners attempt to determine rules and bylaws that will maximize the efficient flow of data to prevent such errors from occurring, even though not all possible errors can be accounted for in advance.

Glitch

Simply put, a glitch is a nice way to say "screw-up." The word derives from the German *glitschen* meaning to slip, the Old High German *gliten,* meaning to glide, and the Yiddish *glitshen,* meaning to slip or skid off course.[51] In computing, a glitch denotes a problematic, annoying, or unintended error that, like the definition of error, tends to be negligible, quickly absorbed by the larger, still-functioning system. For example, a website stalls or fails to load, an online video halts or stutters in the middle of a scene, or strange, unexpected color artifacts splatter across a newly rendered graphics file. When a glitch appears, it indicates a relatively rare moment of unplanned, unprogrammed mediation that, for many glitch artists, provides an opportunity to connect on-screen phenomena with off-screen computational abstractions. My reasons for calling attention to glitch (rather than error, accident, or failure alone) are, again, elucidated through an analysis of emerging trends in media art.

Glitch Art

The glitch art genre is marked by garish, noisy colors. It emerged in the late 1990s and early 2000s through the works of people like John Cates, Rosa Menkman, Paul B. Davis, and Takeshi Murata, and, as I argue in chapter 2, bears strong links to the avant-garde. For this generation of artists and media makers, computer glitches provide the fodder for a new style of art-making. A number of glitch artists and theorists define the genre's source materials along remarkably similar lines. Kim Cascone defines glitch as "a rupture in the continuum of an idealized artifact. . . a subversion of the smooth and technically perfect surface."[52] Olga Goriunova and Alexei Shulgin concur, a "glitch is a singular dysfunctional event that allows insight beyond the customary, omnipresent and alien computer aesthetics."[53]

Some glitch artists further distinguish between "wild" and "domesticated" glitches.[54] Wild glitches are found "naturally" in one's computing practices, including encounters with slow image-processing speeds, low bandwidth, jilted video display, or poor graphics capacities. Wild glitches are spontaneous and undomesticated, they occur unintentionally and without provocation, but after they are detected, they are "caught" and harnessed for use in an artwork by using anti-debugging techniques, a simple screen capture, or graphics editing software (akin to "found art"). In contrast, a "domesticated" or harvested glitch is purposely created and manufactured for artistic use.[55] Examples include data bending and hacking code, alongside numerous image plug-ins and video conferencing software, such as VPS Glitch Bitch, Sugar Bytes' Turnado, Smack My Glitch Up, or CU-SeeMe, which all come with prêt-à-porter glitch effects. Conversely, one could simply apply a filter in Photoshop to achieve a desired glitch effect, avoiding coding issues altogether.[56] In sum, this distinction between wild and domesticated glitches is only useful in some contexts, since, like any distinction, it falls apart the harder we press it. For instance, if we were to reinterpret glitches in terms of

FIGURE 2. Andrew Benson, *Status Update, 2am* (2011). Color video, 36 seconds. Portrait of the artist awake at his computer at 2 A.M. Courtesy of Andrew Benson.

"authentic" or "non-authentic," we would encounter a host of dead-end problems related to computer simulation, the "art object," and image copying. For this reason, my focus throughout lies less with the origins or procurement of a glitch, and more with the unique contextual choices and critical and creative effects accomplished through final results.

As indicated, where a glitch artwork begins and ends can be unclear. Confusion arises in part due to the structural logic of digital media coupled by the difficulty determining the borders of a virtual page, site, or data network. Uncertainty also arises from the ways in which glitch artists intentionally interfere with assumptions about the internet and our experience of it, as implied in the above-noted definitions. Glitch art is made, appears, and disappears within ongoing cycles of deterritorialization and reterritorialization, temporarily providing an opening to see things contrarily or script a "minor literature," as Gilles Deleuze and Félix Guattari put it.[57] Put differently, glitch art engages a rapid game of control and its renunciation; a flirtation with breakdown, chaos, and total immersion in technology, followed by a level-headed bait and switch. In this way, we might even see glitch art's flirtation with failure as analogous to Silicon Valley's, the key difference being the former's incorporation of glitches for their aesthetic merit, versus the latter's attempted obliteration of them.

Glitch art has also been connected to "dirt style," "dirty new media," and the "new aesthetic" that addresses "machine seeing," which I do not endorse. As

FIGURE 3. Jil Sander Navy, "Spring 2016 Ready-to-Wear." This colorful, pixel-patterned top illustrates fashionable glitch styles.

FIGURE 4. *Adventure Time*, season 5, episode 15, "A Glitch in Time" (2013). Special episode directed by David O'Reilly. Jake and Finn are caught in a "glitch" in the source code.

Harvard's metaLAB researcher Mathew Battles notes, the notion bears obvious problems in its romantic projection of human sentiment and "poetic powers" onto computational processes.[58] The desire to see machines as thinking and feeling beings perpetuates naïve mythologies that are of little use here. By the same token, criticality is not intrinsic to glitch art, nor to the way in which many glitch artists talk about their work. An appropriated computer glitch may reveal some aspect of computational processing, but this alone is far from constituting a full-fledged artwork, let alone a critique of the computational ontology governing it. And yet, a number of self-identified glitch artists couch their practice in just such terms, claiming the same kind of political and aesthetic effectivity as the avant-garde. Glitches *may* disrupt convention and cultural fantasies about

FIGURE 5. *Inside Out* (Pixar, 2015). Directed by Pete Docter. Riley Anderson's Imagination— part elephant, part dolphin, and part cat— convinces Joy and Sadness to take a shortcut back to headquarters.

technology, but it is more likely that most of them will become a passing fashion or fad.[59]

Indeed, glitch fashions have been the fate of much of this work, now featured in everything from hip-hop videos to television commercials and the latest runway styles. Examples range from Bing Bong's cubist-inspired shortcut back to head-quarters in Pixar's *Inside Out* (2015), and from "A Glitch in Time," episode 15 of season 5 of the popular television show *Adventure Time,* to the hip-hop mogul Kanye West's music video for *Welcome to Heartbreak* (2009), discussed in chapter 5.[60] In a culture of rich media and ubiquitous data, chromatic glitch effects quickly become passé, "pathetic and prophetic caricature[s] of . . . the repressive channeling of desire," as Jacques Attali writes.[61]

But *how,* exactly, do glitch and noise move from a potentially alarming, disturbing state to becoming complicit with consumer desires? And in the moments just before they do, what sort of political or social critique can they offer? This is discussed in the following pages. For now, consider that in this cycle, glitch art is, unfortunately, largely neutralized of criticality, in the end recontributing to the progressive rationalization of aesthetics in the command-and-control ethos of the twenty-first century.

Failure

Unlike glitch, failure has more complex connotations. These phenomena are "true" accidents to the extent that they exceed meaningful order or intention. They fall under the auspices of what Derrida theorizes as the event: a singular, nonrepeatable, and unforeseeable occurrence. Derrida asks: if a living being undergoes sensation through the body's organic material, then does the body not also iterate and "read" itself to make sense of the experience in a way that a machine cannot do? Unsurprisingly, he sets up and reworks a classic binary opposition between the singularity of the event, associated with a living being, versus a machine's calculable program and automated repetitions.[62] This distinction may ring true on most practical levels but it also perpetuates cultural beliefs in an error-prone, yet self-reflexive, human versus a blind, but fail-safe, machine. Friedrich Kittler proposes a similar theorization of technical media as emerging from a nonhuman basis (as implied in the above definition of media archaeology). Where the human provides spontaneous responses to unforeseen events, the machine is only capable of what has been envisioned for it in advance.[63] I have no interest in maintaining such hardline ahistorical distinctions between the human and machine (because, again, machine noise is always already human-made), but these analytic frameworks nonetheless pose an interesting quandary: is it possible for a machine to think through its experience and simultaneously make sense of it? As a crude machine event, the answer is "no." But as material phenomena that refer back to broader anthropological processes, computer failures can be seen to shed light on the limits of human control.

Failure also tends to shut down a system or situation for more than a merely inconvenient length of time. In the metaphor of the city, failure may be defined as a tragic school shooting, terrorist attack, or ten-car pileup in the Holland Tunnel. In computational environments, failure is more severe than a mere glitch. It could include hacking into a major government agency; an unfixable, heavily degraded video file; or defunct satellite. Failure may be bad for business, but it is good for experimental art (illustrated in chapters 2 through 5). High-tech corporations respond to such failures by integrating "failure systems engineering" to minimize and circumvent the inevitable. Unfortunately, the case of environmental failure has not received such rigorous interventions. Those who desire social and democratic freedoms introduce alternative practices, but these too seem to fail, thwarted by ever more powerful enterprises that make their name by transforming once-alternative views into marketing buzzwords.[64] And thus it is no surprise to find failure and its related instantiations (error, glitch, noise) de rigueur in pop culture and business-speak. Fashionable failure appeals to innovation entrepreneurs, while actual failure is kept at bay. This book's address of failure thus finds more traction in the domains of art and aesthetics, where it is celebrated and repurposed as fuel for advancement.

Trash

Unlike most adults, children love to play with trash. "Picking up junk starts around six," Sierra Club writer, MIT scientist, and urban planner Kevin Lynch explains, "it's very common."[65] Children's enchantment with garbage is personified by *Sesame Street*'s Oscar the Grouch, who lives in a trash can and admits he "loves trash." Similar childlike fascinations with trash figure in *Garbage Pail Kids* (1987) and, updated for the digital trash of the computer age, Pixar's 2008 animated success *Wall•E* and Disney's 2012 *Wreck-it Ralph,* a children's narrative film about a character in a videogame (Ralph) and his sidekick, Glitch, who, true to her name, inadvertently demolishes everything she comes into contact with. Children's love of trash also extends to the everyday, from schoolchildren's transformation of recyclables (paper towel rolls, cardboard) into playful images to toddlers mesmerized by metallic candy wrappers in the gutter.

For at least a century, adults have played with junk as an established avant-garde strategy. Beyond the art world, adults have also been known to collect garbage and put it on display, whether as the raw materials for community building or for environmental and cultural development. In late 2018, the exhibition "Designing Waste: Strategies for a Zero Waste City," curated by Andrew Blum and sponsored by the American Institute of Architects (AIA) in conjunction with New York's Center for Architecture, displayed old milk cartons and images of trash and dumpsters on the city's streets to propose ways to radically reduce New York City's waste by 2030. The exhibition relayed such stark facts as this one: in 2018, over 24,000 tons of trash were produced in New York City *every day.* Multiplied by 365 days, this costs the city over a billion dollars a year, not to mention the environmental havoc caused to the planet, underprivileged communities who remain vulnerable to exposure from toxic waste, ground-water pollution, and proximity to landfill sites

On the other side of Manhattan, we find a number of East Village community gardens. Traditionally home to artists and bohemians, the East Village maintains its eclectic character in places like La Plaza Cultural de Armando Perez Community Garden in an otherwise waste-strewn neighborhood on the corner of East Ninth Street and Avenue C, where, circa 1979, discarded aluminum cans and old plastic detergent bottles were split open and cut in the shape of flowers, decorating the Plaza's small central amphitheater, built from railroad ties and reclaimed building materials.[66] Kevin Lynch defines waste as that which is "worthless or unused for human purpose . . . a lessening of something without useful result."[67] His definition includes a broad range of phenomena from excrement and derelict land and buildings, to literal garbage and garbage turned into art. This spacious definition provides a starting point for my analysis of the afterlife of techno trash, which includes these urban phenomena and, as I will argue: human beings. Environmental scholars have traditionally construed waste as other than human but, as Michelle Yates argues, in capitalism, many people are treated and processed as trash, used up until they are void of labor power and become disposable. A key contradiction emerges herein, she explains, "waste in human form conflicts with capital's internal drive for ever-increasing value, which can only be produced by and extracted from human labor."[68] The faster one can use and dispose of labor power, the higher the profit, but conversely, the less the value of the human life used to produce it.[69] I return to this in chapters 6 and 7, and tangentially in chapter 4. For now, suffice it to note that "playing with trash" is a necessity in a world of reckless consumption.

In sum, my five core concepts are both different and similar. Flexibility is required, since my use of one term always already stands in for at least two others. By theorizing glitch, error, failure, noise, and trash as essential but paradoxical elements of our media culture, I undertake a broader project to reposition these phenomena from a mere eye-candy effect, or negligible aberration to be ignored, to actively relocate them in the foreground of a materialist critique. If these phenomena are intrinsic to the "fundamental social categories of capitalism"[70] then, when they are appropriated in artistic and cultural forms, and analyzed through material, aesthetic critique, they bring to light the contradictions in the so-called "transparent" historical present.

A final note on the book's peripatetic style and softcover format is in order. As the text moves from a detailed analysis of one artist's work to philosophy, to industry-based case studies, to pop culture and back again, the writing performs its own glitch-and-noise philosophy. This results in part from my lack of allegiance to any single discipline or pedagogy (expanded on in the above methods section). Several pages of analysis will delve into the nitty-gritty of Kant's aesthetic sublime (chapter 6 and 7), while the following section of the same chapter jumps to the harrowing conditions of industrial waste in Pakistan and China—only to reconnect them in the penultimate section to photographs by Edward Burtynsky and eco-artist Chris Jordan. Along the way, readers will also encounter a series of passing allusions to disparate artists, designers, genres, and disciplines. While navigating the book's organization and linear trajectory, one should also allow for flexibility in the play between concepts, references, and forms of analysis, in the same way that the glitch-and-noise artists discussed in these pages play with multi-tiered forms of data processing. Lastly, the performative nature of the prose is reflected in what is likely a noisy quality in the resolution of the digitally-printed softcover color images. Those holding the book in their hands will experience the same kind of (potentially invisible) visual noise theorized above and in chapter 4. Such is the state of our most cutting-edge and "democratic" digital printing technologies. Online readers, however, will not have this experience; for them it is all-in for the seductive allure of the liquid crystal display.[71]

V. BOOK OVERVIEW

High-Tech Trash: Glitch, Noise, and Aesthetic Failure analyzes how artists and theorists are placing glitch, error, and noise at the center of their creative practice, and secondarily, how this allows us to critically reflect on a broader ethos of breakdown. While much of the book's content is flagged above, in this section, I fill in some gaps and provide an overview of each chapter's contributions to the book's trajectory.

Part 1 begins with an investigation of the ways in which notions of noise, error, and failure have intersected with the history of Western philosophy, industry, and the avant-garde. Chapter 1 uses the lens of error to map a counter history of Western philosophy from Plato through failure systems engineering, proposing two related theses: first, that noise and error have always been intrinsic to human and human-machine communications, and, second, in the information age, characterized by discrete digital transfer and compression systems, error and noise have become primary agents. Given the prevalence of digital communications systems today, the chapter argues, it is imperative to place error and noise at the center of humanities-based critique. Chapter 2 complements chapter 1 with an archaeology of glitch and noise in the twentieth-century avant-gardes, from the futurist *Art of Noises* through junk art and distortion-based net art in the 1990s. Drawing on preexisting theories, texts, and archival sources, the chapter illustrates how the advent of technical reproducibility in sound and image led to an aesthetic shift toward non-unified forms of abstraction, disorientation, and noise.

In reference to Walter Benjamin's 1917 analysis of "the mark," Judith Butler recently referred to the aesthetic concept of the "unalloyed." In distinction to the relatively closed hermeneutic of the symbol, the unalloyed invokes a state of incompossibility in bringing two distinct pictorial elements together.[72] This non-Hegelian synthesis of nonreconciliation, in Butler's take, forms a correlative to the aesthetic function of abstraction, its development as noise in the avant-garde, and its intensification in glitch art's contemporary strategies. If the unalloyed can operate as a deliberate strategy of anti-compression (whether semantic or epistemological), it can be used to critique dominant systems of visual representation. This is illustrated elegantly in John Baldessari's photograph *Wrong*, and more generally, through abstraction's drive to disorient illustrative norms.

Part 2 (chapters 3 through 5) analyzes how contemporary media artists are using glitch and noise to foreground and critically offset dominant technical systems. This begins with chapter 3's correlations between color as signal / noise and "accidental colors," followed by an investigation of these concepts in Ryan Trecartin's video art. Chapter 4 continues this work by analyzing the photographic glitches German artist Thomas Ruff's work. Ruff's Internet appropriations offer a rich set of materials for discussing digital signal processing and the deliberate introduction of noise into otherwise clear channels of communication. Chapter 5 narrows this analysis to the more developed genre of datamoshing, the stylization of digital video compression algorithms. In it, I frame the analog and the digital as *concepts,* removed from the physical technologies they normatively signify. Doing so allows us to see how the structural logic of either term can stand in for a set of stylistic modalities apropos of the past and present.

Where parts 1 and 2 address breakdown and failure in philosophy and media art, part 3 (chapters 6 and 7) and the postscript move beyond the screen to analyze failure in the built environment. Failure and error are here reconceived as a series of global catastrophes resulting from many years of collective failures to care for our waste and world. Chapter 6 focuses on a precariously inverted aesthetic of the "toxic sublime" in the "offshore" practices of e-waste recycling and shipbreaking, followed by an analysis of the work of Canadian photographer Edward Burtynsky. The decision to emphasize Burtynsky's work (as opposed to a number of other contemporary artists creating visual images of waste and ecological decline), is connected to the way he engages the tradition of the sublime in relation to harrowing environmental realities. What does it mean to deploy beautiful colors in the depiction of such tragic conditions? How does this connect back to our experience of waste and trash in the confines of daily life? Building on this, chapter 7 turns to the twin concept of the mathematical sublime to examine the role of data and statistics in contemporary landscape photography, positioned against a much longer history of environmental, landscape photography. While new approaches to eco-photography adopt data visualization trends to improve the communicative scope of an image, in a growing number of uses, precisely the opposite results: an image incites fear and cognitive breakdown, leaving a viewer incapable of grasping cohesive meanings, let alone undertaking political action.

Each chapter from 4 through 7 focuses almost exclusively on a single media artist's work. My criteria for selecting these case studies was threefold: each artist was to have a unique approach to color; a marked use of noise, waste, or error in relation to high-tech culture; and third, a combination of the first two (a use of color *as* glitch or noise) lending itself to the book's broader mapping of an aesthetic paradigm of failure.

The book's conclusion turns to colored plastic. An old medium by twenty-first-century standards, plastic's emergence as a miraculous techno-substance in the 1930s is juxtaposed with its current toxic ubiquity on the surface of the world's earth and oceans, again foregrounding our failure to adequately care for a substance after its fashionable debut as the latest new media. Taken together, the book's studies serve as a reminder to keep in check highfalutin ambitions to innovate ever-greater, newer, and faster technologies without properly caring for the afterlife of our current ones. An aesthetic of failure may be our most viable option for accepting the realities of the present and a prerequisite for sustained change. Throughout the following pages, readers must keep this fact in mind: *all* computer glitches, errors, or so-called system failures are not episodes of a technology spontaneously acting on its own agency, working against what it has been programmed to do (unless it has been programmed to do precisely this). To the contrary, machines do exactly what they are programmed to do. If and when an "error or breakdown" is perceived, it is because the machine has reached a wall; a limitation in the way *humans* have programmed it. The book's study of high-tech trash is consequently a study of ourselves.

PART ONE

Precursors

1

———

Colors of Error

Innovation and Failure from Plato to Digital
Signal Processing

I. DENIAL

Think only success and ye shall find. This is the anachronistic dictate of the American dream and corporate capital from the industrial era to post-Fordism. "Even thinking about the possibility of failure is foreign to the manager's classic culture," Patrick Lagadec explains of Gerald C. Meyers's business philosophy, president of American Motors from 1977 to 1982. In Meyers's own words: "think success; plan for success; allow no negative thinking; associate with positive people; emphasize accomplishment; and cast off losers,"[1] a credo reiterated by many, including Harold Geneen, president of the ITT Corporation, who, according to Meyers, believed that "once you have set a business objective, you must achieve it. Those who do not do so . . . are not simply poor managers; they are not managers at all."[2] In this ethos, admitting error or failure, let alone a mistake, catapults one into nonbeing.

Forty years later, we no longer live in a society guaranteeing anything that resembles the American dream. Despite ongoing and systematic efforts to deny it, failure colors too many facets of life, from business to family and personal well-being, and the more it is denied, the stronger and more threatening it becomes. This chapter explores these insights through an eccentric mapping of error in the history of Western philosophy and modern American industry. I propose that error, failure, and accident are intimately related and have always been intrinsic to human life and communication. Further, in an era of information overload and frenzied pursuits of "innovation," these phenomena have become key constituents that can no longer be ignored or merely paid fashionable lip service. The chapter begins with a definition of digital signal processing (DSP), illustrating the centrality of noise in it. I do not return to digital processing until the end of the chapter, but it is important to flag it here, because the relationship of signal to noise in DSP sets the tone for the archaeology of error in sections III–IV, from antiquity through the Enlightenment,[3] and foreshadows more recent economic and industrial developments analyzed in section V.

II. FAILURE AS ORIGIN MYTH

In Plato's origin myth, the *Protagoras,* the two brothers Epimetheus and Prometheus are given the task of distributing qualities to animals and men.[4] Epimetheus pleads to take control, assuring his brother he can review it upon completion. After allocating all the qualities—speed and skin to the "brute" animals, strength to the creatures without speed—he realizes he has forgotten humans, but he has no qualities left to dispense. To amend for his brother's mistake and repair humanity's state of "non-being," as Bernard Stiegler puts it, Prometheus sets out to steal the gift of skill (*tēn enteknon sophian*) and fire from Hephaestus and Athena (fire is the means [*amēkhanon*] to use skill). Stolen fire is therefore given to humanity as a prosthetic: a paltry pseudo-godlike power to compensate for what humans are without, but also, an eternal reminder of our fraught existence.

Together, *epimētheia* (foresight) and *promētheia* (afterthought) operate as twin existential concepts: a desire for improvement coupled with inevitable error and mistake. Like the origin myth of *Cura* noted in the Introduction, the *Protagoras* illustrates how human existence is eternally torn between a twofold struggle for perseverance, on the one hand, and the drive to amend for the guilt of being intrinsically error-prone on the other. Taken together, according to J. P. Vernant, we have a "competitive emulation at work," a drive for betterment, paradoxically born from the "lower" motives of jealousy or envy.[5] Human success and advancement are thus just as innate to our eternal wound. This is our primary condition of being in the world, predicated on a prior "défaut," corresponding to the French *défaut* denoting fault, fall, cut, or an originary guilt in being, which, Stiegler insists, is not to be confused with psychoanalytic "lack," or deconstruction's "super lack," but instead a kind of debt owed by virtue of having life at all.[6] Yet it is also possible to interpret this originary falling-short of Epimetheus as a stigma eternally sewn into the fiber of being human. Any attempt to cover over, steal back, or create a prosthetic for our fundamental hamartia is always already tainted by the knowledge that any compensatory gestures (technics and prosthetics) are only ever weak supplements. Under these conditions, we are always already in debt, in a "being towards death," as Heidegger puts it.[7] "Man does not merely stray into errancy," Heidegger writes elsewhere, "he is always astray" in it.[8] The myth's dynamic tension offers a refreshing alternative to our lopsided, goal-oriented, winner-take-all culture, epitomized by attitudes like Meyers's where "even thinking about the possibility of failure" makes one a loser.[9]

The origin myth also offers a metaphor for humanity's twofold struggle between failure and success in communications theory. Here, we find friendly ties with

John Durham Peters's eloquent analysis of the history of communication sys-tems in humans and machines. At the beginning of his book *Speaking into the Air* (1999), Peters identifies an analogous dichotomy in metaphors of "the bridge and the chasm." The bridge model of communication denotes the "dream of commu-nication as the mutual communion of souls," epitomized in conceptions of total mental contact and soulful immersion. Peters's examples include Jesus's teachings (and in particular, the Christian notion of agape); William James's empiricism; Hegel's idealism; nineteenth-century Mesmerism; the "Magic Bullet" theory of media, and, to which I would add, a special brand of techno-utopianism.[10] Like the myth of transparency discussed in the Introduction, techno-utopianism main-tains that new media are clean, totally efficient, and exceedingly productive things, capable of delivering users (consumers, rather) to pure and sanctified spaces, free from the dirt and grime of the material world. Such one-sided belief systems are deeply rooted in American business models and the now global logic of commod-ity capital. As I argue here and throughout the book: ignoring the growing mani-fold of error simply fuels the problem. The richer the media content, the wider the bandwidth, and the higher the fidelity of images, the more glitch, error, and fail-ure there is. Henry Kissinger once noted that in "high office competing pressures tempt one to believe that an issue deferred is a problem avoided; more often it is a crisis invited."[11] The same insight applies to communications technology.

In Peters's chasm, a "nightmare of mutual isolation" ensures that communica-tion is "always breaking down."[12] Noise, error, accident, and disjuncture are the necessary and inevitable results of any communicative exchange, whether internal or external, human or machine, or otherwise. Adherents to this view include post-war information theorists and post-Kantians from Nietzsche through Heidegger, Levinas, Derrida, Serres, and non-philosophers in economics and politics. What would it mean to flip convention and adopt this view, wherein all forms of com-munication (with ourselves, with another, and with machines) would be formed *through* noise, error, and accident as the condition of possibility for innovation and growth? Would this grant a new kind of unforeseen freedom?

The two sides of Peters's dichotomy are inextricably linked, but the vast major-ity of survey histories of technology and triumphant narratives of Western prog-ress seem to focus only on the former's connective bridge. In the spirit of media archaeology, this chapter focuses on the chasm. The first and perhaps most famil-iar example of this is found in the next section's discussion of noise in digital signal processing.

III. DIGITAL SIGNAL PROCESSING

As noted in the Introduction, noise, error, and failure can, in certain circum-stances, qualify as accident, characterized as an unintended, nonmeaningful, chaotic, singular, unrepeatable, or unforeseeable occurrence. This chapter iden-tifies a history of approaches to error and noise as just this kind of undesirable event, arising in tandem with long-standing efforts to manage and control them. The unavoidable presence of noise in digital processing is a prime example. The core function of almost all modern computation systems involves digital signal processing (DSP). DSP is the primary way data travels to and from cell phones, HDTV screens, computer monitors, calculators, scanners, electronic toys, web pages, PDAs, and IMAX screens. Defined as the mathematical manipulation of discrete, informatic signals for the purposes of effective and efficient data transfer, at the core of DSP are signals, but also noise. DSP creates algorithmic numeric bridges for valuable data to travel across channels and between satellites, and noise intervenes as a necessary disruptive chasm. Signal and noise always coexist, like Peters's bridge and chasm.

The origins of information theory elucidate this inextricable relationship. It is by now well established that information theory emerged through Claude E. Shannon's innovative research, working with Warren Weaver, at Bell Telephone Laboratories in the 1940s. The pair drew on Norbert Wiener's studies in feedback and cybernetics to develop a radically new model of communication for telephone systems based on "on or off" pulses or "yes or no" decisions. Shannon referred to these as "bits," a term appropriated from the American mathematician John W. Tukey.[13] The system became known as "binary code," the most appropriate denotation given the way it could break down any kind of quantifiable data into the smallest possible number of discrete units, allowing for greater control and calculations. Shannon had introduced a radically innovative language for the computer age. Unlike other languages, his was an abstract, numerical language capable of communicating anything in the qualitative, phenomenal human world insofar as it could be turned into a series of numerical symbols.

Another major facet of Shannon's innovative system was its ability to optimize "signal to noise ratios," the level of a desired signal relative to the undesired background noise. Optimizing this relationship meant producing greater accuracy and consistency in the transmission and reception of information, regardless of contextual components.[14] Because Shannon's model used a standardized set of abstract numerical symbols (os and 1s) to compress diverse kinds of data across several platforms, an increasing range of cultural techniques could be subject to the same form of binary-based, statistical reduction (compression) and strategic repetition.[15] For example, to illustrate a natural redundancy in the English language, for his definition of "information theory," Shannon wrote:

MST PPL HV LTTL DFFCLTY N RDNG THS SNTNC

The obvious removal of vowels and certain letters provides an excellent illustration of statistical reduction's logic of compression. The sentence is not written in English proper, but it is intelligible in so far as the reader can, eventually, understand what he is trying to say. In order to ensure the fastest and most efficient transmission of symbols through time and space, the translation from data into

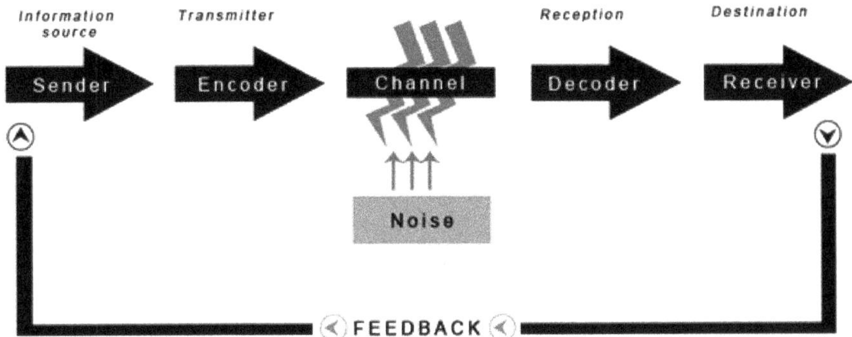

SHANNON-WEAVER'S MODEL OF COMMUNICATION

FIGURE 6. Claude E. Shannon's innovative model of communication for telephone systems, ca. 1948. Binary code was appropriate for the system because it could be broken down into the smallest possible number of discrete units. Figure adapted from communicationtheory.org.

signal was subject to increasing levels of statistical reduction. Any superfluous data was removed that might overload or slow down at channel, or be (perceived) as repetitious or redundant.[16] There are instances of this throughout the media environment, from compressed movie files and cellphone conversations, to "poor" images on social media feeds.[17]

Codecs

Only a few decades after Shannon's pioneering work, a whole range of related DSP compression techniques were standardized as "codecs," or, compression and decompression algorithms. Codecs are complex algorithms engineered into the core structure of digital file formats and they are rarely, if ever, seen. Generally speaking, codecs function to instruct a computer system how and when to display light, color, or sound, but because it is always an industrial engineer's goal to compress information when possible, while still delivering high-quality media (as with HDTV), digital codecs are consistently engaged in a struggle between technological innovation and perceptual comfort.[18] Chapters 3 through 5 return to issues of codecs and digital compression and the ways they have been used to engender a glitch aesthetic. For now, this preliminary definition of signal and noise will suffice.

If we can accept that noise is fundamental to any and all digital communication systems, then we must also face the fact that the greater the range of digitization, the greater the uncertainty in the results. As former Bell Labs' researcher Harry Nyquist explains, when signal and bandwidth increase to allow more data to flow through a channel, the S/N (signal: noise) ratio also increases.[19] The S/N ratio is a standardized way of measuring the amount of signal (valued information) in a

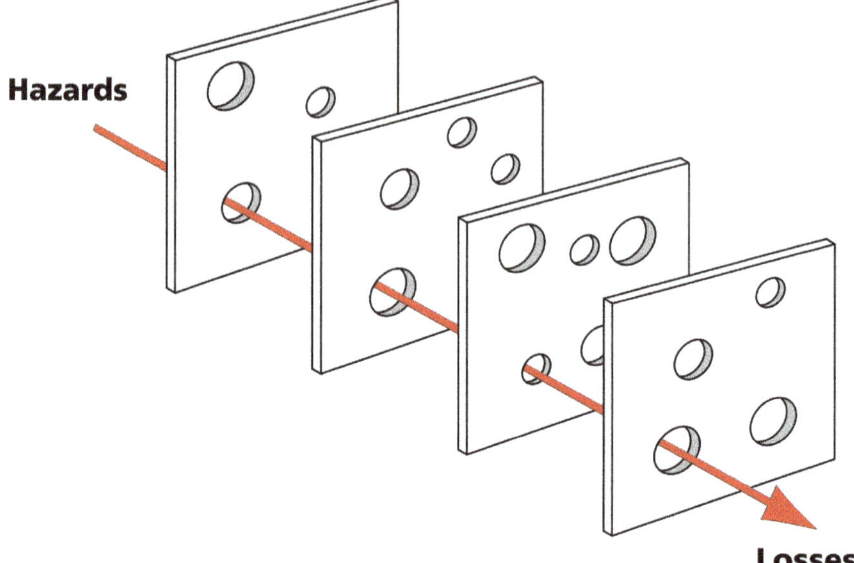

FIGURE 7. Dante Orlandella and James T. Reason's Swiss cheese model offers engineers a method for creating trapdoors to conceal the prevalence of error and noise in complex systems. Figure adapted from wikimedia.org.

system relative to the amount of undesirable noise, whether in the channel or elsewhere. On closer inspection, the inversely proportionate law of S/N also illustrates that signal and noise are actually the same thing, defined by arbitrary and contextually relative rules. That is, what counts as noise in one system may be entirely different in another. French information theorist Abraham Moles concurs, "There is no absolute structural difference between noise and signal . . . the only difference which can be logically established between them is based exclusively on the concept of intent on the part of the transmitter: a noise is a signal that the sender does not want to transmit."[20] In information theory, the problem of noise *is* the problem of information and herein lies the paradox of the "information" age: what comes to matter most is not information, but noise.

Swiss Cheese

Because consumers demand clear image and sound, engineers quite logically seek to increase signal and decrease noise in a communication channel. Dante Orlandella and James T. Reason's "Swiss Cheese" model for cyber security is one excellent example of a strategic endeavor to conceal errors in complex systems.[21] Developed in the 1990s, in the context of safety systems engineering, their model offers engineers a method for creating trapdoors to conceal the growing prevalence of error and noise in complex systems.

Swiss cheese is an apt metaphor because in a single slice there are only a few holes through which a potential error can pass. If several slices are vertically aligned, not all holes meet, making it much harder for an error to slip through all slices. By layering and repeating one's code in the basic design, the Swiss cheese model acts as a buffer to catch and conceal errors in a system, allowing only the most persistent ones to make it through. The genius of the model lies in the way it can conceal a magnitude of errors so that an end-user only registers an error after many have already been caught and only one single persistent one slips through. In sum, in order for a DSP system to succeed, engineers must create complex algorithms to conceal error.

Now consider that a similar logic rests at the heart of Western culture. In both culture and DSP, we find the same tension between the bridge and chasm; signal and noise; Epimetheus and Prometheus; and failure and innovation: two eternal and ambivalent forces inextricably bound to the nature of existence. I return to digital error in the penultimate sections of this chapter, where the centrality of noise in failure systems theory is found to be largely analogous to the role of error and noise in critical theory after the 1960s. For now, we jump to a very different tradition of error established in antiquity and active through the Enlightenment.

IV. ERROR IN ANTIQUITY

In this and the next section, I discuss holistic and binary conceptions of error in Western epistemology and philosophies of sense perception, from the Socratic era through the Enlightenment. Section V turns to our contemporary, albeit obfuscated, relationship to failure and noise in the industrial and postindustrial present.

According to Nicholas Rescher, the fifth-century B.C.E. Greek philosopher Parmenides of Elea proposed that error was connected to a dynamic sense of being, rather than nonbeing.[22] Error was a way of diverging from what already is, akin to Epimetheus's accidental forgetting in the *Protagoras*. As a natural part of being, error did not point to what was wrong or missing in life, but rather suggested only how things could be different from the way they were. In this way, error also creates possibility; an opening for the new and yet to be.[23] This early, integrative conception of error was later adopted in experimental media, as discussed in chapter 2, though it remains largely antithetical to philosophies of error in industry and technology. This holistic approach to error-as-facet-of-being is also foreign to the majority of Western philosophers, beginning with Plato and Aristotle.[24]

For Plato, the ambiguity of error was problematic. According to Rescher, Plato believed that error was characterized by "nonexistent non-facts," versus a more generous account, which might have viewed error as merely an "incorrect characterization" of actual facts. Rescher provides an example from *The Republic* where Plato's character Thrasymachus lands himself in trouble after "refusing to acknowledge the doctrine of sovereign immunity, which establishes that a true ruler cannot commit error."[25] While the claim is invalid from a logical standpoint (anyone can commit an error), Thrasymachus's error, in this context, lay in his refusal to accept the letter of the law, which is to say, a deliberate negation of cultural and political hierarchy even *after* he is given "correct" knowledge of how and why it should be one way and not the other. Thrasymachus is of course a sophist so it is his job to be provocative, but nonetheless, his disobedience sets forth one of the first binaries between the erred human and so-called objective law.[26] Error is henceforth an epistemological and ideological tool for differentiation and judging one's failure to obey the law.[27]

A second example of error is found in Plato's *Theaetetus* (369 B.C.E.). In a dialogue regarding the conditions that can lead to knowledge formation, Plato determines that knowledge can't develop through "self-production" or direct sense perception, but only as a "reflection" of these two.[28] The world imprints itself on a subject's senses and these imprints must then be refined through a learned process of reasoning that necessarily moves beyond one's (faulty and erroneous) sense perception. Skipping over the faultiness of perception as an initial step, yet simultaneously relying on it to produce knowledge thereafter bears an obvious contradiction that many poststructuralist and deconstruction theorists have noted. In Plato, we encounter the beginning of the decline of holistic notions of error as natural and integral to life and being. Plato provides a new foundation for error rooted in what would become the long-standing metaphysical gap between good and bad; true and false; and eventually, signal and noise.[29]

Aristotle was less concerned with Platonic epistemology, and in some ways, gestured back towards holistic, pre-Socratic views. In chapter 25 of his *Poetics,* he distinguishes between two kinds of error: poetic errors that intentionally break rules and accidental errors made in representing the world. In the latter, it is out of ignorance that a painter "portrays a female deer with horns."[30] In the former, a new frame of assessment is required, opening the door to rhetorical genres of persuasion, storytelling, and other forms of art and "sophistry." Here, error as an intentional practice is accepted as part of art-making, not as a false or failed attempt to "copy" truth from Form, but as a valid creative strategy. Granted Aristotle's theory of error is related more to classical aesthetics, it nonetheless illustrates a key pivot from the Platonic approach. If one were to pursue this trajectory further, through a genealogy of aesthetic representation, one could inquire into the history of the Western concept of the Beautiful, from Plato's discussion of the Good and Beautiful in the *Symposium,* through St. Thomas Aquinas's *Summa Theologiae* ("for beauty three things are required . . . integrity or perfection: those things which are broken are bad")[31] to its breakdown in modern thought.

V. ENLIGHTENMENT ERROR

In the years bridging antiquity and the Enlightenment, numerous ambiguous and religiously inspired philosophies of error emerged. One is found in the work of

St. Augustine who, in the fourth century C.E., argued that the "visible absence of perfection in the universe" comprises a negative space through which divine perfection and wholeness could be imagined.[32] Error, for St. Augustine, existed as that which could point to what was not. In the thirteenth century, St. Thomas Aquinas theorized three major "defects" in human cognition: "ignorance, error, and heresy," which meant that is was possible to be "ignorant without passing judgment on the things we are ignorant of," whereas with error, Rescher explains, we judge and incorrectly accept the false in place of the true.[33] The Scottish Franciscan friar Duns Scotus (1266–1308) believed all error was the result of human will, relative to the divine. In sum, the responsibility of error clearly fell on man and evidence of this abounded in our mistakes of judgment, false propositions, and human inadequacies.[34]

The ancient skeptics held that if we cannot confidently claim to know something, we should refrain from asserting it to be true. For Descartes (1596–1650), as for Plato, all sensory experience was suspect. This hard line, binary view of error acquired great momentum in Descartes's philosophy. In his *Meditations on First Philosophy* (1641), error is at once central to the discussion, and yet, also a liability in any aspiration to truth: "In so far as I am not myself the Supreme Being and am lacking in countless respects, it is no wonder that I make mistakes. I understand, then, that error as such is not something real which depends on God but merely a defect."[35] For Descartes, God is true and the "self" is fundamentally at fault. The irony—the presumed "I" who bears this insight is somehow mysteriously excluded from the "I" who makes mistakes—did not escape him. The logical contradiction, as John Roberts explains it, became the ground on which Descartes came to doubt all knowledge.[36] So while Descartes "inherited Plato's distrust of the senses," Roberts continues, the production of knowledge in the pursuit of pure thought was still "stripped back to a bare-boned skepticism."[37] To avoid error, Descartes would have had to withhold all judgment, which is to say, purport nothing at all. If philosophy ever saw an apogee of epistemological breakdown, this would be it. To reiterate, Descartes's contradiction is similar to Plato's, both are thick with self-doubt. Since they are also both icons in the Western tradition, their outright dismissals of error as a mere defect of reason has, unfortunately, affected the many legacies that have extended from them.

At the same time, and counter to popular accounts of the Enlightenment as the apogee of metaphysical separations between body and mind; subject and object, and such other binaries, David Bates argues the era was actually much more ambiguous than has been historically understood. On the one hand, the era's rejection of "first principles" created a void that was filled by finite philosophical systems and unfettered beliefs in progress and reason. And yet, figures like Hobbes, Spinoza, Leibniz, Locke, and d'Alembert, all key thinkers of the Enlightenment, ground their philosophical edifices on the precarity of error.[38] For Hobbes, error was not logically inconsistent, but a reasonable and coherent conjecture that only turned out to be wrong in the future.[39] Similarly, Spinoza argued that error was not located in the perversity of human judgment, as it was for Descartes, but rather, in misunderstanding. "Being ignorant and being in error are two different things," he explains, a misnomer on the "canvas of knowledge" that could just as easily be adjusted with a new coat of paint.[40] Leibniz also "rejected the Scotist-Cartesian view of error" as a fundamental human flaw. For him, error was a mere stepping off the mark, which "does not depend on the will" but was an accidental "misjudging rather than a mis-willing."[41] If one knew better, one would not have made the mistake. Likewise, John Locke theorized error as a "premature claim" unrelated to axiomatic truths, though he did connect it back to the divine. Without "divine inspiration," Bates explains, Locke believed that "the mind was prone to lose its way among the plurality of ideas" and would thus make inaccurate connections among them.[42]

In Jean le Rond d'Alembert's essays on the elements of philosophy and principles of human knowledge, he conceived of error as a "productive blindness." Any desire for direct illumination or foundational first truths were seen as the seeds of "intellectual aberration". As a precursor to Nietzsche, d'Alembert argued that the wandering mind was enticed by both the false light of error and occasional flashes of authenticating truth.[43] For his protégé Nicolas de Condorcet, unnecessary reflection led to error, but risking error was also what provided greater reward.[44] Errors stimulated exploration, wandering, and provided an opening to the new, in many ways the equivalent to a romantic muse.[45] Take Diderot, who regarded pure unmediated knowledge as impossible. Diderot also drew on dynamic metaphors of wandering and the peripatetic to describe his philosophical inquiries through a disorganized, unpredictable world. One "stumbles" into knowing, he argued, only by first wandering astray.[46] Étienne Bonnot de Condillac's late encyclopedia entry on error likewise argues that it is intrinsic to human nature. A man may be able to get over one illness or setback, but given his intrinsically "feeble temperament,"[47] he would inevitably only "fall into another."[48] One could never manage to fully separate oneself from error entirely, though one could exchange old errors for new ones.[49]

In sum, despite common conceptions of the Enlightenment as metaphysically rigid and truth-obsessed, we see from these cumulative perspectives that the issue of error was in fact widely considered by Enlightenment figures. Discussion of truth, rather, was rare, and made only "fleeting appearances."[50] Where Descartes contrasted error with reason, Locke and others of his generation modified it could serve as a new foundation from which a science of investigation and inquiry could be built. Accordingly, it was also error—not truth—that provided the necessary preconditions for the production of knowledge, just as noise in information theory is the necessary and unavoidable cost of processing a signal. How then did error and failure become so intensely stigmatized once again, associated today with debt and nonbeing? To answer this, we turn to the role of error and breakdown in Kant and Hegel.

Kant's Communication Breakdown

The prolific contributions to Western philosophy of Immanuel Kant (1724–1804) are beyond the scope of this or any single volume. Here, I examine only his systematic theorization of the gap between knowledge and error.

Often referred to as the "Copernican turn," Kant's formal intervention in Western philosophy reversed the classical privileging of claims to objective "worldly" knowledge with a more "modern" notion of the subject as the origin and source of (mediated) knowing. On the one hand, as John Roberts points out, Kant adopted the "anti-sense apparatus" of seventeenth-century epistemology, characteristic of Locke and Descartes.[51] He argued that a rational subject's knowledge is dependent on the world in which they exist in. That is, any inquiry into knowledge must begin with the question: how does one's experience of the world acquire any certainty at all, when existence is itself fragmented and precarious?

A subject begins the process through empirical, sense experience. Any proper knowledge claim can then only be acquired after, through the application of what Kant called "concepts," a priori cognitions that lie above the sphere of daily experience and that humans possess as imminent mechanisms of consciousness. Concepts are prerequisite for the formation of knowledge. Thus "the senses do not err," Kant writes, "not because they always judge correctly, but because they do not judge at all." Put differently, human *reasoning* errs, not sense perception. In the *Critique of Pure Reason* (1781), he expands: "illusory appearance[s] as the cause of error, are only to be found in a judgement, in the *relation* of an object to our understanding."[52] If a priori cognitions are the matter of consciousness, then the problem is not matter itself but the way in which we, as reasoning human subjects, are capable of organizing these sense impressions to make meaning of them; "in a cognition which completely harmonizes with the laws of the understanding, no error can exist."[53] Perception is thus freed from erring, though it remains incapable of generating objective truth. Many of Kant's radical interventions in the history of philosophy were not appreciated until well into the twentieth century (by Heidegger, Wittgenstein, Foucault, Deleuze, and Derrida, among others) and thus when we turn to Hegel in the next paragraph, it will appear as if we are taking a step backward, to mistrust the noisy and faulty senses once again.

G. W. F. Hegel

In 1793, idealist philosopher J. G. Fichte declared the French Revolution a "dreadful spectacle" that had gone too far. He leveraged a resentment that, according to Roberts, relegated such errors "back in[to] the realm of shadow darkness."[54] Shortly after Fichte, G. W. F. Hegel (1770–1831) drew on the French Revolution to expound an idealized theory of historical determinism that, ironically, Roberts points out, is structured on the concepts of error and failure.[55] Hegel saw error neither as an unfortunate human shortcoming, like Plato or Descartes, nor as innocent, as I have suggested of Kant. Instead, like many early Enlightenment thinkers, he viewed it as a necessary "gateway" to the truth of being.[56] As a gateway, error was subordinate to truth as a stepping stone on the path to historical unfolding. This is clearly illustrated in Hegel's *Phenomenology of the Spirit* (1807), where—like Plato—he argues that one must always begin with the error and falsity of sense perception, only in order to surpass and overcome it (*Aufheben*) to reach truth.[57] Only in the negation of failure and error can truth and the more desirable ideals of abstract reason emerge as part of the larger apparatus of historical development. Error in Hegel is thus not to be avoided or denied, only miscounted and distrusted. Error—like noise in relation to signal, and color in relation to form—provides the fodder for reason's capacity to overcome it in the pursuit of seemingly more estimable goals.[58]

Hegel relocated Kant's valuation of the relationship between sense impression and reason to the domain of history. Kant's notion of error systematized the anti-Cartesian break and moved towards an inclusion of the world in theories of knowing and being, in many ways remaining "locked in the cognitive constraints of the autonomous subject." By contrast, in Hegel, error is contrarily "removed from the auspices of the autonomous rational subject" and "placed in the realm of history proper."[59] That the actual, material events of war, revolution, and trauma inspired Hegel's idealism is not surprising or unique. Horror and bloodshed have time and again evoked radically new visions of a better society to come.[60]

Thus far, this chapter has charted theories of error in early Western thought and digital communication systems. Much of this has concerned theoretical developments only, failing to consider the cultural, psychological, and technological contexts shaping these developments. The remainder of the chapter amends for this as the next three sections address the advent of new technology and the way in which they led to a quasi-Hegelian shift in the theorization of error and failure, from the inadequate human subject to the wider registers of history and techno-culture.[61]

VI. FAILURE IN THE "CONTROL" REVOLUTION

Prior to the industrial era, social, economic, and political change happened gradually. New ideas and new technologies stuck around for millennia. Adam Davidson notes that a type of hand axe devised in Africa 285,000 years ago still maintained its basic shape and use 250,000 years later.[62] Likewise, during the Middle Ages, major advances in agriculture, warfare, and building technology remained in use for up to a century at a time. Even the largest and most developed economies ran "at a human pace," James R. Beniger observes, with processing speeds enhanced only slightly by animals, wind, and water power.[63] A dominant technology remained unchallenged for many years, like the African hand axe that became one of the longest "fail-proof" human technologies, consistently resisting obsolescence relative to newer devices.[64]

The stability and longevity of a technology, Davidson also perceptibly points out, is intimately connected to a culture's appetite for risk. Demands for growth and innovation during the agricultural era were minimal because people needed to rely on offspring and the land's consistency as a source of income. To abandon this and attempt some new and "untested innovation" was too great a risk.[65] Insofar as a technology is "fail-proof," it has proven itself in a culture that either experiences minimal levels of innovation, or simply has no interest in it. What does this say about our era, ostensibly so full of innovation and "game-changing" developments, but still somehow locked into the same few platforms (Google, Amazon, and Apple)? As to whether or not we are in an age of actual innovation or merely inflated discourse about it is a complex question. One way to determine this is to compare our situation to the culture of innovation from a century ago, again with a focus on truth, error, and failure relative to innovation and success.

During the golden age of entrepreneurship (1908–20), developed nations experienced massive growth and change in such a short period of time, it is difficult to focus on any one development without concurrently addressing another. During the Industrial Revolution, inventors like James Watt (1736–1819) and Eli Whitney (1765–1825) helped establish key mechanical technologies for mass reproduction and automation, leading to a host of innovations: the steam engine, the spinning jenny (1764), the Bessemer steel-production process (1856), and the telegraph. New industrial methods improved the accuracy and speed of production, unleashing a cultural ethos of unfettered progress. Accordingly, cycles of failure and innovation quickened, and the slow culture of nineteenth-century agriculture transformed into an economy of streamlined efficiency, perpetually and fatally dependent on the introduction of new things and techniques.[66] Beniger refers to this shift as the "control revolution," epitomized by Frederick Winslow Taylor's reprograming of the most basic human movements to conform to an idealized "system-level rationality." Mechanizing, quantifying, and fine-tuning the minutiae of human work and isolating assembly-line gestures seemingly allowed a factory owner to produce at maximum efficiency. One could break down activities into "elementary operations and motions" and then control them, "eliminating all false movements."[67] In the same way that redundancy and noise are removed to optimize signal processing, superficial gestures were systematically removed in the Taylorization of industrial labor.

Not surprisingly, in practice, Taylor's ideals of total efficiency failed. How could they not when error-prone humans are the object of mechanical standardization? His processes were eventually deemed repressive and led to a number of problems resulting in the system's downfall. Moreover, Taylorization was immersed in a broader culture colored by new forms of mechanization ranging from cinema to cars, trains, and the marketplace. The radical shift to mechanical logistics in work and home life forced the sudden adoption of new behaviors and perceptual experiences, often leaving masses of people fearful and uncertain of what or whom they could rely on. As growing numbers of people found themselves facing social and financial insecurity, the industrial era witnessed new levels of poverty, labor exploitation (child labor in particular), noise and air pollution, and eventually, the Great Depression.

As a remedy, citizens were advised to seek stability in economic registers. They were instructed to measure and gauge themselves in relation to financial growth models, providing an indication of their relative success or failure.[68] Credit-reporting agencies (agencies that determine the "worthiness" and capacity to "trust" an individual) were developed in response to the United States' first economic crisis, but as early as 1837, Sandage explains, New York's Mercantile Agency (later Dun & Bradstreet) had already begun offering a new service to help unfamiliar businesses and individuals decide who was trustworthy or not. As a result, more and more people came to identify their "worthiness" by credit ratings.[69] Unlike pre-Enlightenment notions of error or failure, where wandering and wavering away from a goal was to some degree accepted, error and failure were henceforth ingrained as existential stigmas attached to an individual's self-worth.

The reification of the modern subject in the form of a credit report was not lost on Karl Marx, Max Weber, Daniel Bell, Émile Durkheim, and Arnold J. Toynbee, all of whom explored the growing dangers of subjective failure in these new socio-economic systems.[70] Marx wrote extensively about the eclipse of the human and diminishment of social values in the mechanical age, and Durkheim identified the cost of transitioning from an intuitive, qualitative world to one ruled by bureaucratic machines, statistics, and algorithmic optimization.[71] Even Sigmund Freud (1886–1939) resisted reducing the richness of human experience to systematic and controllable laws. In his 1910 essay on "Errors," he recounted three mistakes he had made in his own book: "I was responsible for a series of errors in historical, and above all, material facts, which I was astonished to discover after the appearance of the book. In a closer examination I found that they did not originate from my ignorance, but could be traced to errors of memory explainable by means of analysis."[72] Freud identifies error as integral to modern experience and seems to enjoy doing so. At the same time, he does so only in so far as they do not belong to his "knowledgeable" self but rather, to "the suppressed fantasy [that] falsified the text of my book."[73] At least he took responsibility for them.

Writing before Freud in the 1880s, Nietzsche argued that all truths and so-called objective facts were fabrications, proposing instead a radically new way of understanding human language and culture through metaphor.[74] His work, as noted in the Introduction, clearly paved the road for poststructuralism in the 1960s, and deconstruction in the 1980s. Nietzsche also inspired Heidegger's work and in particular, his nuanced views of error and truth. In his 1930 essay, "On the Essence of Truth," Heidegger proposed that epistemological errors were "the most superficial" ones; only one facet of a much larger phenomenology of failure and declension. Humans do not fall into error, as they would "into a ditch," he argued, rather, all life "start[s] from error . . . errancy belongs to the inner constitution of Dasein."[75] Heidegger's German verb *irren,* "to wander," from the Latin root *errare,* means "to wander from the right way," and only secondarily to "fall into error," as David Krell contends. By proposing a nonbinary, holistic meaning of error, Heidegger reclaims its Greek origins in the modern context. Void of guilt, shame, or subjective lack, Heidegger's phenomenology runs orthogonal to hegemonic accounts of error as sin (biting the apple, being tempted by woman, or opening Pandora's box); epistemological lack, as argued by Plato, Descartes, and Kant; or subjective failure (Sandage, Davidson, Marx). This is also why his elegant yet romantic humanism has influenced numerous philosophers since, including the theories of error offered by Michel Foucault and Bernard Stiegler.

Foucault's brazen acceptance of error colors his Introduction to the work of the biologist Georges Canguilhem (1904–95). "Life is what is capable of error,"[76] Foucault writes, summarizing his insights into Canguilhem's work in establishing a theory of evolution organized through the concepts of failure and mutation. Canguilhem argues that all biology depends on genetic change, which is to say, anomaly and the mistranslation of code. The ongoing capacity for a species' adaptation in order to sustain life is contingent on the capacity for errors to emerge. "Error," Foucault concludes, is "at the root of what makes human thought and its history."[77]

In sum, humanity is perpetually caught between a fallen world of base matter and an intrinsic but unfulfilled desire to go beyond it. Modern philosophers of error no longer viewed it as a shortcoming in the pursuit of a single truth, but rather as this dynamic, nonlinear mode of exploring our complex being-in-the-world.[78] As digital technology progresses, however, simply acknowledging this existential ambivalence is not enough. In our post-industrial climate, we have witnessed how the factory has transformed into an "open concept" workspace, in which machines are responsible for assessing their own shortcomings—independent of and alienated from human contact. We humans are no longer the sole focus or exclusive scapegoat for error, rather, our new social and economic responsibility is not to own error, but to manage it.

VII. FAILURE MANAGEMENT

Managing error extends to humans and machines alike, but by far the greatest "risk-mitigating institution," Adam Davidson argues, was the midcentury corporation.[79] The corporation introduced a safety valve against personal and cultural failures in the postwar era. A steady job meant a company or corporation agreed to pay its employees regularly and provide them with a sense of stability and security. General Motors was the first modern corporation to introduce pensions and retirement accounts, made possible through stricter management. The corporation created a consistent consumer base for its goods, ensuring a win-win for both parties. As individuals learned to capitalize on the buffering system of the corporation, they hedged their bets in entrepreneurial ventures that minimalized chances of work-related accidents or career failures. What the Swiss cheese model is to failure systems engineering, the corporation is to economic safety in midcentury America.

Why, then, did this model fail? For one thing, large corporations tend to view innovation as too risky relative to the stability of products that have already been tested on the market. This conservativism leads to another problem: truly transformative, "game-changing" innovations are far less likely to transpire in a culture prioritizing security and safety over experimentation. During this midcentury moment of "Great Compression," as Davidson calls it, when the wage gap between the rich and poor was at an all-time low,[80] prosperity abounded but experimental R&D budgets were cut and safe bureaucratic order became the name of the game. Innovation dissipated. This is a lesson learned time and again in the annals of the history of technology. The fates of once-experimental think tanks like Bell Laboratories, DuPont, and Xerox in the late 1970s and 1980s are all cases in point.[81] In this ethos, corporate success depends on "safe" and "conservative" ventures, high product turnover, and shareholder profit.

By the late 1960s and early 1970s, another factor came into play. Unstable cycles of innovation and failure were unleashed through the Nixon administration's detachment of the U.S. dollar from the gold standard, resulting in higher risks on the international market. The dramatic abstraction of the U.S. dollar, as David Harvey has shown, earmarked a new age of flexible accumulation characterized by the removal of stable jobs from the labor market, replaced with temp work; less regulated financial markets through the circulation of "fictitious capital"; and a general a shift in employment from manufacturing to service.[82] Furthermore, cheaper and sometimes better products began to emerge from other countries around the world, global trade continued to flourish, and domestic companies, Fred Turner explains, "began to rely on temporary workers" and "project-based labor forms," alongside emergent tendencies to "outsource production, causing massive deindustrialization across states like Michigan, Ohio and Pennsylvania."[83] The innovation-and-failure loop was shortened again, this time from generations to a decade or less. And even so, the greatest challenge to personal and financial security during this time, Davidson argues, came from computers.[84]

Older media paved the way. Long-distance technologies (telegraphs, telephones, railroads, and automobiles) pioneered the abstraction of social life into rationalized systems of economic assessment, from credit exchanges used as standards for measuring progress and success, to the delivery of media and entertainment.[85] In finance, face-to-face encounters, handshakes, and social interaction were supplanted by a credit agency's reductive, binary choices and a project's success or failure was negotiated using the same intangible statistical systems of analysis, blind to context and the nuances of humanness.[86] Where people in agrarian cultures were directly connected to visible phenomena like war, weather, and diaspora, factory and office workers' predominant access to the world was through media screens, reports, and other abstractions. More and more people began to experience the "booms and busts" in personal and economic life as mysterious events with undefined origins. The mass media (cinema, television, magazines, and radio) only exacerbated things by focusing on attention-getting spectacles of crisis, reaffirming a new climate of fear and insecurity.[87]

The introduction of computer automation and network communications in the 1970s not only intensified these abstractions from real world events and face-to-face communications, they also began to replace jobs. As discussed at the outset, because digital machines calculate and analyze numbers in ways far superior to human capacity, their implementation has thus led to an uprooting of professional jobs and related forms of job security. The loss of human jobs to new forms of computer automation was first experienced by those in so-called low-skilled, low-pay jobs, like factory workers and secretaries, or bookkeepers, who had to compete with the machines. Many responded with Luddite-like vitriol, but at the end of the day, they were still rendered powerless. The gamut of professions uprooted by computer automation has since expanded to higher-paid "white-collar" professions from accounting to design, editing, and publishing. As recently summarized on National Public Radio, if your job can be taught to someone else in only a few minutes, chances are it will eventually be replaced by a robot.[88] If so, then who is really managing failure?

If corporations introduced stability and consistent growth in the early and mid-twentieth century, in the last quarter of the century, computers were doing the opposite. Decentralized, flexible computer networks made innovation precarious. Demand now turns on the capacity for ever newer networks like Facebook, Instagram, Uber, or Kickstarter to connect individuals through flexible and decentralized hubs.[89] In high-tech, cycles of innovation and failure spin at astounding speeds, fueled by currently fashionable metrics—from Google stats and big data analysis for brand awareness, to "Influencer" likes, sustainability issues, and vanity platforms (Facebook "likes," YouTube "views," and Twitter "followers"). If cycles of failure and innovation in the twentieth century could be measured in decades,[90] in the current era of hyper-accelerated media, Davidson notes, many entrepreneurs will work years to face a product lifespan as short as a season.[91] The internet aids in the acceleration of these cycles in everything from policy, law, and health care, to self-care and international relations. Widespread economic and political volatility ensure heightening forms of mass fear, anxiety, and a lack of confidence in oneself and one's job, or what used to be called a career. As soon as a product or company is no longer valued in the marketplace, thousands of workers may potentially be laid off, raising unemployment, divorce rates, and forcing unwanted moves and career stagnation. In a culture that defines success through economic prosperity, but eliminates the circumstances for achieving it, we are all "born losers."[92]

VIII. CONCLUSIONS: FAILURE IS HERE TO STAY

In summary, two general models of progress fueled changing conceptions of error in the history of Western philosophy and modern industry. In the late eighteenth century, the development of radically improved machinery for factories coincided with the diffusion of Enlightenment notions of history as a record of progress.[93] Here, science and technology were seen in the service of liberation from political oppression. In the late nineteenth and early twentieth centuries, this changed. In the modern notion of progress, improvement and innovation were intrinsically linked to technology again and the Enlightenment values of justice, freedom, harmony, and self-fulfillment become secondary to technocratic ends. As the technological model of progress severed connections to holistic registers of life and being, it landed us in a new pseudo-scientific practice of measuring (things and ourselves) as indications of value and success. Put differently, improvements in power, efficiency, and rationality become ends in themselves, typified by figures like John D. Rockefeller, Andrew Carnegie, Thomas Edison, Frederick Winslow Taylor, and Henry Ford.[94]

Henry Adams, Thorstein Veblen, and a host of others objected that this means-ends industrial model fell short when imposed on actual life and practice. Taylor's theory of scientific management, Leo Marx observes, "embodies the quintessence of the technocratic mentality" and "'the idea,'" he continues, quoting the economic historian Hugh G. J. Aitken, "'that human activity could be measured, analyzed, and controlled by techniques analogous to those . . . applied to physical objects.'"[95] Inevitably, such idealized mechanisms fell asunder when applied to the eternally forgetful and accident-prone human being.

Unsurprisingly, we now find ourselves inundated with human *and* machine failure. Lauren Berlant offers a valuable critique of the prevalence of failure in the present, articulated through her concept of "cruel optimism." Since the 1990s, she argues, optimism has held "less and less traction in the world." There is less professional and personal success, but conversely, more desire for it.[96] We cling to fantasies of what it means to be happy, but the reality of acquiring it is increasingly scarce. This defines the condition of cruel optimism, experienced when the "thing that you desire is actually a problem in terms of its practical attainment." This is life as usual for an increasing number of Americans (and people around the world) and yet, Berlant observes, a remarkable number of people, institutions, and public bodies fail to see it, clinging to anachronistic visions of freedom and the American dream. For Berlant, Davidson, myself, and many others, failure is no longer an exception but the norm. Can we accept this as the starting point for life in the years to come, and learn how to "fail again" and "fail better," as Samuel Beckett once suggested?[97] Could doing so somehow appease our relentless appetite for material "success" and force a reconsideration of our personal and cultural values?

The next five chapters offer answers from experimental media art, beginning with chapter 2's analysis of error and noise in the twentieth-century avant-garde. Here, we see an active embrace of error (rather than its rapid denial) as the condition of possibility for the progeny of media art histories.

2

———

Avant-Garde Glitch

Red Noise, Purple Haze, Black Box

What does it say about the present that our visual media actively mobilize so much multivalent dissonance in the form of polychromatic noise and digital artifacts? These are not the classic principles of visual communication—optical precision, linear perspective, and proportional balance—but fragments of sensory chaos otherwise pushed aside because they offer nothing but raw and immediate affect. If such acts of anti-communication are political or pedagogical, then what kinds of things do glitch, noise, and colored distortion mark in our historical moment, and why would a creative producer be driven to use state-of-the-art technologies only to negate their capacity to reproduce verisimilitude?

Glitch and noise are well established techniques in the avant-garde. Throughout the twentieth century, scratching, desaturation, illegibility, and broken materials were used to mark something askew in psychic and social registers. Such anti-communicative strategies were quickly rationalized into mainstream cultural styles. This was the fate of the avant-garde from Dada and Surrealism, to the experimental cinema of the 1960s, through glitch art today. What has not yet been given proper scholarly attention, however, is the way in which twenty-first century acts of visual discord symbolize broader economic, psychic, and environmental failures, generating a registry of unrequited longing in the age of information. This chapter considers an archaeology of glitch art precursors in key selections from the twentieth-century avant-gardes.

As noted in the Introduction, approaches to error and noise are treated differently in industry and Western philosophy than they are in the creative worlds of art and design. Chapter 1 provided a philosophical and cultural history of error.

48

This chapter examines the opposite: its brazen acceptance, and in some cases, active pursuit. This is especially true in the avant-garde, where error is required to maintain the field's expansion through time. As John Roberts notes, art must continually remake itself by transgressing its own preestablished rules and conventions.[1] Accordingly, in what I here call "glitch art history," I employ the lens of "abstraction" to connect contemporary gestures of anti-communication to a longer history of the avant-garde. Defined as the defamiliarization of immediately recognizable things, forms, or figures, abstraction employs fragments of color and line to undermine expectations of accurately rendered visual forms. Pioneer abstract artists include Wassily Kandinsky through Rothko and Jackson Pollock. In a sense, all modern abstraction could be construed as proto-glitch, and to some extent this is precisely the chapter's thesis. Both modern abstraction and glitch art involve the defamiliarization of normative viewing experiences. But to what degree is total abstraction (Kandinsky, Rothko, Pollock, Mondrian) helpful in glitch art's challenges to media culture? Not much, I argue when I return to this question in chapters 4 and 5. For now, the chapter considers this legacy through a genealogy of medium specific abstractions. I consider how noisy, low-resolution or, "poor images," as Hito Steyerl terms them,[2] have a natural tendency to "abstraction," therein aligning contemporary glitch with visual art's wider history.

Section I, "Red Noise," addresses abstraction and fragmentation in early twentieth century art, including Arnold Schoenberg's *The Red Gaze* (1910) and Fernand Léger's neglected machine aesthetics in his and Dudley Murphy's *Ballet Mécanique* (1924). Section II, "Purple Haze," addresses the lo-fi hum of electronic media saturating the 1960s and early 1970s. If mechanical art invokes red-hot metaphors of iron, steel, and the vibrant rhythms of the industrial age, electronic art lands us in a purple haze of cool synthetics. Section III, "Black Boxes," positions glitch art in the computer age, where glitches become less visible as code, but increasingly insidious, often only detected by way of the spectral colors glitch artists use to bring them forth on screen.[3] In sum, the chapter offers an aesthetic critique and material archaeology of glitch art that moves across media genres. The interdisciplinary mapping of glitch aesthetics here in no way satisfies the disciplinary demands of art history, just as chapter 1 makes no such claims vis-à-vis traditional philosophy.[4]

II. RED NOISE

Red is the fiercest of the twelve hues in the standard color circle. In contrast to other colors, it hits the eye first and incites immediate, physiological responses hard-wired in our bodies through thousands of years of evolutionary biology.[5] In Western culture, red is associated with danger and fear, especially of the feminine; blood; murder; violence; and the explosive ecstasy of being. Red is also the most challenging color to reproduce in print and electronic form. Due to its intensity, it easily leaks or "bleeds" across borders and edges. As a result, red pigments and lighting require higher levels of engineering, making them costlier and more difficult to work with. This is also one of the reasons video tends to look more greenish. In science, red is affiliated with high frequencies, like infrared radiation or long-wave electromagnetic spectral energy. Long-wave light energy travels far, but cycles slowly, making it useful in devices from remote controls to military weapons ranging from lasers to automatic rifles.[6] The midcentury Canadian media theorist Marshall McLuhan describes "hot media" as a media technology that traveled outward to an audience in (what was then perceived to be) high definition, like radio, film, or the hustle and bustle of industrial life in the early modern city. The perceived "hotness" of these media, like an F-sharp, is ex-static and unequivocally red; aggressively pushing out from its material substrate towards a presumably more passive viewer or recipient. In music, red translates into "top" notes like F-sharp. I picture the sound of red like the cut of a rusty knife. All of the above figure in my concept of "red noise," beginning with the edgy abstract art that emerged in Europe in the interwar period.

The Red Gaze

Disruptive circumstances engender disruptive action. In Paul Virilio's account, during World War I, "two men face off" at the mouth of the Somme river in northern France circa 1914. They are Georges Braque and Otto Dix, the "same two men who later brought us . . . the fractured collages of Cubism" and the broken tones of German expressionism.[7] By extending this correlation between war and expression, this section articulates how the quality of red noise corresponds with this moment of cultural breakdown.

Early twentieth-century expressionism aimed to reject both the harmonies of nineteenth-century impressionism and naturalism's mimesis of nature, taking up instead a *discord* between expression and experience.[8] A prime example is Arnold Schoenberg's *The Red Gaze* (1910), a close-up painting of a man's face.[9] The side of the subject's skull is blurred by browns and yellows that fade off into the background while hollowed-out, reddened eye cavities and yellow pupils convey a mix of horror and ghostliness. Thomas Harrison argues that the eyes, masked in haunted shadow, seem to be on the brink of disappearing as the pupils reflect illness and bloodshed, premonitory of the impending horrors of World War I. In contrast to classical painting, which attempts to resolve opposing tensions through higher unities and formal symbolism, *The Red Gaze,* like other works of its time, uses abstraction to articulate a state of perpetual struggle; a dynamic and irresolvable tension akin to red-hot noise. Harrison also suggests that the *Red Gaze* is a visualization of Schoenberg's "emancipation of dissonance," a term the composer proposes in his 1911 *Theory of Harmony,* denoting the *willful* disruption of harmonic order. If consonance is the pleasing resolution of clashing tones, dissonance, he argues, is the opposite: the willful disruption of harmonic order.[10] Consonance, for Schoenberg, avoids movement as it fails to "take up the search," settling for

FIGURE 8. Otto Dix, *Kriegskrüppel* (*War Cripples*) (1920). According to Paul Virilio, Dix's troubled broken-line aesthetic reflects his World War I experience. © Estate of Otto Dix / SOCAN (2019).

what is already given and expected. In contrast, his theory of atonal composition proposes that changing melody and harmony into a formal language bereft of tonal resolution or (classical) consonance allows for sustained dissonance, that is, noise, in sonic or visual form. In *The Red Gaze*, this takes the form of blurred colors, indistinct shapes, hollowed-out and uncertain eyes, and a vacant subjectivity. In this way, Schoenberg's dissonance also speaks to a much broader fragmentation in modern life and subjectivity. The distressed red eyes, presumed to have witnessed a "battle-torn world," personify a cultural condition of atonal, dissonant being, visualized through a "death-like vacuity."[11]

Beyond war, the rapidly changing conditions of modernity introduced unforeseen forms of noise and confusion on the canvas. This is illustrated throughout early modern painting, and most notably, the work of Die Brücke and expressionists Richard Gerstl, Oskar Kokoschka, Egon Schiele, and Carlo Michelstaedter. Edvard Munch's *The Scream* (1893) has personified modern psychosis for over a century.[12] Wassily Kandinsky's work offers a milder form of visual noise, meticulously depicting modernity's chaos and fragmentations through soft colors and gentle abstractions. After attending one of Schoenberg's concerts in 1911, Kandinsky was inspired to break from the representative constrictions of visual art and "liberate" the signifying possibilities of painting from the depiction of the so-called objective world.[13] Despite associations with Gestalt, Kandinsky deploys line and color

FIGURE 9. Arnold Schoenberg, *Der rote Blick* (*The Red Gaze*) (1910). Close-up of a man's face with red, hollow eye cavities. The sides of his skull fade into an ambiguous background. © Estate of Arnold Schoenberg / SOCAN (2019).

in "atonal" ways, creating jagged, linear vectors that cut across rounded shapes, or alternatively, patches of primary and secondary colors combined in ways formerly considered disharmonious. Kandinsky describes his approach as a series of "clashing discords, loss of equilibrium, principles overthrown, unexpected drumbeats, great questionings, apparently purposeless strivings, stress and longing . . . opposites and contradictions."[14] He juxtaposes shape and color to reflect a fundamental gap in his culture's ontology, a red-hot break between subject and object, spirit and matter.[15] What Schoenberg did for music, Kandinsky did for painting.

Other noteworthy examples of red-hot visual noise in modern painting and sculpture include Giacomo Balla's *Dynamism of a Dog on Leash* (1912); Carlo Carrà's *The Red Horsemen* (1913); Juan Gris's *Man in a Café* (1912); Umberto Boccioni's sculpture *Unique Forms of Continuity* (1913); and Marcel Duchamp's *Nude Descending a Staircase No. 2* (1912) and *The Bride Stripped Bare by Her Bachelors, Even* (1915–23), because of the prominence of broken glass in its final state. All of these works illustrate dissonance and visual noise by deliberately using abstraction to depict a "great inner unrest" in the zeitgeist or, as Wilhelm Worringer puts it, "an awareness of temporality, contingency, and . . . state of abject terror."[16] Their gestures mark literal breakage and foreground it on the canvas, resulting in a double breakage: a literal rupture and noisy abstraction seen by a viewer, coupled with an uprooting of aesthetic tradition, where, as noted, the deliberate use of misalignments and "incorrect" renderings do not result in actual failure, but rather, in the discipline's longevity.

The Art of Noise

As noted, the modern spirit of fragmentation was largely inspired by music. The futurists celebrated dissonance and atonal aesthetics in their "Art of Noises." The Italian futurist Luigi Russolo actively engaged noise as a kind of music, utilizing his "intonarumori" (noise intonator) machines and accompanying 1913 manifesto, *The Art of Noises,* in which he argued, noise not only counts as an art form but is in fact aesthetically pleasing.[17] "Let's walk together through a great modern capital . . . we will vary the pleasures of our sensibilities by distinguishing among the gurglings of water, air and gas inside metallic pipes, the rumblings and rattlings of engines breathing with obvious animal spirits, the rising and falling of pistons, the stridency of mechanical saws," Russolo wrote to F. T. Marinetti in 1909.[18]

Russolo's desire to orchestrate the eccentric sounds of military and industrial life characterize this avant-garde's heated zest, complemented by the punchy, abrasive rhythm of the machines he used. As I argued in chapter 1, noise has always been fundamental to life; it is simply that the kind and quality of it changes over time, retroactively constituting what we call a culture's aesthetic. Schoenberg and his contemporaries recognized this in mechanical fragmentation and introduced themes of dissonance and declension in visual art and music. Russolo and his colleagues did the same using industrial-era machines, as did Fernand Léger in cinema.

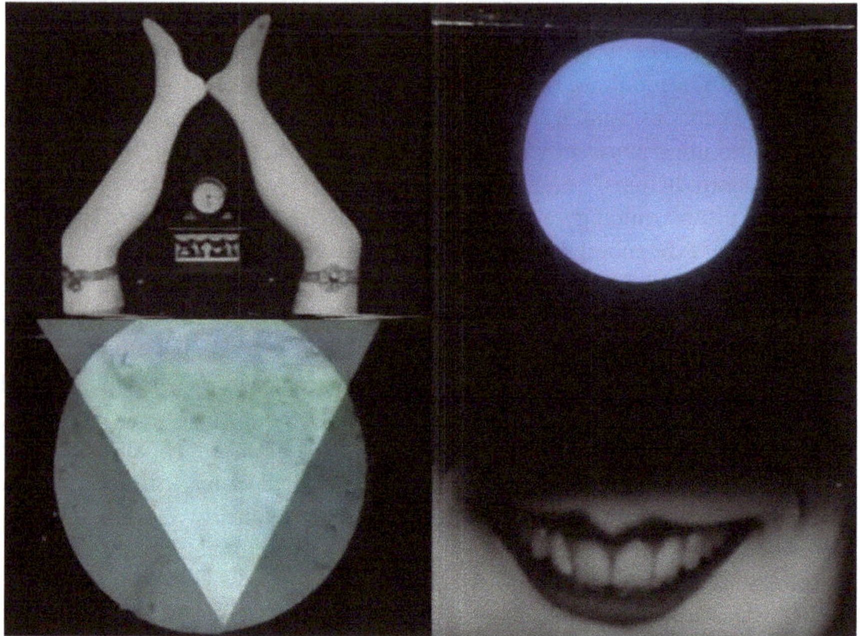

FIGURE 10. Fernand Léger and Dudley Murphy, *Ballet Mécanique* (1924). 35mm film, black and white, silent, 12 minutes. Stills. © Estate of Fernand Léger / SOCAN (2019)

Machine Aesthetics as Proto-Glitch

Machine-era fragmentation could not be more central to cinematic aesthetics. Not only is cinema itself a fragmented technology of rapidly moving twenty-four images per second, it also engenders a new set of distorted visual techniques ranging from scratching, burning, dodging, overexposure, and other uncommon and, at first, non–commercially viable "noisy" effects. Perhaps the most effective technique of fragmentation is montage. Because we are largely desensitized to montage cuts today, it is difficult to imagine what it must have been like to watch the eloquent but radical montage sequences in an original screening of *Battleship Potemkin*. For this reason, turning to a non-narrative, experimental example of early montage helps us to re-render the disjunctive power of early cinematic perception back into the foreground. Many examples could be used to illustrate how montage figured as a proto-glitch aesthetic. Fernand Léger and Dudley Murphy's nineteen-minute avant-garde film *Ballet Mécanique* (1924) offers a particularly interesting case, not only of montage, abstraction, and compositing but also, a stylized human-machine aesthetic.[19]

Created with the composer George Antheil, visual artist Man Ray, and co-directed with Dudley Murphy, Léger's *Ballet Mécanique* consists of a series of black and white images of machine parts mixed with close-ups of a woman's lipstick, decapitated legs, cars, carnival rides, pistons, mass-produced crockery, and other industrial phenomena, animated into a chatty, upbeat montage. The film begins with an allusion to classicism (the ballet, a young—non-decapitated—lady in a swing), but the pace is quickly overtaken by punchy cuts, resulting in a dynamic rhythm—an "innervation," as Walter Benjamin terms it—between viewer and medium. The montage style is far from subtle or nostalgic; a hot fragmentation imbued with a machine-age optimism. If classical ballet and portraiture were concerned with preserving the preciousness of organic forms and lines, the machine-age aesthetic devours it with a voracious appetite for speed.[20]

Among other works of its time, *Ballet Mécanique* introduced new techniques of discord and broken visuals, rooted in abstraction, compositing, and accelerated editing and montage. The stuttering, frenetic language, speaks to the red-hot changes of early to mid-twentieth-century life wherein a new kind of beauty was to be found in the "convulsiveness" of the industrial or, "not at all," as surrealist André Breton put it in his pivotal novel *Nadja* (1928).[21] Mass fears of failure in the face of a new generation of machines, as discussed in chapter 1, were creatively reconceived as the gateway to the new century's aesthetic.

Junk Art

Across the Atlantic, Jasper Johns and Ed Kienholz were fascinated by found objects, debris, and junk as the raw materials for creating visual noise. "Junk art" became popular in the 1950s and 1960s, especially in the New York School, exemplified by the American sculptor John Chamberlain, construed here as a proto-glitch artist insofar as he built his career by recycling trash into colorful sculptures. Chamberlain created his sculptures by crushing automobile body parts and then reconfiguring and repainting them into visual abstractions.[22] Noteworthy European precursors include the techno-assemblages developed by the Swiss sculptor Jean Tinguely, the cybernetic artist Nicolas Schöffer, and more recently, a whole host of "zombie media" artists and practitioners.[23] Tinguely, French American artist Arman (Armand Fernandez), and *affichiste* Jacques Villeglé incorporated urban debris into their art. In London, Gustav Metzger included destructive random noises and degraded machine objects.

"Auto-Destructive Art," Metzger argued in his 1959 manifesto of the same name, is "a form of public art for industrial societies." Despite its emphasis on breakdown, it is conceived of as a "total art," unifying broader, disintegrative processes. His *Liquid Crystal Environment* (1965), for example, embodies this concept using heat-sensitive liquid crystals placed between glass slides and inserted into projectors. The slides are then rotated to create movement within the liquid and as the crystals heat up and cool down, their luminous colors shift accordingly. The abstract patterns produced in each slide are then projected onto screens in the

FIGURE 11. Gerhard Richter, *Familie nach Altem Meister* (*Family after Old Master*) (1965). © Gerhard Richter 2018.

exhibition space, coordinated by a computer program, highlighting the mirrored relationship between chaotic destruction and random regrowth. Metzger was also key to the Destruction in Art Symposium (DIAS) held in London in 1966, a conference that bolstered growing interest in aesthetic destruction and noise.[24]

German artist Gerhard Richter can also be viewed as a proto-glitch artist, though he did not work with hardware or broken machine parts. Richter's paintings often display such visual artifacts as blurs, overexposures, or high-contrast obfuscation. *Familie nach Altem Meister* (*Family after Old Master*, 1965), for instance, alludes to traditional portraiture while obfuscating its depicted referent through a heavily blurred image and dulled "authorial" brush, a technique the artist is well known for. Imperfection, transience, and incompleteness, for Richter, are natural and given characteristics of memory and experience, and thus, his goal, according to the artist, is to make "everything equally important and equally

FIGURE 12. Bruce Conner, *Breakaway* (1966). 16mm film stills.

unimportant."[25] Relative to the prevalence of blurs and glitches in contemporary media, his aesthetic may seem mundane but, fifty years prior, these ambiguous hazes eccentrically called attention to our always already mediated and imperfect acts of perception.[26]

Postwar Glitch

Experimental art and cinema thrived in the postwar era, much of it through the legacy of fragmentation and glitch charted above, albeit in a more conceptual fashion. Both Nam June Paik's *Zen for Film* (1962–64) and Aldo Tambellini's *Black Films* (1965–67) used clear leader as their "content." The former's *One for Violin Solo* (1962) also invoked noise and destruction as a violin was slowly lifted over the artist's head, held still for a long time, and then crashed down on a table. George Maciunas's *Fluxfilm No. 7: 10 Feet* (1966) projects ten feet of blank film, "with no camera" on the screen, and Andy Warhol, in his first use of film in 1963, intentionally allowed light to leak into some of the unprocessed film by not completely closing the viewfinder of his 16mm Bolex camera.[27] Generally speaking, this postwar expanded cinema prioritized techniques otherwise seen as industry or commercial failures: scratching, dying, hand painting, pure color fields, and especially, hyperaccelerated animations that challenge the viewer's relationship to the medium.[28]

Drawing on the human-machine motif noted above, Bruce Conner's 16mm epic *Breakaway* (1966) presents an upbeat version of mechanized human-machine choreography, also in montage style. With music by Ed Cobb and dance and vocals by Toni Basil (Antonia Christina Basilotta), the five-minute film captures Basil's exuberant moves contained in a highly contrasted, small, dark space. Conner shot the film at single frame exposures as well as 8, 16, 24 and 36 frames per second, and then rhythmically interspersed sections of black leader with sections of Basil's jumps. The result is a frantic but celebratory embrace of cinematic movement, as a hybrid human-machine system. Two-and-a-half minutes through, the image and sound are reversed. The human spirit does not fall under the machine's weight and unexpected inversion, but rather grows refreshingly hotter and more vibrant. Like the above-noted examples, Conner's *Breakaway* uses the materiality of the medium to produce glitches and stutters in cinematic experience, often creating a sustained and irresolvable noise at the edges of this technology's human-machine capacities. Essentially, many avant-garde works could be cited as precursors to what has become the rapid pace of an MTV and now internet video aesthetic.[29] I have, however, only highlighted those that explicitly call attention to limits of the medium through either material disruption or destruction of viewer experience (the literal *and* psychological glitch).[30]

III. A SEGUE THROUGH CONCEPTUAL BLUE

Claude Shannon's pioneering work on the relationship between signal and noise (see chapter 1) was increasingly popular among experimental artists and musicians after World War II. In music, his influence emerged in the experimental compositions of John Cage, Erik Satie, Edgard Varèse, Karlheinz Stockhausen, and Pierre Boulez (Boulez was also inspired by Russolo and Pierre Schaeffer's adoption of the latter's techniques), whose 1948 broadcast, "Concert of Noises," for example, consisted entirely of recordings of train whistles, spinning tops, pots and pans, canal boats, and percussion instruments. Schaeffer's work also helped pave the way for *Musique concrète,* a genre defined by its inclusion of multiple source materials, including synthetically produced electronic noise, found noise, and almost any nontraditional sonic form.[31]

The work of John Cage was largely informed by that of his teacher, Arnold Schoenberg, who, as noted above, systematically broke with harmony, melody, and the "teleological implications of tonality." Cage, born in Los Angeles in 1912, developed his own method of avoiding classical attributes and devoted a number of performance pieces to support the notion that noise exists in silence. By 1938, he turned to the principles of chance and randomness to explore the capacity for any and all noise in a sound environment to structure the "content" of a work, most famously translated in *4'33"* (1952–53).[32]

4'33" was composed for any instrument. It was first performed by David Tudor in 1953 in Woodstock, New York, where Tudor sat at the piano and did nothing but acknowledge the beginning and end of the composition's 4 minutes and 33 seconds. At the end of the demarcated time, he closed the piano's lid. The "content" was the random noise and movements in the space, everything but typical sounds from a piano. The piece was inspired by Robert Rauschenberg's *White Paintings* (1951), created under an apprenticeship with the colorist Josef Albers.[33] The *Paintings* consist of seven large, white, oil-painted panels that act as "hypersensitive" mechanisms, absorbing and reflecting the surrounding light, dust, and shadows wherever they are installed. In this way, the pure white is "dirtied," not by gestural abstraction, but by the dust and shadows of the world that houses them, resulting in a series of paintings with constantly changing, marginally visible, content. This is also why Cage refers to Rauschenberg's blank white panels as "landing strips" that must await actualization by a spectator.[34]

The pieces by Cage and Rauschenberg both enact a dematerialization of authorial concepts, lending themselves to another register of failure: the pseudo-renunciation of the artist-genius's control of the creative process. By introducing randomness and chance, they seemingly relinquish personal touch and put the onus of the work on the viewer and the context of viewing. In this, we find evidence of this generation's exhaustion with the older artist-genius paradigm, and an interest instead in motifs in chance, error, and the aleatory noise of the computer age. John Roberts argues that postwar art is in many ways defined by this reversal of the conventional relationship between control and chaos; and errancy and truth, or simply, the failure of the myth of the artist as sole author of a work.

This new breed of conceptually minded, rational artists, drew on the structural logic of computer programing to redefine postwar artmaking as anonymous, desubjectified "research" into open "systems" and flexible "communication networks." Oddly, Roberts also argues that the best example of this is found in Jackson Pollock's paintings, which result from a seemingly arbitrary splattering of paint across the canvas. Pollock's genius, he maintains, was his avoidance of identification with the expressed self or any stable sign-making attributes. Through the "delirious signs" of his aleatory lines, he articulates a chaos that is both personal and anonymous, universal and indecipherable. An artist needed to be out of control to be in control, Roberts explains, or at least present the veneer of the former.[35] The same is the case, as we will see, with issues of control and chaos in digital glitch art. In sum, in the postwar era, there is a cooling down of red noise, pacified by a brave new world of level-headed analytic humans and machines.

IV. PURPLE HAZE

The disintegration of the historic avant-garde and myth of the genius artist occurred alongside the rise of mass advertising and eventually, the popularization of personal computers. As a result, the 1960s were colored by the lo-fi hum of electric guitars, color television, pastel colored cars, appliances, and other buzzing devices set to the 60 Hz standard.[36] The piercing red F-sharp morphed into a cool B-flat. The new concept-driven artist, influenced by Cage and a new culture of computer programming, was only responsible for "setting up" a system, as Rauschenberg put it in 1965, and after that, "chance deals with the unexpected and the unplanned." Roberts argues that this systematic destruction of nonpositivistic reason reflects Western capitalism's progressive assimilation of modern art.[37] This may be true early on, as suggested above, but by the end of the 1960s, the avant-garde's driving logic seems to have dissipated into an electro-psychedelic mysticism. In this section, I analyze the purple haze characteristic of glitch in this style of postwar experimental media art.

With the introduction of electronic audio synthesizers in the 1950s and 1960s, additional forms of sonic experimentation emerged through the work of pioneers like Reed Ghazala, considered the "father of circuit bending." Ghazala observed how shorted-out amplifiers emitted a series of "synth" sounds, which he began to reproduce in his work. An iconic example is his short-circuiting of the *Speak & Spell* toy, rewired to bring about a disconcerting robotic voice.[38] Artists have since explored related sonic qualities by modulating everything from children's electronic toys, to using existing equipment in unanticipated ways and building sound instruments from household items. Also in the 1960s, synthetic sounds were adopted in noise rock and linked to pop through guitar-based electronic distortion.[39]

Purple haze colored the culture's aesthetic of noise by centering on two core effects: feedback and distortion. Both are connected to a noisy signal passing through a sound circuit. The former involves the back-coupling and perpetual rerouting of a signal through the same circuit and is one of the core principles of cybernetics established by Norbert Wiener, largely influential to Shannon (discussed in chapter 1). The second, distortion, involves small pick-ups on the guitar that react to the sound of an amplifier in what was at first a "distortion" of normative, clear sound but, in noise rock, quickly stylized as a trademark of the genre. One of the first deliberate uses of these effects can be traced back to Link Wray's "Rumble" (1958), but ultimately, Torben Sangild argues, it was garage bands like The Kingsmen, The Kinks, The Who,[40] and, of course, master of purple haze, Jimi Hendrix who "constructed a whole catalogue" of virtuous noise effects through his "blues-inspired rock compositions." Such techniques track the cultural moment when noise and fray were just that: noise, with no convention or established meaning. Today, such noise is merely cliché; definitive of the genre's most standard aesthetic.[41]

Corresponding visual noise saturated Nam June Paik's 1960s electro-cybernetic video art. Like Cage before him, Paik was heavily influenced by Schoenberg. After studying music, art, and history at the University of Tokyo in the 1950s, Paik wrote his thesis on Schoenberg and several years later, moved to New York to join the downtown avant-garde. Because I have discussed Paik's work at length elsewhere,[42] suffice it to note here that his style is marked by abstract, electronic glitches that consistently catch viewers off-guard. Classic examples include *Magnet TV* (1965), which consists of a cathode ray tube (CRT) television with a magnet on top. The magnet is powerful enough to draw and detract the high-speed electronic phosphors shooting through the electronic gun, actively deforming the "normal" broadcast image into colorful traces and abstract patterns.[43] *Magnet TV* is an example of visual abstraction void of signal or signification. Pure noise as pure medium.

Made in collaboration with Jud Yalkut,[44] Paik's *Beatles Electroniques* (1966–69) involves the manipulation of pop icons and images from mainstream culture. In this three-minute piece, Paik and Yalkut use a magnet to disrupt the black-and-white video footage of a television broadcast of the Beatles' *A Hard Day's Night* (1964), produced during a series of experiments taping the monitor of a Sony videotape recorder. The accompanying soundtrack by Kenneth Lerner—originally called "Four Loops" because it derived from four electronically altered loops of Beatles' sound material—complements the repetitively discordant abstractions. As black-and-white images of John Lennon and the Beatles were processed through numerous synthesizers, the figures and sounds were simultaneously engulfed in a cool blue ooze. Where Léger's *Ballet* juxtaposed the human and machine in an upbeat, jazz-age rhythm, Paik's electronic-era glitches imploded distinctions between the human and machine through infinite cybernetic feedback loops.

Two other pivotal, proto-glitch electronic artists are Steina and Woody Vasulka, who, like Paik, were the "first of a generation to 'open the box.'" Their work explores the material noise of the video medium, sometimes in the images, at others times by literally "ripping apart pre-set commercial, manufactured media systems."[45] Joan Jonas's *Vertical Roll* (1972) and Mary Lucier's *Dawn Burn* (1975) and *Bird's Eye* (1978) offer three other examples. *Vertical Roll* is a video-performance piece including mirrors, masks, and the intentional offsetting of the vertical blanking signal on the analog video camera. Using a metal spoon to bang on the head of a microphone, Jonas uses sound and image to depict a misalignment between self and mediated subjectivity.[46] Mary Lucier's *Dawn Burn* and *Bird's Eye* provide empirical records of the distorted optical effects of light burned directly on the video camera's "eye." For the former, Lucier aimed the camera's lens directly at the sun, burning the camera's vidicon tube in real time and inscribing it with calligraphic abstractions of light. In *Bird's Eye*, she aimed a laser directly at the camera lens, producing an analogous but visually distinct effect. The result is just over ten minutes of a single concentrated light, occasionally split and bent through various kinds of distortion. The rhythm is slow and soothing but, when coupled with a relatively high-pitched electronic noise running throughout the soundtrack, a tension is created between the seemingly alien perspective and a familiar noisy light.[47]

In sum, relative to the chatty red noise circa 1910, purple haze is cool and cognitively distant. Delivered through the nascent rhetoric of a "global village" and visionary theories of mediated cosmological connectivity, this avant-garde witnessed one last burst of color, just in time for its obfuscation in the dark age of so-called transparent digital media.

V. BLACK BOX BREAKDOWN

Now that digital computing has been around for over half a century, the postwar metaphor of the black box may seem outdated, especially in lieu of our prosaic candy-colored (1990s) and metallic-toned (2000s) computers. The trope is nonetheless invoked here as a rhetorical device to signal the gap between code and interface underpinning all digital media. The distinctness of the color metaphor (versus the red and purple glitches that precede it) also allows us to demarcate how digital glitch aesthetics are materially and symbolically distinct from their precursors. Namely, where prior media glitches involved a hands-on hacking of a canvas or media platform, in digital media, we necessarily move to a systems-level glitch where visual noise can, typically, only be generated by way of manipulating nonvisible, abstract code. Put differently, the black box creates a boundary around the media that prevents it from receiving a direct inscription on its material substrate, as analog glitches (painting, photography, film, and television) could. The vast majority of digital glitch art demands intervention on the level of abstract code. In this sense, a digital artist is not an artist at all but rather, a programmer.[48]

Net Art

One early example of digital glitch art comes from the pioneering genre of "net art," formed by an early generation of artists who experimented with the internet and computer media in the 1990s. As defined in the Introduction, glitch art is the deliberate aestheticization of what is otherwise deemed to be an error in digital processing. For hackers, net artists, and glitchers, however, these otherwise unwanted phenomena are valued as raw material for art making.[49] The net art duo JODI—Joan Heemskerk and Dirk Paesmans—have made deliberately glitchy, error-prone net art in the Netherlands since 1994. After attending Silicon Valley's electronic arts laboratory CADRE at San Jose State University in California (Paesmans also studied with Nam June Paik at the Kunstakademie in Düsseldorf), they turned away from industry to nonprofit new media art. Like Léger, Duchamp, Dada, and Paik before them, Heemskerk and Paesmans are remix artists. But rather than mash-up music and television clips, or juxtapose magazine images and typography, JODI appropriates code from HTML, the Mac OS, hexadecimal values, and various other forms of computational data. Like much new media art, JODI's work exists in between the luminous screen and the code that generates it. Using the logic of the otherwise obfuscated "backend" code, JODI foregrounds nonsensible hacks and computer glitches, setting the tone for newer generations of digital artists. I analyze two of JODI's works here: *My%Desktop* (2002–10) and *All Wrongs Reversed © 1982* (2004).[50]

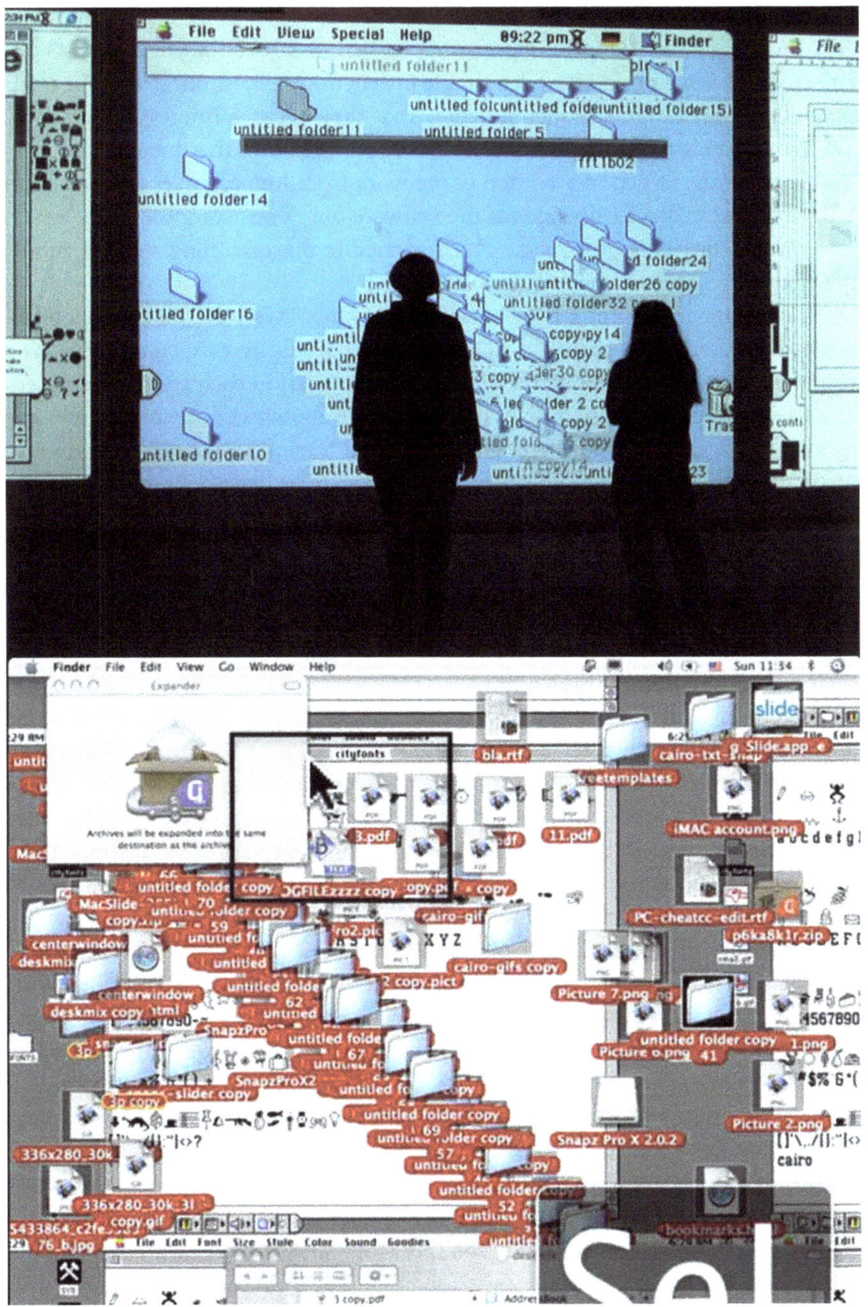

FIGURE 13. Jodi, *My%Desktop*, OS 10.4 2 c (2002–10). A user launches a website that results in the appearance of out-of-control errors.

My%Desktop was the centerpiece of JODI's first American exhibition, "INSTALL.EXE." In the spirit of postwar, post-authorial art, the piece consists of a large four-channel projection with simple instructions: play around with the icons on a computer desktop to such a degree that they become interesting to watch. The result yields a chaotic desktop-as-movie performance that incites confusion and fascination. To access a version of the work from home, a user enters a given URL that automatically downloads the software onto one's computer, after which "everything start[s] to go wrong. . . . If you tried to do something about it, it only got worse."[51]

Numerous viewers took issue with *My%Desktop*. "We were punished a number of times for that website . . . the host server would receive complaints. As a result, we had to move the website to a different location each time," Heemskerk and Paesmans explain. Their Brechtian maneuver operates in much the same way as the avant-gardes before them: errors are used to rupture a user's unconscious assumption about viewing and consuming media. Their dysfunctional glitch effectively functions in the form of discord, just as Godard's jump cut once did in the French New Wave, or Léger's cuts did in his early cinematic montage sequences. The fact that many viewers, especially students, find this piece frustrating attests to its effectiveness as glitch art. Years after its initial release, JODI still receives "emails with corrections and pitiful remarks from their audience concerning 'mistakes' in their work," Josephine Bosma notes.

Peter Weibel, director of the ZKM Center for Art and Media in Karlsruhe, even approached the artists after a presentation of the work to inquire, "What went wrong"? Paesmans explains the set-up prompting Weibel's inquiry: "[*My%Desktop*] took a picture of your desktop, which was then manipulated into different variants. If you tried to stop it, it would take you to a different variant each time. There was, however, no real manipulation of the computer at a deeper level."[52] In short, *My%Desktop* is only a simulation of the OS's breakdown, used to create the illusion of failure. If one presses "Command-Q" to quit the piece, the chaos ceases and the artwork shuts down, as with any other software application.[53] By toying with culturally conditioned responses to technical glitches, *My%Desktop* stages our human-computer anxieties while remaining under tight control.

Jon Satrom's 2010 witty remake of *My%Desktop, Windows Rainbows & Dinos* is a thirteen-minute single-channel work presented as a comedic-video drama about OS malfunctions that take place entirely on a Macintosh desktop. The piece is more entertaining than *My%Desktop*, primarily because it caters to an eye-candy spectacle and fails to post any real danger, whether actual or illusionary. Similarly, JODI's *All Wrongs Reversed © 1982* (2004) is a forty-five-minute performance piece involving a vintage ZX Sinclair Spectrum computer from the 1980s, using BASIC programming language. In the performance, one sees streams of seemingly nonsensical data, numbers, counters, and hexadecimal code running on screen without a foreseeable end.[54]

For this pioneering generation of net artists, the *work* of the digital artwork was to articulate the constantly shifting relationship between code and interface. N. Katherine Hayles refers to this relationship as a series of "flickering signifiers,"[55] implying both terms are unstable but inextricably bound.[56] Another way to describe the strange relationship between screen signal and abstract, numerical code is to consider that code is only readable by machines, not humans. We may read and write code, Friedrich Kittler argues, but regardless, it is mostly incomprehensible, having been "encrusted" with layers of architecture that render it inaccessible.[57] In other words, code *shouldn't* make sense to most of us. We shouldn't be able to see or read the back end of the system as it boots up. This code is not meant to be visualized as an image in and of itself, but by doing so in *All Wrongs Reversed*, JODI calls attention to this relationship by inverting the "two-tiered" structure between the code and the interface conditioning all digital media.[58] Much early net art had this basic task in mind.[59]

We are now three decades from these humble "net art" origins and significant transformations in digital media aesthetics have been under way. Glitch art events, screenings, and festivals are now held in numerous cities and online venues, coupled with tumblers and online discussions. VJing performances are also popular among glitch artists, merging audio and visual glitches, particularly at conventions and symposiums such as the annual new media festivals GLI.TC/H and BYOB.[60] GLI.TC/H co-founder Nick Briz notes the rich diversity at the festival, a balance between commerce and hacker-punk types. It's "evident from all the debates," he writes, that "glitch.errz partake in glitch art for very different reasons. We had plenty of 'punks' present but we also had designers who work at ad agencies."[61] The *Bring Your Own Beamer* (BYOB) festival was developed by Anne de Vries and Rafaël Rozendaal in 2010. It involves a series of one-night events and is now held in over eighty cities around the world. With the rise of mobile and personal computing, social media, and screen culture writ large, digital glitch aesthetics have become an increasingly salient feature of our social landscape.

To close the chapter, I turn to one final example of digital glitch not exclusive to computational code, but apropos to social and racial black-boxing in the twenty-first century. In Sondra Perry's beautiful *Double Quadruple Etcetera Etcetera I & II* (2013, both are two-channel, silent video installations), one sees a digital animation of the dancers Danny Giles and Joiri Minaya moving individually in the corner of a white-painted studio. The body of each dancer is blurred by rapid movement. The only clear lines emerge from the intersection where the wall meets the floor and the performer's swaying head of dark hair is contrasted with the white walls. Using the "content aware" function in Photoshop, Perry replaced the presumed "content" of the "natural" human dancer (the body, flesh, and limbs) with the studio's walls and corner space enclosing it. The content aware function in Photoshop allows a user to select a "patch" of an image, from either the background or foreground, and then apply this selected "content" to another area. This results in the "body" of the performer appearing to be emptied out and re-filled with the background "content" of the walls. The dancer's movement is also sped up and treated with a fairly standard glitch effect. In the final works, the viewer sees a hyperactive and frenetic dancer perform at a seemingly inhuman speed, filled up with the matter of space.

Seen within the above-noted lineage of human-and-machine relations, from Léger through Conner and Paik, we can see Perry's interventions as aesthetically affiliated but also distinct. Léger's and Paik's ballets mime and celebrate the uppity rhythms of mechanical and electric machines, respectively; and Conner's dancer ecstatically attempts to "break away" from mechanized time. They do so through an embrace of the machine spirit, paying homage to the elegance of the human in it. In contrast, Perry's dancers are trapped. Like them, we are all also placed in a "box" marked by race, gender, and socioeconomic status, let alone the many other algorithmic classifications engendering high-tech being. Perry's dancers know and live this, but instead of responding with dismissal defiance, they generate a refreshingly bold reflection of it. Gone is the visionary spirit of the 1960s counterculture and the progressive utopianism dowsing modern art. Instead, we have error and breakdown as prosaic building blocks of being, of living with too many difficulties, identities, representations, and desires (double, triple, and quadruple) culled into a black box with no exit strategy.[62] Perry's work shows us yet another devastating failure to move beyond pigeonhole classifications, intensified through algorithmic automation. This is our culture's socio-computational glitch, glimpsed inside another, larger black box. Such frustrations appear everywhere today. Perry's happen to do so in the shape of a frenetic dancer caught in the corner of a whitewashed cube, hollowed out and resigned to do nothing but perform quadruple spins over and over again. At least she had the wherewithal to bring the walls and floorboards with her.

The next chapter considers "color as noise" in the work of digital video artist Ryan Trecartin.

PART TWO

Bring the Noise!

3

—————

Color as Signal / Noise

I. "A GRINDER AND MIXER OF MULTICOLOR DRUGS"

Ryan Trecartin was born in Webster, Texas, in 1981, and since his undergraduate years at the Rhode Island School of Design (2000–2004), he has produced eccentric, performance-based digital video and installation art with his troupe "The Experimental People Band." Soon after graduating from RISD, he emerged as a "rising star" in the art world and beyond, receiving media coverage in the *Wall Street Journal* and solo exhibitions at the Los Angeles MOCA (2010), MoMA's PS1 in New York (2011), the Musée d'Art Moderne in Paris (2011), and the Museum of Contemporary Art in Miami (2011), all before the age of thirty.[1] He is now represented by the Saatchi gallery in London and the Elizabeth Dee gallery in New York. But given his in-your-face, gauche pop culture aesthetic, catering to what Wayne Koestenbaum coins the "bubble brain gestalt of the identity surfer"[2] in an "attention-deficit Internet culture,"[3] how does one account for his swift success in the upper echelons of the blue-chip art world?

Trecartin is undeniably "a grinder and mixer of multicolor drugs," as Plato put it in reference to artists in general.[4] His fashionable use of digital media, fast-paced editing, belligerent makeup and costume, and chaotic, broken, and synthesized dialogue, echo his unforgiving color juxtapositions. His work also emerged during a time in the early 2000s when the art world was embracing a trickle-down of academic trends in post-media, post-identity politics, and queer theory. Accordingly, Deitch Projects founder Jeffrey Deitch compares his fragmented aesthetic to the "multivalent structures" of Cubism,[5] while Linda Norden places his "commercial leveling" on plane with Andy Warhol's use of Day-Glo colors to acclimate a postwar art world to a new culture of advertising. Likewise, I argue here that Trecartin's work analogously sanctions the colors of a newer world of selfies, social media apps, the internet, and automated-effects plug-ins.[6] One set of arguments in this chapter proposes that Trecartin's over the top aesthetic from the 2000s acts as a precursor to the now ubiquitous social media apps and automated digital offerings—from Snapchat to Auto-Tune—allowing the once-gauche and noisy to become prosaic as pop culture kitsch.[7] At the same time, at the beginning of the twenty-first century, Trecartin's noisy colorism offers a refreshing strategy for coping with Western culture's progressive applications of digital signal processing. Instead of compressing data to produce the least amount of noise and the most amount of signal, we find a playful, campy embrace of noise and anti-compression techniques to undo myths of transparency and streamline efficiency held too sacred in a world realistically void of them.

In this chapter's analysis of Trecartin's work from the 2000s, I identify three key tenets of his style: a transgression of categories and ways of classifying the world in favor of noise and ambiguity; an aesthetic category I theorize as "accidental color"; and his use of whacky stops and pauses—in the tradition of the avant-garde—to incite subject disorientation and criticality. While each tenet is distinct, they often overlap and feed into one another. The chapter also extends Kevin Lynch's definition of trash as something "worthless or unused for human purpose" (see Introduction), to uses of color in visual communications. Specifically, I theorize how "color as noise" in Trecartin's work corresponds with what I have identified as an aesthetic paradigm of failure, marked by a total and irreversible cross-disciplinarily, post-media, pansexual, polycultural everything, including traditionally queer, class-based, and gendered subjectivities. There are no boundaries to break, let alone adhere to. Trecartin's work embodies this landscape of imploding axioms, and for this reason, it provides the most potent case study for this chapter's analysis of color as signal and noise. While I analyze his work primarily through the lens of media technology and aesthetics, I also encourage readers to explore queer and gender-based interpretations of his work elsewhere.[8] Before jumping into this work, however, it is first necessary to establish a set of distinctions between color as signal versus color as noise.

II. COLOR AS SIGNAL AND NOISE

In *Chromatic Algorithms*, I analyzed the role of synthetic color in computer art after 1960, contextualized within a longer history of countless attempts to isolate, harness, and control color as a stable object of inquiry. Such efforts inevitably fail, I argued there, because color is always on the move, shifting, transforming, or escaping the rules and protocols that attempt to contain it. Colors of any sort may be placed in a box, inside a frame, dyed into a fabric or placed on a chart, but its transgressive essence ensures it will not remain there for very long.[9] On its own, color tends toward the ephemeral and shape-shifting. This is its nature. Colors fade, oxidize, bleed, and change their appearance based on their surroundings.[10] As Bauhaus colorist Josef Albers puts it, "in visual perception a color is almost never seen as it really is—as it physically is. This fact makes color the most relative medium in art."[11] Over time, a strain of artists, philosophers, and scientists have gravitated towards this subjective approach to understanding color. As a phenomenon of individual perception, color is fundamentally strange and estranged, inconsistent, noisy, and unreliable.

For others, all of color's shape-shifting amounts to an ancient fear dating back to the origins of Western metaphysics. Sophists, rhetoricians, and painters are "creator[s] of phantoms,"[12] Plato argued, "technicians of ornament and makeup." But by far the most poisonous of simulacra was color: a cosmetic and false appearance that, like the Sophist's "gaudy speeches" and "glistening words," seduces the listener with its "ambiguity and deceiving sparkle."[13] Unlike words, however, color does not even have the benefit of carrying a signifying capacity beyond itself. In short, color holds to nothing and to no one, and herein lies the source of its perceived danger and fear.

For Plato, the most sensible way to deal with this "color problem" was to relegate it to the realm of artifice, cosmetic, and appearance. Likewise, for Immanuel Kant, a preliminary solution was to codify "a mere colour" as "charming" so its seriousness or threat could be disregarded.[14] As a marginalized phenomenon, color is sanitized, safely associated with nothing beyond decorative charm or mimetic supplement.[15] Hence its association with women, racial and ethnic minorities, and the fluffy and whimsical. As secondary and marginal, color can seduce the senses through deceptive means, but it will always be excluded from the hierarchy of the beautiful and the sublime, let alone the formulation of truth and reason.

For centuries now, color has had to maintain this secondary, subordinate status as "Other" linked to falsity, defect, ornament, and décor or, to quote David Batchelor, "some 'foreign' body—"usually the feminine, the oriental, the primitive, the infantile, the vulgar, the queer or the pathological."[16] Insofar as color can never constitute an original truth, Jacqueline Lichtenstein argues, it can never be the object of genuine value or recognition, and thus its uncontrollability ceases to be a problem for "real" philosophical inquiry. Banished from metaphysics, transcendental truth and logic, color remains just where Plato left it: as a simulacrum on the walls of a cave, growing stronger there, amplifying and intensifying the dangers and shadow-inspired fears that instigated its expulsion in the first place.[17]

Color, like trash and noise, only returns to upend the system from the inside out. Herein color and noise find their shared terrain. Put differently, color as color has always been a kind a noise.[18] Through a long history of culture and communication, however, color has been molded into a series of signals. For example, when encountering a red stop sign while driving, one slows to a stop, and then continues driving. This is color as signal because the communicative meaning of the red is clear. Because red stop signs are cross-cultural and pervasive, decoding them tends to be more automatic than deliberate.[19]

What happens when the signal is not the normative red but, say, purple? One might stop because the sign bears the same octagonal shape, text, and positioning on the road, but the odd color introduces a temporary disorientation in experience, a kind of *visual noise*. It is unclear to the driver how it can or should be interpreted through existing convention. This is how color operates as noise, at least in this first, naïve encounter. As noise, a color halts unconscious processes of data interpretation and in so doing, opens up a space of questioning. On a deeper level, color as noise is akin to a "conceptual glitch," discussed in chapter 2, or Duchamp's *In Advance of the Broken Arm* (1915), illustrating the concept in a framework entirely divorced from color. In this piece, one finds a single, basic snow shovel buttressed against the wall of the gallery. At first sight, its vernacular meaning seems obvious, but as an *artwork*, its meaning is unclear (i.e.: conceptual noise). After reading the title, however, one is able to connect the work to its implied meaning as a human prosthetic, instantiating a relationship between hand and tool analogous to that between an art object and its caption. *In Advance of the Broken Arm* makes preliminary meanings ambiguous and in so doing, generates a conceptual glitch that forces a moment of pause, followed by a resignification of the object's meaning. The power of color as noise holds the same potential in the visual field.

Unleashing the powerful yet traditionally feared capacity of color as noise has been an understudied theme in a visual tradition stretching back through Turner, Van Gogh, Monet, Seurat, Signac, and Francis Bacon through James Turrell, Olafur Eliasson, Pipilotti Rist, and Jeremy Blake. In interior and graphic design, one can find tangential correlatives in Russian and Art Deco poster design, the work of Pushpin Studios (Milton Glaser, Seymour Chwast, and Edward Sorel), Verner Panton, Ettore Sottsass, or more recently, David Carson and April Greiman. These artists and designers use color as a form of free-floating noise—at times for political ends—and yet they do so elegantly, without losing sight of our aesthetic and cognitive need to find meaning in the world.

At the same time, color as noise can just as easily prevent critical questioning and self-reflexive pauses. Consider certain print or television advertisements. If the goal is to capture and sustain attention, then the use of bold and abstract color becomes one of the most effective strategies for maintaining "eyeballs" and stringing a viewer along. Color still operates as color, which is to say, noisy and "liberated" from narrative, convention, or structure, but unlike avant-garde techniques, the goal is much less to call attention to the materiality of the media apparatus or the politics of viewing than to simply project as many images, logos, and brand names in as quick a time as possible.

Lastly, the difference between color as signal versus color as noise is in no way fixed or universal. In order to be, become, and sustain itself as noise, color must be worked and reworked; released and liberated from subordination to line, form, convention, or structure using deliberate and medium-specific strategies. Once a cipher for decoding meaning is provided, a noise ceases to be noise and instead communicates as signal. *In Advance of the Broken Arm,* the "shovel" attains new value as a communicative signal once it takes on the implication of a human prosthetic. In my stop sign scenario, a driver might take into account the placement of a purple stop sign (e.g., in a graffiti-strewn neighborhood), and whether there is a special occasion for it, like Halloween. Reestablishing symbolic connections catapults a once-noisy color back into its role as signal. Definitive meaning is restored and color communicates exactly what it was intended to.

In short, color as noise is in no way divorced from the world that gives it shape and meaning (or a lack thereof). Further, my binary distinction between color as noise / signal does not propose a universal, ahistorical, acultural, or apolitical definition but rather, recognizes how this binary is constantly shifting and changing according to context, perspective, circumstance, memory, lighting, and numerous other factors. In the art and design work noted above, what might have appeared as noise at one point in history is now conveniently canonized as signal, as argued of avant-garde glitch in chapter 2. In the case of Trecartin's noisy colors, we encounter them on the cusp of their appropriation into mainstream media cultures.

III. COLOR AS NOISE: RYAN TRECARTIN'S WORK FROM THE 2000S

To expand on Deitch's description of Trecartin's work, briefly cited above:

> [It] incorporates almost all of the innovations of twentieth-century art, literature, and performance to break into the twenty-first. His works' multivalent structure alludes to Cubism. His scripts fuse Gertrude Stein with infomercials. His eccentric, vividly painted characters draw on a vanguard tradition stretching from Weimar Berlin to Jack Smith. His community of collaborators, living and working with him in a Los Feliz McMansion that looks like an abandoned swingers' club, fuses elements of Warhol's Factory, the Wooster Group, and MTV's The Real World.[20]

All of this is accurate, and yet, there is much more at stake in the substance of the work itself. For one thing, there is a systematic transgression of categories and ways of classifying the world (i.e., nouns become adjectives and vice versa); second, there is a stylized use of what I theorize as "accidental color;" and third, a use of zany stops and pauses to incite disorientation in contemporary subjectivity. We begin with the first.

Noise in the Epistēmē

In his 2009 essay on Trecartin's work, director of New York's New Museum of Contemporary Art Massimiliano Gioni, described the artist's style as one where "information is speaking the characters, rather than the other way around."[21] Gioni's witty reversal of the normative assumption that people utter information temporarily appeals to the nonsense-making at the core of Trecartin's work, but to my mind, it is much more that the characters speak a highly critical noise in the midst of their multilayered, chronologically overlapping universes. This is illustrated in Trecartin's work early on, *A Family Finds Entertainment* (*AFFE*), presented as his 2004 BFA thesis at RISD. Ever since, the plot has been interpreted ambiguously. Ricardo E. Zulueta analyzes it as a parody of the classical family mellow drama; *New York Times* critic Roberta Smith argues it is a "coming out" narrative; Dennis Cooper claims it is a story about "Skippy, a clownish but terrifyingly psychopathic boy."[22] There is some truth in all of these interpretations, and it is this ambiguity that keeps the work alive, unclear and muddy, simultaneously thriving on multiple registers.

This same incapacity to find any single interpretive meaning for the plot is illustrated in Trecartin's 108-minute single-channel video *I-BE AREA* (2007). In one early section of the work, the character named Pasta (played by Trecartin) drives with her friend Wendy MPEGgy / sen-teen (played by Alison Powell) to the house of the characters Amanda / Hunter (Kelly Pittenger) and a character who appears to be named Charity (actor unknown). So far so good; the viewer is given a loose narrative structure—Pasta gets in a car, drives to a house, parks, gets out, locks the door, goes inside, the girls have fun, and the evening is over—but what is actually expressed on screen is something else entirely.

Rewind and replay: from out of nowhere the video jumps back in time to the inside of character Pasta's car. Like the protagonist I-BE 2 (also played by Trecartin), Pasta is an "ambiguously gendered . . . mixed-media humanoid."[23] Pasta's face is painted opaque yellow with blue, purple, red, and white smudges circling her eyes and nose. Her irises are also yellow, those of a kind of human jackal in a hyperactive trance, both scary and smiling. Retro 1990s computer-generated snowflakes dance across the screen as pink and purple lines recede toward a floating vanishing point to the pop song "Kiss Me" by *Sixpence None the Richer* (1998). The song, for its part, is synthesized to a barely recognizable pitch, matching the over-the-top makeup, both of which are then juxtaposed with Pasta's exceedingly conservative suburban outfit: light blue mom jeans with a crisp white, short-sleeved button-down shirt tucked into them.

Ricardo E. Zulueta and Kevin McGarry shed light on Pasta's origin story: stolen as child named "Jango," Pasta has since "developed herself" into another person. And yet, McGarry continues, "Jango the child continues to live in temporal coexistence with Pasta the adult, perhaps unaware of Pasta yet destined to one day invent her."[24] Zulueta offers a somewhat distinct take on the narrative logic: "I-BE Area follows the peripeteia of I-BE 2, a self-claimed 'real life mixed media,' clone of I-BE, the first 'total original.' [I-BE 2] is in the midst of an existential crisis as he desperately seeks to abandon his original incarnation in pursuit of other

FIGURE 14. Ryan Trecartin, *I-BE AREA* (2007). Digital video, color, 1 hour, 48 minutes, compilation of video stills.

identities to assume."[25] The plot, whether explained accurately or not, matches the confusing and genre-defying mixture of graphics, CGI, and characters (actors, performers, and/or real life characters). Some fragments and phrases are familiar, but for the most part, the combined whole is deliberately estranged. This is boilerplate Trecartin.

Trecartin's noise becomes literal and conceptual in its consistent transgression of pre-established categories of being and knowing, undone through his trademark campy defiance. As critics like Zulueta note, Trecartin's eccentric merging of perspectives and subjectivities compound into a multisensory cacophony of "cyberqueer," interpreted here as a techno-mediated estrangement that extends beyond sexuality.[26] As Trecartin describes it, "[i]t's important to me that the work invent new or alternate meanings in the context of something familiar, rather than merely demonstrate something already known."[27] This is key because, in making art, one does not want to make a piece *too* strange and *too* chaotic, leaving no foothold for a viewer, and thus one simply dismisses the work altogether (discussed in chapter 5 as a "botching" of the Deleuzian "diagram"). And, rest assured, Trecartin leaves some such signals amid this onslaught of noise; we just have to do a bit of work to get to them.

To return to *I-Be Area,* as Pasta's car moves, highways and streets are nowhere to be seen. Car windows open to a depthless, perspectiveless computer maze of animated graphics and QuickTime files. High-speed aerial zooms show computer-generated mountain ranges, mixed with abstract color lines and tiled images of Amanda and Charity, floating backwards and forwards in a no-space space, featured on an outdated QuickTime player.[28] As Pasta jerks forwards and backwards in her car, she laughs. The laughter echoes through the synthetic maze and an (otherwise) noneventful drive is transformed into a hallucinogenic trip through a hybrid world of photography, infomercials, video game glitches, and rudimentary computer animations (already offering a blueprint for what will become a conventional Snapchat segue in an episode of *Keeping up with the Kardashians*).

It is night outside when Pasta arrives at the house, where she greets Wendy MPEGgy, who has made a brief appearance in the car along the way but disappears before Pasta reaches the destination. Wendy MPEGgy sports thick green eye shadow with blue around the edges of her teeth. Once inside Amanda and Charity's house, the girls, who appear to be "normal," unadorned, but highly affected American preteens, announce the "media people are here," by which they mean the internet, or the video they will be producing for it (one must cease to look for singular meanings). Pasta and Wendy MPEGgy perform for us, and the camera, and the media people, and the young girls. The ambiguity, again intentional, complements the blurring of boundaries between genders, genres, narratives, data space, and physical space. Trecartin calls this a "continuous 360-degree situation," inferring an obfuscation of temporalities, epistemologies, and just about anything and everything in between.[29] Pasta is also the girls' former baby sitter, now hired by the girls as a media producer, along with Wendy MPEGgy. Pasta and Wendy announce themselves as cofounders of "Instant action . . . Life reproductions." The drama hits the heightened pitch of an afternoon talk show. The team boasts being "On top of shit. Always in the moment. Always. Always. Always . . . Right now." In the style of a cliché infomercial, they repeat their "instant" proclamations in Trecartin's signature staccato style, never resting on a scene, face, persona, or sound bite for longer than a couple of seconds.

The content of the dialogue further echoes this belying of linguist categories. By inverting nouns and verbs, using props as characters and remaking behaviors into objects, one begins to question unconscious assumptions about things and their relationship to one another.[30] Examples abound in *I-Be Area:* from the title, which implies a person is a space, to the character Pasta, which is something we eat, to Wendy MPEGgy, whose last name is an acronym for an algorithmic compression scheme. Even such casual remarks as "I don't know you need to delete your birth mom" or, "No, it's not, it's about how the world ended three weeks ago. Starting now," further illustrate the semantic play. "Maintenance" is the term Trecartin uses to describe this technique where categories and classes of things are emptied out just enough to open them up to questioning—like the noise engendered by the purple stop sign hypothesized above.[31] While working, "we might try to interpret a car commercial as a hairdo," Trecartin explains in conversation with Cindy Sherman, "an ideology as a designer skin tone, a banking situation as a cheekbone, copyright issues as a jaw line, or maybe an application as a facial agenda."[32] Nouns become adjectives and verbs become both, and vice versa. The deliberately crafted mumbo-jumbo prevents sustained attention, at least on the level of logic.

On the level of surface experience, however, it enhances it. "Trecartin understands how a concentration on distraction can ironically enhance absorption," Linda Norden writes, citing Wayne Koestenbaum.[33] Distraction—noise in so many forms and formats—becomes the germ and seed for a new order and rhythm. I return to this in this chapter's conclusion on the "pacified sublime," and to the concept of the sublime in chapters 6 and 7. For now, let us consider how the *quality* of this kind of empty but persistent absorption echoes models of mainstream media consumption.

Jodi Dean has theorized this media landscape under the rubric of "communicative capitalism," which, she explains, is chock full of noise and failed communications. For Dean, this "noise" is fundamental to our communication infrastructures and yet, it's also the very thing that hinders actual communication from occurring. Her paradigmatic example is the "democratic" internet with its ubiquitous data flows, falling under the guise of "communication" but failing to communicate anything of substance. She recounts the contesting discussions surrounding the second Iraq War. Insightful reports, commentary, and critical voices were seen and heard, from independent news media to blogs and beyond. As the march to the war grew closer, thousands of bloggers commented on each step but mainstream U.S. news outlets failed to cover the mass demonstrations and protests.[34] The White House and president acknowledged the existence of such voices but failed to directly respond to their critical content. The mere acknowledgment that such disparate voices existed constituted for them a sufficient response. Everyone had the "democratic opportunity" to voice opinions, but no actual "messages were received" by the people they aimed to communicate with. The same could be said for numerous television talk shows, news programs, and podcasts. Trecartin's work echoes this growing dynamic of communicative capitalism, with its broken dialogue, stilted relations and vapid characters who seem to respond, not to the person who spoke before them, but to their own solipsistic, internal agendas. The difference is that once it is subject to analysis, as is done here, noise can be reconstructed as critical signal. To cite Hito Steyerl again, writing in a different context, we might say that Trecartin's work, "In addition to a lot of confusion and stupefaction," also creates the possibility for "disruptive movements of . . . thought and affect,"[35] however politically active or benign they may be. Unfortunately, no such process appears on the horizon for politics or the popular press.

Accidental Color Aesthetics

The second facet of Trecartin's style deals with "accidental color," a turn of phrase used by editor and publisher of the *Pantone View Colour Planner*, David Shah, at the 2017 color planners meeting in London. In an exchange with an "American forecaster in the room" (A) the exchange proceeds as follows:[36]

> Shah: What is the zeitgeist going on in the United States about color? Are they big colors? Are they strong colors? Prime colors?
>
> A: I think what's going on in the United States now is that it's all happening. It's almost reflective of the conflict going on around us—where you're not having one definite color correction, but you're seeing examples in various areas. I think it's mostly about mixes.
>
> Shah: So it's not about solids. It's about how you put colors together?
>
> A: Exactly, and different from what it's been before. It's almost like a counterculture type of a feeling—you deliberately use colors that would not ordinarily work together.
>
> Shah: Accidental colors
>
> A: That's a good way of putting it, yes

In the context of this book, accidental colors are also noisy colors. The distinction is that accidental colors must then be skillfully transformed into an ordered, stylized set that retains an *aura* of accident or noise. In other words, the strategy aims to make the colors in a set *appear* off, wrong, ad-hoc, or unexpected. *Intention* is key, since it differentiates an actual color accident from the deliberate and consciously produced appearance of one. For example, one might encounter a purple stop sign and experience what I refer to as "color as noise." This does not count as accidental color, however, because it is not deliberately designed as an aesthetic object. And herein lies the contradiction at the heart of accidental color aesthetics: there is nothing accidental about it. I provide some concrete examples below, after reviewing accidental color's antithesis: *conventional* color systems.

In art, science, and the world at large, there are numerous conventional color systems, all established through a history of media (neon colors, electronic colors, televisual colors, etc.); fashion and interior design (textile standards, Pantone colors); physics (the seven spectral colors of the rainbow); or any discipline that involves visual perception. In most art and design curricula, the standard twelve-hue color circle explicates these basic complementary pairs: purple appears opposite to yellow, and orange appears opposite to blue, forming complementary pairs. Trichromatic color is another example. Normative in humans and the vast majority of electronic devices, trichromatic color consists of the primaries: red, green, and blue, and all other possible colors derive from these three. In nature, we find established color systems through cliché associations with the beauty of nature, almost always tending towards complementary pairs such as a light blue sky and orange sunset, or red flowers rising from fresh green grass. The human perceptual system has a natural tendency to create balance, so when we are exposed to one hue for an extended period of time, we naturally begin to crave its opposite. In short, conventional color systems extend across media and have ingrained themselves in society through thousands of years of culture and habit.

In contrast, accidental colors are marked by the appearance of being unconventional or "off." This veneer of a half-hazard design choice in some ways works to dismantle conventional color systems by opening up new possibilities. This is also why I refer to accidental colors as a set and not a system. It should also be noted that, as with noise and glitch art, their capacity to disrupt is not guaranteed but always contingent on context. One example of accidental color could include light pink and baby blue placed with the strong contrast of black and white. Using two pastel colors paired with a monochromatic contrast, the set is acceptable but slightly off, since the two different systems (pastel and monochrome black and white) don't necessarily belong to any recognizable color system or conventional use. In this way, accidental colors are also antithetical to color matching. Accidental colors are undefined, unexpected, and incomprehensive *as a unified system*. In essence, the set is an anti-system, and in this way, it is also anti-modern.

To identify where and how accidental color exists in the world, one can perform this test: does this group of colors fit with any pre-established color convention in color theory, biology, or the natural environment? If the answer is no, we can press on to analyze it for additional correlations. A second set of qualities to consider concerns context. Accidental color panders to a façade of accident and happenstance and yet, very much like glitch art, maintains tight precision and control over design choices, from start to finish. Furthermore, once accidental colors lose their novel front (also like glitch art), they become mainstream trend. So-called accidental colors fade into standardized colors as they find their permanent home in a slot as one of the "64 colors arranged into nine distinct palettes" in the *Pantoneview Colour Planner*—a prêt-à-porter aesthetic for designers and cultural producers in the years to come. No longer deemed accidental at all, they are now formulaic. Until this occurs, however, accidental colors can and will operate as a low-level noise in the background of media and visual culture. As practitioners and theorists, it is our responsibility to pay attention to these transitions in the media environment. Doing so allows us to see how and when a new set of color relations is deemed too edgy, versus those on the brink of cliché. Because accidental color aesthetics are endemic to Trecartin's work, the concept provides a fruitful analytic tool that can now be brought into a discussion of his work.

Trecartin's Accidental Color Aesthetic

Almost any sequence from any of Trecartin's works (which he calls "movies") could be used to illustrate the accidental color concept. In almost every scene of every one of his works, one finds bizarre color combinations: a haphazardly painted yellow face, a white wall attacked with red, a mismatched outfit, white teeth that bleed blue, yellow skin, yellow eyes, and so forth. All of these constitute deliberately stylized, accidental color, used to stun, shock, or undermine color convention. Nonetheless, I focus here only on one of the opening scenes from one early work: *A Family Finds Entertainment* (*AFFE*; 2004), a 42-minute epic horrification of the "after school special" genre.

In an early scene in *AFFE,* we find four Caucasian twenty-somethings sitting in a living room. The room's interior is decorated in a lime green and dark yellow color scheme, alluding to the folksy get-together culture of a 1960s family interior. One plain-faced boy (by which I mean he is not wearing an apparent costume or makeup) sits on a stool, while another, equally unadorned white male in cozy red socks rests on the arm of the couch, knees tucked in and guitar in hand. He begins to play as the first boy begins to sing, "I will hold on, I will hold on . . ." A character named Veronica (played by Veronica Gelbaum) gazes longingly at him, and when he is done, she responds, "Oh, Ben, that was so romantical. . . . I love that more than anything." The mellow drama is both forced and raw.

The strangeness is echoed by Veronica's makeup, which is not comprised of complementary colors but instead, a series of black-and-white outlines where color would (normatively) be found. A close-up of her face reveals her opaque white lips, outlined in a thick black pencil, mirrored by a white teardrop outlined in thick black below her right eye, and a streak of white (which appears grey) on one side of her black head of hair. The technique undoes the normative role of makeup as a filling in and coloring over, replacing it with a series of outlines to indicate color's absence. This "bad" makeup job deliberately covers nothing, save its self-revelation as an empty artifice.

And then there is the strategically developed bad accident of color matching in the room's interior design. Veronica is sitting on the couch in this scene, wearing a lime green velvet dress to match the lime green and yellow interior of the room and couch pattern behind her. The matching is far from subtle, begging an inquiry into why or how it doesn't seem right. If "matching" by definition is an

FIGURE 15. Ryan Trecartin, *A Family Finds Entertainment* (2004). Digital video, color, 41 minutes. Noisy colors mark the set design of the opening scenes.

FIGURE 16. Ryan Trecartin, *A Family Finds Entertainment* (2004). Video still. More noisy color.

attempt to fit things together in likeness and kind, according to the dictates of "good design," then here we encounter its inversion: matching taken to such an extreme it becomes a mockery of so-called "good" taste. The matching becomes so "off," it forces a viewer to refocus attention from the drama to the colors composed on the surface of the screen, allowing these visual motifs to perform a complementary comic relief alongside the characters and their eccentric drama.

The characters, for their part, act like zombies. Their lines are delivered in stilted isolation, even though they are sitting in the same room, sharing the same intimate space of the velvet couch and stool. Some of this is explained by the fact that Trecartin deliberately refrains from giving lines to actors up until the moment they are to deliver them. "I don't let most performers see the script ahead of time, because I like them not knowing where their character is going," he says. "I tend to feed the performers their lines one or two at a time, and thus their performances often capture the feeling of still figuring out what a line is about, even as they're saying it."[37] Trecartin believes the tactic allows the actors to remain open and spontaneous when delivering their lines, and hence, the appearance of stilted connections between them. An apt example occurs in *AFFE* after the singing has ended and the band members inform Veronica they are going on tour. The camera cuts to a close-up of Veronica, who turns to the red-and-white-clad character beside her and says, "Penny May, I hate you so much." Not only is the communal after-school special genre turned on its head, but so too are any allusions to a connected, 1960s folk culture. Instead of friendly singing or emotional support, we witness bitterness, jealousy, and the characters' alienation from each other. This peculiar lack of belonging is iterated again when we next cut to an image of Skippy, who has "locked himself in the bathroom" to perform a series of parodic suicidal bloodbath incidents, refusing to go downstairs to meet the others.

Taken together, these scenes operate on multiple registers as parodies of a serious "coming out" narrative; an undoing of the cheap poetic endemic to folk culture; and kitschy first-year film projects, with their excessive use of fake blood and gore. "It's not blood, it's red," Jean-Luc Godard declared in a 1965 interview, by which he meant cinematic blood is one facet of a larger cinematic apparatus that is itself an artifice used to generate a set of seemingly coherent and "transparent" signifiers in the mind of a viewer. Here, though, it is red (or fuchsia) that is meant to signify *not*-blood, not the other way around. Transparency is undone and artifice is laid out to dry. Furthermore, instead of cliché nostalgic flashbacks, featured in undersaturated "super-8" color, typical of such "retro" styled pieces, Trecartin delivers an uncomfortable eeriness that pervades the "real" characters as they deliver broken lines, seem dazed and confused by the guitar, and, aside from some mania and bitterness, are otherwise bored and vacant. Veronica's white lips with black outlines speak the same language of boredom as her zombie-like character: anything laying claim to the authentic or serious catapults her and her "family" members, into attention deficiency.

The next scene cuts to a character named "Snow White Girl" (played by Trecartin). Snow White Girl is falling down a snowy hill, outfitted with opaque white hair and face paint, save for blotches of fuchsia (presumably meant to signify blood, but so far off from the actual color of blood that the effect is comic), and white and light yellow clothing (again, a comic affront to the ostensible purity of snow white).[38] The screen splits into four quadrants, each one depicting a variation of Snow White Girl in her white costume and makeup, simultaneously engaging in different activities with different people. Each quadrant also has a soundtrack. Mostly screeching and screaming is heard—or is it singing? One can barely make out the words to Bonnie Tyler's 1983 pop hit, "Total Eclipse of the Heart." One faintly hears, "Forever's going to start tonight . . . Forever's going to start tonight . . . " The voices overlap, but even together, the audio is barely intelligible. The sequence then cuts to Snow White Girl alone inside a room. The mood grows somber. She is bent over on the carpet, still with an opaque white face, an off-white top and a yellow skirt. She appears to be having some sort of hallucinogenic trip, or is it a transcendental religious awakening? She slowly rises up from the floor in a slow-motion gesture, her eyes rolling back in ecstatic joy, and her hands and arms slowly extending upward as she appears to reach Nirvana-qua-psychosis.

On the one hand, Snow White Girl's colorful accidents need no further explanation. There is nothing pure or white about this character, drenched in fake blood and psychosis. All colors *appear*, at least at first, to be inconsistent with what or how we expect to see representations of blood, transcendental experience, or the iconic Snow White. Taken a step further, the sullied and accident-prone Snow White Girl (and the obsessive limes and greens in the "family" room), feed back into the piece's broader meta-reflection on the failures of utopic mythologies, from hippie folk cultures to youthful transcendental awakenings and "serious" drama. The celebrated artifice of color and these deliberately staged "bad accidents" boldly proclaim dead the older paradigm of single genres and authentic relations. Witnessing these pretentious edifices fall to the ground is how and where this family finds entertainment.

One final example of accidental color in *AFFE* is found midway through the piece. Cliché color-matching techniques are again pushed to such an extreme they begin to implode. Obsessive matching results in a lack of matching altogether. This occurs through a series of brief cuts through three different characters: Linda (Lizzie Fitch), Phalangena/Coughdrop (Alison Powell), and Shin (Ryan Trecartin). The scene cuts from one face to the next, and each character utters brief soundbites. Shin takes the lead, a character wearing a red wig, with a face painted in opaque yellow, red, and blue, and without apparent gender or sexuality. Faint traces of green can be seen around her upper eyelids. Her hair is orange and she dons a purple-and-white plaid shirt. She also holds a bottle of Naked Juice. With the label facing forward, it suggests a blatant tie-in to her color scheme. The background—is it wallpaper or a bedspread?—also conveys the same saturated yellows, reds, blues, and greens. An animated zigzag line suddenly cuts across the center of her face. Unsurprisingly, these animated colors also bear the same kind of bold red and blue with black-and-white boundaries—like face, like backdrop, like wig, like bottle, like shirt. When this degree of overmatching is used throughout, it becomes a stylistic device that could not be further from any actual accident.[39] As a staged accident by way of costume and set design, it undoes preconceived notions of what is implicitly deemed "tasteful."

In sum, the accidental color aesthetic discussed in these scenes deliberately defies norms of visual representation and cultural practice (that an image should be clear; makeup should not be noticed on the face; matching should be subtle; folk culture is intrinsically communal and friendly, etc.). The aesthetic of failure is deliberate, and herein lies the internal contradiction of glitch art and related noise genres: it bears a veneer of error, all the while maintaining the opposite. Indeed, a majority of Trecartin's colors, costumes, makeup, and editing effects are planned out in advance.[40] The work is not a random free-for-all or happenstance documentation of last night's party (one of the artist's critiques of a common reception of his work). Rather, they are designed to work in the guise of anti-design. In this way, Trecartin's designed accidents connect him to a legacy of colorists mentioned earlier—from Turner, Van Gogh, Monet, Seurat, Signac, and Bacon to Paul Sharits, Pipilotti Rist, Jeremy Blake, and Paper Rad. For them, colors speak as noise, or at least they did during one moment in the history of visual art. Today, many of these artists' colors no longer seem loud or garish because they have been acclimated through decades of canonization. Trecartin's colors have also begun their move into the prosaic. With so many social media apps and plugins (Snapchat, Instagram filters, etc.), what was once "gauche" about his monstrous deformations of image and sound have already entered mainstream culture as kitsch, less than a decade out the gate.

*Stops, Pauses, and Ruptures (as critique of
contemporary subjectivity)*

This brings us to a third and final facet of Trecartin's work: stops, zany pauses, brakes, and ruptures as a critique of contemporary subjectivity. On the one hand, insofar as one aims for continuity, seamless editing, and narrative cohesion, this repertoire of devices can be classified as producing an aesthetic of failure. Insofar as one does *not* follow the dictates of Hollywood or mainstream narrative media, but draws instead from precursors in the avant-garde (as discussed in chapter 2) breaks, pauses, and fragmentation can become a vehicle for exploring the materiality of the medium, or for critical questioning. To be clear, a critical pause does not automatically result in any one of these things, it is merely a possibility inserted into an otherwise conventional use of a medium. It should also be noted that Trecartin is not interested in formal or medium-specific experimentation, but instead with the destruction and stopping power of the absurd and zany, even as his visual strategies foreground a (human) failure to keep up with our media.

The first example is taken from the 2006 saga *(Tommy-Chat Just E-mailed Me.)*, also produced as an advertisement for the 2006 New York Underground Film Festival. The characters named Beth (played by Lizzie Fitch) and Tammy (played by Ryan Trecartin) appear in their messy but abstract art-clad apartment. Tammy, dressed in the epitome of accidental color sets: a blue dress, blond wig, and white face paint with blood-colored makeup smeared across the left side of her neck, gets an email from Tommy (also played by Trecartin) who has conflicting plans for the evening. Beth asks whether they should invite Pam instead, but Tammy hates her. The solution? Beth and Tammy do a Google search.

The mere suggestion of online activity triggers a camp hysteria. Graphics begin to fly across the room to upbeat music. They enter the keywords: "great lesbian subversive underground ugly . . . " into the Google prompt. Tammy asks Beth: "Why don't you become a lesbian for me?" "You know why," Beth replies in a high-pitched synthesized voice. Tammy looks directly into the camera, the pace slows as Beth with boyish grin pleads, "I don't know why." The image catapults into rapid-paced cuts, complemented by haphazard exchanges and bad accident sartorial choices. Being a lesbian *for* Beth, Tammy implies in this isolated instant, is as seamless as finding something on Google. This is not so much a performance of "clip-on identities"[41] as it is an articulation of what is already multiple. Media-savvy socially engineered millennials do not—cannot— revert to essential or existential notions of a "self" in any singular, static, or unmediated way. Who they are is how they use their media. In *Tommy-Chat,* Trecartin plays three roles simultaneously: Pam, a lesbian librarian with a screaming baby in an ultramodern hotel room; Tammy who lives in an apartment filled with installation art with Beth (who also plays the character Bolivia); and Tommy, who is "only seen in a secluded lake house in the woods."[42] The ability to inhabit multiple identities, sexual preferences, and gender roles and to put them on public display for each other through social media becomes an accurate reflection of the multichannel environment young people inhabit today. At the same time, Trecartin's work is not all multichannel noise and rupture. Rather, his stops and stutters push away meaning up to the point when they open up an alternative route for reformation.

Two last examples from Trecartin's *K-CoreaINC. K (section a)* (2009) and *Center Jenny* (2013) illustrate this point. *K-CoreaINC. K (section a)* is a 33-minute single-channel video in which we encounter another campy plot circling around an "unending business meeting."[43] The participants are a group of young actors known as "Koreas," pronounced "careers," held together in a "lightly allegorical cloud," as Kevin McGarry puts it.[44] They wear blond wigs, ample makeup, and tongue-in-cheek office attire which Trecartin refers to the look as "work face." The Koreas perform as exaggerated, hyper-professional characters, colliding in corporate carnival scenes held in offices and airplanes that seem less like any traditional office environment than a "bump and grind" party. Accordingly, the Koreas' aim is to "assimilate cultural stereotypes and reductive international relationships as individual basic operating procedures." But their jargon-clad business-speak, repeated at the highest of possibly bearable pitches, and cut to Trecartin's trademark staccato editing, thwarts the pretense of any actual business occurring.[45] As McGarry describes it, each of the Koreas' individuality is "subsumed into the group" and collectively reflected as a homogeneous drive for "diversity."[46] The characters are so deeply immersed in this world of constant change and professionalization that they conform to the rhetoric of diversity in order to accomplish sameness. The phrase "my career" is repeated so many times, it begins to morph into a darkly humorous battle cry for the ways in which all of their individual subjectivities have been subsumed into this "diversifying" discourse of the global economy.[47]

For Sianne Ngai, Trecartin's work embodies the aesthetic category of the zany, first and foremost based in an intensely affective character associated with camp and theatricality. Ngai's key example is Lucille Ball's *I Love Lucy*,[48] though the character type has a much longer history with the Italian *zanni*, she explains, a comic character or "itinerant servant" associated with the working or immigrant classes in sixteenth-century Italy.[49] The zany "type" has since developed into a number of familiar media icons and, for Ngai, persists in contemporary media culture as a direct response to new demands for worker flexibility, apropos of the post-industrial economy.[50] In *I Love Lucy*, as also recounted by Rebecca Porte in her review of Ngai's work, the character Lucy Ricardo quixotically transforms from episode to episode, from ballerina to saleswoman to bellhop in "an undifferentiated, chaotic swirl."[51] The zany character is a natural response to a set of rapidly changing social and political conditions. In the context of this book, it is the impossible demand to shift seamlessly between things and states (channel surfing, multitasking, overlapping identities, etc.) in order to survive in an increasingly algorithmic world. As error-prone humans, we must fail. Trecartin's Koreas reflect this contemporary inevitability in the tension between our culture's demands to do too much, too fast, and in too many "innovative" and "diverse" ways, while also somehow being "true to oneself."[52] The result? "One" becomes like every other cookie-cutter office-worker, seeking "outside the box" solutions and "creative destruction" strategies that all end up looking and sounding the same.

The second example of this kind of zany in Trecartin is taken from his 53-minute video *Center Jenny* (2013), the first piece he created after moving with his troupe to Los Angeles. The city plays an unspoken presence in the piece. Hollywood has long privileged actors, Western notions of beauty, and living one's life for the camera (as Warhol ingeniously depicted several decades prior). But, instead of depicting a group of attractive young female actresses who naturally find fulfillment on screen and incite the attention of a (male) director, *Center Jenny* inverts this trope to show its underside: a black comedy of vapid females vying like wolves in a pack for the (unavailable) attention of a solipsistic male director. The set design, with its lack of polish and half-built walls and furniture, reinforce this X-ray glimpse into Hollywood's underworld.

The Jennys' cliché goal is to differentiate themselves from each other to attain idealized beauty and stardom, but the result, again, is homogenization. As they compete against each other, they all end up looking the same, all equally unattractive in their selfish ambitions. The male leaders/directors of the Jennys are equally self-involved: stereotypically misogynistic, they preach self-righteous platitudes void of substance or context. In *Center Jenny,* as in Hollywood, differentiation is based on nothing in particular but used to justify everything. Every Jenny always already fails to be unique, being instead "basic," just like everyone else who also strives to be unique. The contradiction of embodying both is zany, yes, and potentially tragic, if it were not treated with such comic absurdity.

IV. CONCLUSION: PACIFIED CONTINUOUS SUBLIME

In sum, throughout Trecartin's work, these three aesthetic tenets prevail: the undoing of conventional epistemologies; a deliberately forced accidental color aesthetic; and overlapping, multiple identities. Together, they help manifest the uncomfortable realization that ongoing confusion and uncertainty color the state of affairs today. But the effect of color and/or color as noise, as we now know, is never permanent or eternal. Seeing color and allowing its noisy madness to do some damage, in the end, opens up only a brief play, one that will soon dissipate into mainstream commerce and convention. As noted, we already see this in a number of the plug-ins and "distortion" apps readily available on a myriad of social media platforms. Moreover, given that Trecartin's work was produced in the early 2000s, and these distortion effects have only become popular in the past few years, we can also conclude that his once gauche and noisy aesthetic has helped to transform this brand of cultural noise into mainstream kitsch. To paraphrase Raymond Williams, the avant-garde acts as the forearm of capitalism. Future aesthetic innovation depends on identifying and extracting similar moments of color as noise, prior to their appropriation as monolithic signal. My concluding illustration turns to a recent installation produced by Ryan Trecartin and his long-time collaborator Lizzie Fitch.

In their 2016 exhibition at the Andrea Rosen Gallery in New York, *Lizzie Fitch / Ryan Trecartin,* the duo presented a series of new single and multichannel videos, large-scale installations, and densely layered soundscapes carefully crafted into a cave-like labyrinth inside the Gallery's luxurious multi-room space. The subject of the exhibition, the "comfort cravings of the American psyche," was embodied by the inclusion of physical space as an integral component of the exhibition, in what they call "sculptural theaters," dark coves that expand the on-screen work into an "environmental panoramas."[53] The many installations inside the gallery offered comfortable seating and expansive rooms for visitors to watch the "movies" for extended periods of time. The setting matched the aesthetic of the work itself: colorful gym mats, fake plastic rocks that one might find on the set of a movie production, slabs of carpet, and comfortable movie theater seating.

Sound also shaped the space. By deploying layers and fragments of voices, nature sounds (birds, trees), and other abstract sounds, the artists created a continuous yet fragmented soundscape throughout the space, heard as one wandered from enclave to enclave. As described by McGarry for the Andrea Rosen press release, the effect generated a "kind of numbed, placid continuity."[54] But this is not the same kind of placidness one might associate with trendy meditation practices. Traditionally, meditation involves a quieting of the mind and body, a "Zen out" from the noise and chaos of the world, a reprieve from work and the stresses of everyday life. Here, however, these layered sounds and noises lend themselves to the opposite: a unified, trancelike narcosis resulting from a *lack* of quiet and stillness. As an allegory for the noise of the high-tech world, or simply the busy Manhattan Street from which one exits in order to enter the gallery, pacification is actually *stimulation,* which is to say, fuel. The concluding insinuation: we have become beings who require constant stimulation and overlapping, attention-grabbing devices to maintain any semblance of peace.

This chapter drew on Ryan Trecartin's work to offer a set of metaphors and aesthetic concepts to make sense of the images and practices of our noisy and chaotic present.[55] It also built on my earlier work to substantiate digital colorism as an aesthetic category in its own right, locating it in a new paradigm of aesthetic failure. I introduced the concept of "accidental colors," theorized as akin to "color as noise," insofar as both designate an emergent aesthetic that no longer demands clear-cut meaning or definitive signification but rather, systematic abstraction and flux. Together, the noisy color and trashy noise inundating Trecartin's "multivalent structures"[56] and "myriad" of "narratives," as McGarry puts it,[57] offer an accurate metaphor for our otherwise noisy and (tragically) trash-filled lives.

4

Visual Noise in the New Photography

I. THE UNCLEAR

Once photography achieved the level of precision and accuracy that painting and illustration had sought for centuries to accomplish, a breed of talented artists needed to find a new tune. Impressionism, expressionism, and related forms of twentieth-century image making henceforth emerged. Now that photography and filmmaking have matured, their capacity to capture and display realistic representations of the world has become banal. This chapter explores one of the most recent outcomes of this legacy: photography's turn from realism to visual noise in the digital age. To connect visual noise to the broader media ecology of twenty-first-century communications, the chapter focuses on German photographer Thomas Ruff's experiments with noise and digital distortion in the late twentieth and early twenty-first centuries. Three core tenets of visual noise are identified in Ruff's work, all derivative of a larger media aesthetic rooted in technological failure. The first is a renunciation of classical norms of visual representational and pictorial convention. Photography is an especially intriguing platform for exploring this because it has been implicitly associated with visual truth, realism, and authenticating documentary capacities for over a century. I argue that the development of the New Photography genre in the 1970s foreshadows styles of visual ambiguity operative in twenty-first-century glitch art and that Ruff's aesthetic trajectory, from his early training to his more advanced work, mirrors wider shifts in the development of contemporary aesthetics.

The second tenet of visual noise in Ruff's work analyzes the obfuscation of clear meanings by building on correlations between color as noise established in chapter 3. Here, a noisy, anti-communicative aesthetic correlates with Judith

Butler's notion of "incompossibility," referred to in the Introduction. The deliberate failure to provide hermeneutic closure has a long tradition in twentieth-century theory and practice. In digital art, hermeneutic breakdowns tend to manifest as an inconsistency between an image's appearance on screen and its source code, examined here in Ruff's work, though equally operative in chapter 5 and in Jodi's work, discussed in chapter 2.

The third tenet, discussed only briefly, concerns cultural and psychological projections of failure onto machine technology, coupled with a consideration of our motivations for doing so. Examples include a website stalling, failing to load, or a cell phone spontaneously shutting off or dropping a signal. From the machine's perspective, it is operating in precisely the way it was programmed to respond to this situation. There is no failure. Disparity arises through the cultural expectations for efficiency and undisturbed visual content that we unconsciously project onto it.

The chapter begins with an overview of Ruff's early work and training, followed by a definition of the New Photography. Section III addresses Ruff's *nudes* (1999–2012), drawing on Greg Hainge's discussion on the topic. Section IV turns to visual noise in Ruff's *jpegs* (2002–), which includes a technical exegesis into JPEG compression. My conclusion points to the persistence of visual glitch styles in popular culture, construed as budding artifacts of unfulfilled desires in a world of high-tech. As in chapter 3's analysis of Ryan Trecartin's work, my focus here lies less with identity politics, pornography, or catastrophe journalism (though I touch on all of these) and more with communicative breakdown, and the ways in which it resonates with the aesthetics of visual noise in twenty-first-century media culture.

II. THOMAS RUFF AND THE BECHER SCHOOL

Thomas Ruff was born in Germany's Black Forest region, in Zell am Harmersbach, in 1958. In 1977, he attended art school at the Staatlichen Kunstakademie Düsseldorf, where he later became a professor from 2000 until 2006. He found early success as an international art photographer, exhibiting his work at such esteemed venues as Documenta 9 and the Venice Biennale (in 1995 and 2005). He is represented by the Gagosian Gallery and David Zwirner in New York, and his work is now included in the permanent collections of the Metropolitan Museum of Art, the Hamburger Bahnhof Museum for Contemporary Art, Berlin, and the Art Institute of Chicago.

As a student, Ruff attended classes with other nascent international art stars, including Thomas Struth, Candida Höfer, Axel Hütte, and Andreas Gursky. Together, they benefited from the teachings of the well-known artist couple Bernd and Hilla Becher, esteemed for their serial photographs of industrial-era objects (like refineries and factories) in a flat documentary style.[1] The Bechers had a lasting influence on their students, many of whom continue to reproduce their matter-of-fact, distanced style, developing it into what has now become known as the "Düsseldorf School" (or sometimes the "Becher School") of contemporary photography, typified by a direct, seemingly uninvolved and aloof "objective approach" to image making. The stylistic approach can be contrasted with the "freer pictorial language" one finds in highly emotional commercial or journalistic practices.[2] Even many art students who did not study with the Bechers associate themselves with the Becher School and its method, and at times, German photography is on the whole incorrectly conflated with it.[3]

In line with the Becher School's approach and progeny, Ruff's early photographs are cool, detached, and aloof. They consistently deny symbolization, thwart narrative structure, and avoid personalization. One of his very early series, *Interior* (1979), for instance, consists of a set of frontal color images of the dwellings of friends and family from his native Black Forest region. At first glance, the images seem flat and boring, perhaps because no event or action is occurring. They read as banal documents of one's personal space, with no theme or subject beyond this. Unsurprisingly, when Ruff first showed the *Interior* images to his mother, a homemaker who grew up on a farm, and his father, a technical director at a ceramics factory, they said, "Perfect. That's exactly how it looks in our house."[4] They saw them as just this: flat, straightforward documents of interior spaces. They did not see the images as "art," but rather as precise, faithful reproductions of reality. "I think my parents didn't realize that I went to [school to] study art," Ruff explains. "They thought, Thomas is going to study photography," a good profession with direct, unpretentious, practical sensibilities. Their reaction to the photographs points to the subtlety of the Becher School's preference for "flat and dry anonymity," as Daniel Birnbaum puts it.[5] They were not the only ones who needed an explanation for how and why its aesthetic looked the way it did.

The crux of the Becher School's aesthetic can be identified by the way it goes *almost* unnoticed as "art."[6] Another illustrative example from Ruff's early work are the now well-known *Portraits* (1981–87), a series consisting of several large-scale color photographs of friends and colleagues at the Art Academy. Each person featured in one of the images was photographed alone, head-on, without expression or emotion. The same framing technique is used throughout the series, emulating the often-rigid guidelines for passport photographs.[7] The flat and banal approach again mimics the "objective," quasi-scientific style of technical photography, while also foreshadowing a machine-like detachment that develops in Ruff's later work.[8] The *Portraits* were shown at galleries in Germany while Ruff was still a student, followed by exhibitions at important institutions in Europe and elsewhere.[9] And yet, despite the early success of this work, the artist remains dissatisfied with them and is irritated by particular viewers' interpretation of his *Portraits*.[10] It is not the specific meaning that people project on them that disappoints him, but rather, the imposition of *any* meaning at all. To amend the situation, in 1986, he enlarged the format from 18 × 24 cm to 165 × 210 cm and replaced the individually selected background colors with evenly lit, monochrome gray ones. Although the changes were minor, they effectively removed the possibility of linking the images to any expressive meaning or poetic content. The new series refocused viewers' attention on the frontal poses only, intensifying the anonymity, inexpressiveness, and serial nature of the "larger-than-life faces," as Ingrid Hoelzl and Remi Marie out it.[11] For Birnbaum, it is this absence of personal affect and involvement that effectively marks the artist's "objective" style, coinciding with the School's aesthetic.[12] I return to Ruff and his noisy digital transformations after further contextualizing the German School alongside the equally detached aesthetic of the mostly American New Photography genre in the next section.

The New Photography

The denial of meaning, hermeneutic closure, and comprehensive communicative transactions are tried and true marks of experimental art and photography from Duchamp and Warhol through John Baldessari and Jeff Wall (as they also are of media archaeology and postwar aesthetics, as discussed in the Introduction and chapter 2, respectively). What distinguishes the Becher School and Ruff's work in relation to the history of photography is their unique role catalyzing the development of the "New Photography" movement and its embrace of pseudo-objective scientific methods.

For French art critic Jean-François Chevrier, the New Photography emerged in the 1970s at the moment when the "photograph" in the traditional sense became a *tableau* (painting or picture), as Michael Fried notes.[13] In the context of media archaeology, the New Photography performs a deadness in the image, meaning a mood that emulates a death-like vacuity. For example, the new approach required artists to adopt an attitude of neutralization and quasi-scientific stance to their subject matter, in contrast to the highly emotive poet/artist pathos otherwise key to the history of painting and much of modern art. William Jenkins, curator of the defining 1975 exhibition *New Topographics: Photographs of a Man-Altered Landscape*, held at the International Museum of Photography at the George Eastman House in Rochester, explains the "viewpoint is . . . anthropological rather than critical, scientific rather than artistic."[14] His observation is insightful in more ways than one. Telltale signs of the genre include the now vernacular large-scale color print and photographs produced for a gallery or museum, rather than a magazine or newspaper. Robert Adams, Lewis Baltz, Joe Deal, Frank Gohlke, Nicholas Nixon, John Schott, Stephen Shore, Henry Wessel Jr., and the pioneering Bechers were among the artists featured in the exhibition. Once arriving in front of one of these massive prints, Fried observes, the viewer is confronted with a new kind of aesthetic experience. These images do not draw on straightforward methods, he explains, nor do they aim to communicate direct experiences (and herein lies the irony of Ruff's parents' "straight" response to his work). If the images seek to communicate anything, it is a rhetoric of anti-communication, intended to undermine century-long assumptions linking photography to notions of transparency, authenticity, and visual realism. Moreover, because the New Photographic artists primarily depicted the post-Nature landscapes of suburban and urban America, their work could not help but invoke an archaeological deadness in both style and content.

What then appeared to be the largely unannounced goals of the New Photography genre—like those of the Becher School—incited visual and historical ambiguity, *without appearing to do so*—at least not explicitly. By producing moments of apparent "openness and contradiction," as Chevrier puts it, the genre eschewed modernism's reactionary impulses for grand narratives of social, political, and technological progress.[15] In the same way that the cultural context of the late 1960s and 1970s brought about increasing forms of political disillusionment and sociocultural disappointments, he suggests, this new breed of seemingly dead-pan photographers sought to dismantle outdated responses to expressionism and delusions of grandeur. In creating an awkward distance between the image (object) and an individual's (subjective) aesthetic experience of it, as Chevrier suggests, both the New Photographers and the Becher-led German School echoed broader forms of cultural alienation and sociopolitical segregation between a subject and the world they lived in.

Early on, Ruff played a central role in the formation of the Becher School's aesthetic and in turn, was equally influenced by the New Topographic artists. In his later work, however, he has moved in a new direction, away from the pseudo-objective, and towards experimental techniques that lend themselves more directly to digital glitch, noise, and blur. In the 1990s, Ruff began investigations into various techniques utilized in the reproduction of digital images, from the stereoscope in his *Stereo-photos* (1994), to the telescope in *Stars* (1989–1992), and the Minolta Montage Unit (an image-generating machine for the creation of composite faces used by police departments in the 1970s) in *Portraits* (1994 and 1995). His more recent engagement with digital practices range from composite picture making to the use of night-vision technologies, hand tinting, digital retouching, photomontage, and appropriated imagery from such dissimilar sources as scientific archives, newspapers and more recently, the internet. He has also since addressed disparate genres and imaging conventions in the history of photography from collage techniques in *Newspaper Photographs* (1990–91) and *Retouched* (1995), to scientific imaging in *Stars* and *Machines* (2003).[16] In sum, true to his training, Ruff's style remains rooted in exceedingly controlled methods to ensure a lack of interpretive depth. His more recent work remains void of personal psychology though it bids adieu to the quasi-scientific objectivity that both the Becher School and the New Topographic artists implicitly sought.

III. RUFF'S *NUDES*

In the 1990s, Ruff stopped using a camera altogether. He produced instead a new series of works barely resembling the documentary style of his earlier training.[17]

This work drew on prêt-à-porter methods of appropriation, namely, foraging and mining the internet for pre-existent images. The *nudes* series is a prime example. He began the series in 1999, five years after the launch of Netscape in 1994, during a time when internet cultures were beginning to bubble. A friend of his suggested it might be interesting for him to turn to the subject of the nude but, after facing his lack of interest in traditional approaches (such as working with live models), he began researching the subject of the nude on the internet.[18] The first set of examples he encountered were the classics, nudes taken by well-known fashion photographers like Helmut Newton and Peter Lindbergh, carefully composed photographs that were not especially inspiring to him.

Ruff next decided to try expanding his search terms. The results produced an astounding mass of internet pornography. "There were so many [pornographic] images," Ruff explains, images that were "much more honest than all the artistic nude photography . . . I had seen previously."[19] For early internet media, pornography was (and still is) prosaic, inviting divergent critiques beyond the scope of this discussion.[20] To skirt the issue entirely, however, would be negligent. At the very least, it can be agreed that pornography is candid, showing a lot and holding back very little. In contrast, the erotic image can be said to play more subtle games with visual mystique, perception, and hiding and revealing. In photography, the distinction between "the naked and the nude" is often used to distinguish between porn and erotic art. Some will likely disagree with this quick delineation and, of course, the harder we press them, the more quickly any distinction between pornography and erotic art, or the naked and the nude, will fall apart. Nonetheless, a loose contour is drawn here to show how Ruff moves between them, further challenging their constructed distinctness.

Ruff was drawn to the pornographic images he found online, not for their sexual nature, he explains, but because of their "low-resolution pixel structure."[21] He found that the unintentionally noisy aura cast across the majority of them resembled the abstract compositions he had been toying with on his computer. The key difference was that the noisy appearance of internet porn was due to its low resolution and excessive copying, whereas the abstract compositions the artist had been experimenting with were deliberate abstractions. Nonetheless, the visual parallel guided his decision to move forward with the topic and create a series of related images, which eventually became *nudes*.

Using the techniques he had already been experimenting with at home (software-based distortion effects, modified color, and the removal of intrusive details), he transformed his downloaded selections to the point where the pixel structure and representational content were highly ambiguous.[22] In other words, he enlarged the "found" internet images as much as he could, without completely eclipsing the capacity to loosely recognize the content from afar. By maximizing the size of an already extremely low-resolution internet image ("blocks of eight-by-eight pixels") it was inevitable that any additional noise or digital distortion would further obfuscate their readability. This was especially the case "at close range," where all of the images became "unreadable representationally," akin to the dots in a pointillist painting.[23] This was precisely the effect Ruff sought, one he had previously attempted to emulate through more contrived means. It also marked an important break with the medium's conventional use and the straightforward realisms of the Becher School, which now seem to fit more squarely in traditional histories of the medium.

Ruff produced his final results by smoothing over the rawness of the stark source material, producing a whimsical, blurry-pixel eroticism; a Gerhard Richter for the internet age. Abstraction softened and accentuated the images' visceral and graphic qualities, shifting their collective identity from "bad Internet porn," to deliberately staged imagery that appeared to look like "bad art."[24] Greg Hainge offers a detailed argument of Ruff's images, discussing the various techniques the artist uses, including cropping and reframing an image so that bodies and limbs bisect the entire space, sometimes vertically, as in *nudes ga 08,* and sometimes diagonally, as in *nude ree07* (2001), *nudes ez14* (1999), and *nudes dg06* (2003).[25] In the latter, one leg creates the base of the diagonal bisection, framed by an overlapping folded leg, creating an arrow towards the top left-hand corner of the composition.[26] The lines are further accentuated with the white shoes, deepened again by the back seams on the subject's translucent stockings. In other images, Hainge notes, body parts are used to horizontally frame the image, such as *nudes noe 09* (2000) and *nude gu 06* (2000), where an inserted dildo is seen at the very center of the image, tracing a line out to the left of the frame with a stroke of brilliant red and translucent blue. This same kind of dissection reoccurs in *nudes ez 14* (1999), where a "dark space between the profiles of two women about to kiss" creates a fuzzy visual tension by activating the negative space.[27]

As noted, the *nude* series also utilized visual techniques in blur and ambiguity to play with historical tensions between the naked and the nude. Where the former suggests a cruder, raw depiction of a naked body (i.e., porn) the latter slides (or attempts to slide) into the domain of "the erotic," often affiliated with art. In other words, if the naked is akin to the straightforward style of the pseudo-objective Becher School, then the nude (and by extension the erotic) denotes a somewhat nuanced and more seductive mode of simultaneously revealing and concealing in an image. Is this a tenet of glitch aesthetics? Possibly. In traditional pornography (and photography), being out of focus, focusing on the wrong object, or missing the "money shot" definitively indicates failure in a work or series of images. This is illustrated in John Baldessari's black-and-white photograph *Wrong* (1966–68), discussed in the Introduction. Here, however, this genre-defining convention is rewired into a new circuit that curtails a clear signal to produce instead ambiguous visual noise. Put differently, the failure to show too much becomes an entry point for a poetic language of ambiguity; a *seeming* accidental transformation of signal into noise. It is also at this point that Ruff's work gestures towards the

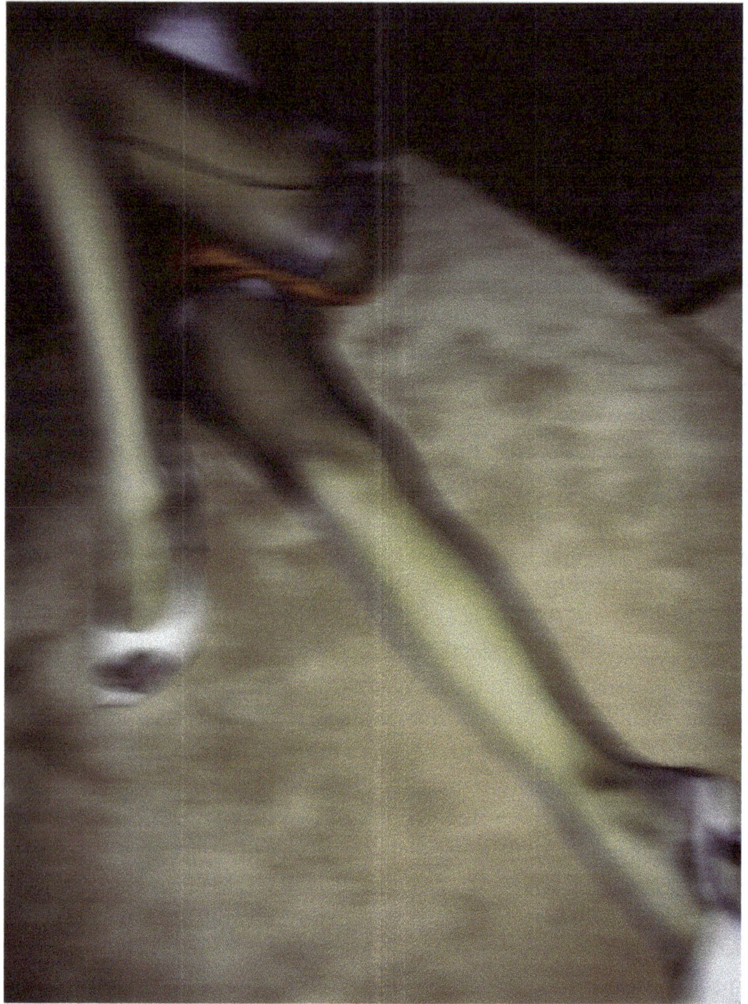

FIGURE 17. Thomas Ruff, *nudes dg06* (2003). Visual noise fuses barely stockinged legs with a beige carpet in the background. © Thomas Ruff / SOCAN (2019).

first and second tenets of failure noted above: the use of noise to deny cultural norms for clear visual communication, coupled with a deliberate introduction of uncertainty in the development of a visual rhetoric of anti-communication. This further underscores how nudity itself operates in the series as an allegory for the ambiguous haze of perception, as such. Unlike his predecessors, Ruff's new work begins to draw on twenty-first-century techniques that rely on optical ambiguity to reflect new cultural concerns with obfuscation, transmission, and comprehension.[28]

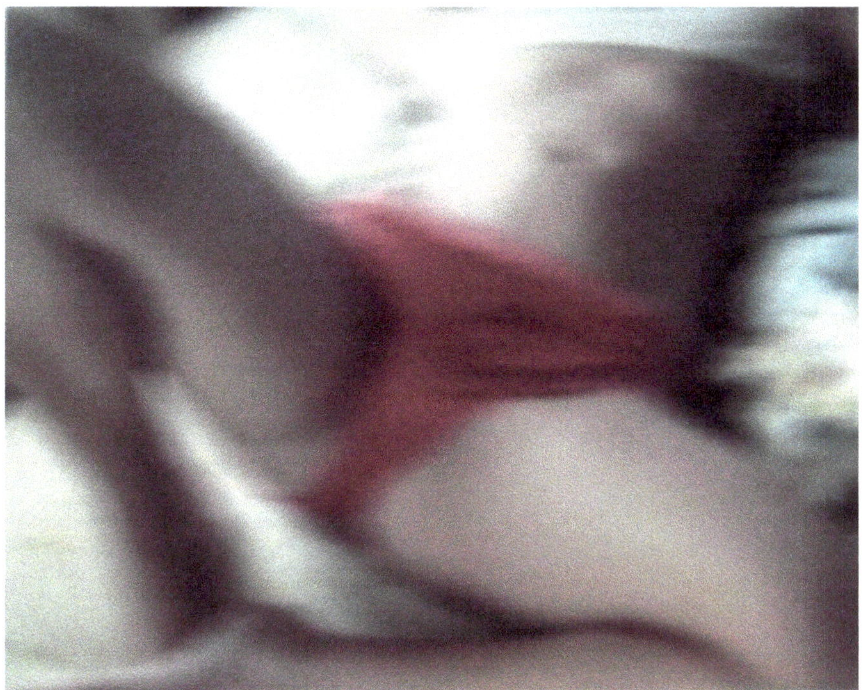

FIGURE 18. Thomas Ruff, *nudes ree07* (2001). Photo noise softens the candidness of a classic "money shot" pose. © Thomas Ruff / SOCAN (2019).

We can also identify in the *nudes* an explicit attempt to undermine classical traditions of representation and, Hainge notes, unified theories of perception, such as those presented in the markedly German tradition of Gestalt.[29] Defined as a psychological and holistic approach to artistic creation, in Gestalt all aspects of a work play a necessary and vital role in the formation of the whole. Many Gestalt tendencies derive from the work of Bauhaus artist Wassily Kandinsky[30] and extend through colorists Josef Albers and Johannes Itten, Russian formalism, Mondrian, the architecture of Le Corbusier and Bruno Taut, and the interior design of De Stijl and the Eames. On the whole, Gestalt is linked to modernist tendencies and telltale signs of Ruff's effort to work against this tradition, Hainge argues, includes the use of cropping to cut off certain body parts, especially head and eyes, off-center compositions, and produce deliberately "off" color combinations (like neon green and white).[31] In this way, some of the *nudes* qualify for the "accidental color aesthetic" discussed in chapter 3. Finally, the open structure of each image, with hands, heads, and limbs cut off, allows us to see how the motif of consistently severed body parts echoes the postmodern sentiment of the moment, with its insistence on the fragmentation of perception and modern life, always already

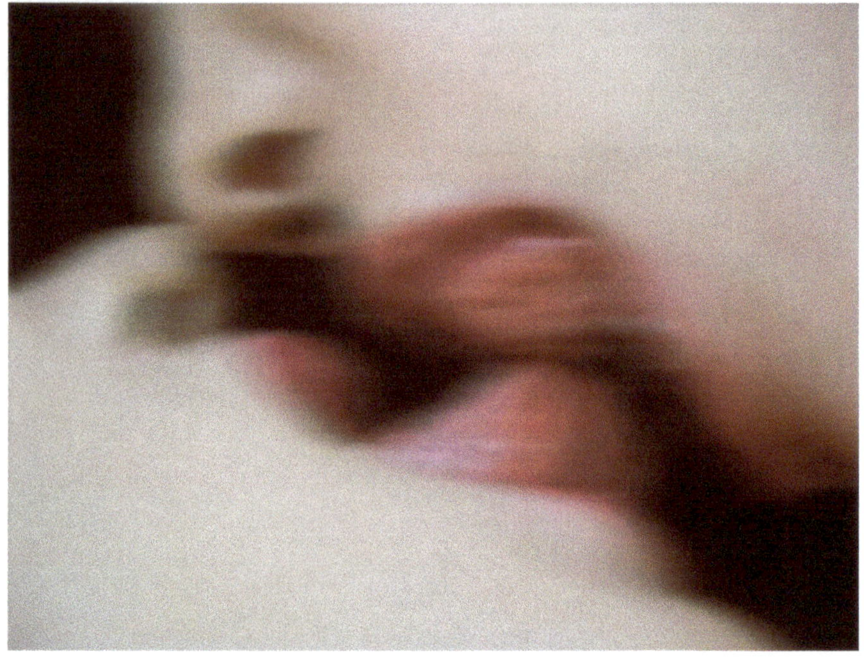

FIGURE 19. Thomas Ruff, *nudes ez14* (1999). The two sets of blurry, painted lips create a tension in their mirror-image. © Thomas Ruff / SOCAN (2019).

mediated by new media technologies. Noisy color becomes the primary means to most accurately reflect this paradigm.

Michael Fried goes so far as to suggest that Ruff's color treatment has an affinity with fauvism and German expressionism, given that both movements concerned themselves with "garish color," as he puts it.[32] However, both fauvism and German expressionism use bold and saturated colors, while Ruff's colors are always at least a bit muted and unsaturated. This occurs in part because of the technological limitations in forcing such extreme enlargements of low-resolution digital images, but also as a result of his artistic choice. Ruff's colors are loud, but they do not overtake the image, as one could argue of fauvism. In fact, if Fried were to seek a more appropriate digital correlative for the bold colors of fauvism or German expressionism, he might turn to the racy colors of datamoshing, discussed in the next chapter.

Regardless of the relative weight of color in the *nude* series, the work as a whole exhibits a proclivity for blur and noise as its primary motif and mode of expression; noise as surface phenomenon is conflated with the signified content of the images. Visually unclear shapes and objects speak a language of uncertainty that is in fact more accurate and "honest"—to borrow from Ruff's description of internet

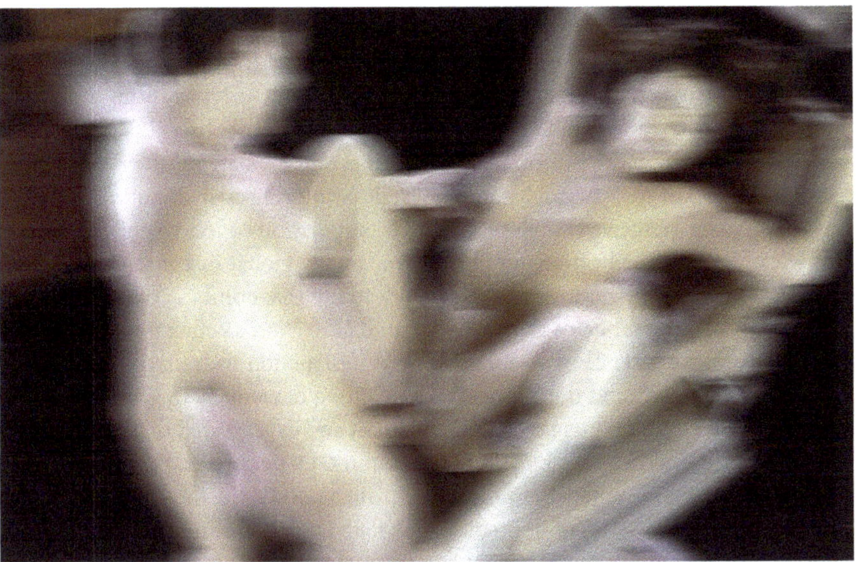

FIGURE 20. Thomas Ruff, *nudes emo8* (2001). Bodies are blurred and repeated to suggest an abstract elegance in mechanical movement. © Thomas Ruff / SOCAN (2019).

pornography—than the perpetually deferred promise of clarity, the fulfillment of desire, or any other such industry-derived rhetoric around "crisp and clear" digital colors. Ruff's colors are candid about their falsity, they do not attempt to communicate anything beyond themselves, and this, in turn, makes them "honest." This is also why Ruff's use of color is void of nostalgia. As I argue in chapter 3, color-as-color or, color-as noise always carries a balance between signified imagery and its material form of appearance. Similarly, in an interview with Paul Pfeiffer, Ruff explains his goal to "reflect the medium in the image itself" (i.e., Wollen's fore-grounding), one must "always be aware of the medium while using it."[33] Chromatic noise, again, becomes the primary technique to accomplish this, not because the color is bold or outlandish, but because color and shifts between light and dark are the only vehicle through which pixels *can* collectively resolve themselves as data on screen, whether as clear, communicative signal or fuzzy and ambiguous noise.[34] Here, the first tenet of Ruff's work—the failure to instantiate norms of visual communication—takes on the cool, slightly distanced approach from the Becher School and New Topographics, and in so doing, segues into the second and third tenets: the intentional blockage of meanings and failure to provide a comprehensive communicative exchange, often by way of technological mediation. The next and penultimate section of this chapter further considers the third tenet, where visual noise operates through the graphic attributes of the JPEG image while also speaking to a set of low-level human fears projected onto them.

IV. RUFF'S *JPEGS* (2000–)

We now turn to Ruff's noisiest series: the *jpegs* (2002–). Like the *nudes,* the *jpegs* do not gesture towards nostalgia in the slightest. Rather, in typical Ruff-style, they adopt a cool disposition akin to the detached eye of a scientist observing phenomena under a microscope, which, I argue, also becomes a blank slate for the projection of cultural fears.[35] The *jpegs* began in 2002 as a series exploring crisis, failure, and breakdown, using the (perceived) "failure" of JPEG compression codecs to do so. To create this work, Ruff focused on scenes of disaster, usually global in consequence, from the crumbling of the twin towers in New York to the U.S. bombing of Baghdad; the Iraqi Army burning oil fields during the second Gulf War; satellite photos attempting to prove the existence of weapons of mass destruction in Iraq; the Russians in Georgia and Grozny; and the Khmer Rouge's killing of civilians in Cambodia.[36] He gathered low-resolution images from the internet and exacerbated their grainy, low-res appearance by downsampling them to about 100 kb per image. He then enlarged them again to a monumental size ranging from 188×188 cm to 297×364 cm. The result was a uniform series of dramatically pixilated and blurry images of barely recognizable scenes of disaster, rendered at a whopping 1.3 GB per image file. As with the *nudes,* by significantly increasing the compression artifacts in the already low-resolution images, he accentuated the pixel structure to intensify visual noise, highlight blocks of color, and obscure objects and elements depicted therein. In the artist's words: "I had to re-scale the files to a very small size and then compress them as the worst possible quality JPEGs."[37] The technique appears to be the same as the one used in *nudes* but, according to the artist, in the *nude* series, he used blurring because the "material was so ugly,"[38] while in *jpegs,* pixilation techniques were used to investigate the material logic of the compression scheme itself, to which we now turn.

JPEG History

In 1987, the Joint Photographic Experts Group (JPEG) produced the first single standard of image data compression for web users. Between 1986 and 1994, the committee created the first international standard for still (single-frame) image compression, intended to ensure global compatibility. The "Joint" in JPEG refers to the link between the International Standardization Organization (ISO), which develops standards in a wide range of fields, from freight container dimensions to ISBN numbers for books, and its specialized partner organizations, the International Electrotechnical Commission (IEC) and the International Telecommunication Union (ITU).[39] The publication of the JPEG codec as a joint ISO/IEC standard in 1994 coincided with the launch of the first commercial web graphic browser, Netscape Navigator, a merger foreshadowing the centrality of digital images in today's media culture.

At the same time, and as scholars have recently noted, algorithmic compression is in no way unique to digital media or the internet. To note only one example,

FIGURE 21. Thomas Ruff, *jpeg wlo1* (2006). Tight cropping leaves a viewer uncertain as to where or when this destructive event occurred. The compressed title barely gives a clue. © Thomas Ruff / SOCAN (2019).

recall Filippo Brunelleschi's fifteenth-century demonstration of linear perspective which necessarily involved the compression of three-dimensional space onto a two-dimensional plane, as also noted in the Introduction. Decompression occurs when any viewer uses the synthetic processes of perception to decode visual information.[40] To press this a step further, we might also draw on Alexander R. Galloway's recent proposition that the history of media *is* a history of compression. For Galloway, and I would agree, we are undergoing a progressive "cataclysmic compression of modern life." This applies to multiple aspects of culture, from visual art to philosophy and economic theory. He gives a range of illustrative examples from the compression of thought in philosophy, to the notion of "the roundoff" in engineering, denoting the process of digitizing data so that the nuances of analog information are "rounded off" to the closest digital integer. Galloway also notes the treatment of redundancy and ornament in minimalism, where the gradual deletion of surreptitious material becomes a definitive motif of the entire genre.[41]

Both Philip Agre and Bernard Stiegler have proposed similar theories, largely complementary to Galloway's. The notion of "grammatization," which Stiegler borrows from Derrida, denotes how human experience and activity are compressed into units or "grammars of action."[42] Similarly, Galloway notes, recent scholarship by Luciana Parisi on the "incompressible" and by Hito Steyerl on the "poor image" do much the same work. One could also include recent studies of increasing repetition in pop music, inadvertently leading to an overall compression in the genre.[43] In one sense then, Galloway's theory of compression is compatible with dominant tendencies already known and accepted in the media environment. His focus on the gradual *reduction* of information, rather than industry-driven discourses of constant improvement also falls in line with the aims of media archaeology.

To return to the JPEG, it is a compression algorithm known as a codec. A codec regulates how information is compressed and decompressed within digital technologies (see chapter 1).[44] The particularity of the JPEG codec derives from its capacity to compress continuous color images of "real-world" subjects, as found in conventional photography and paintings. Color is the name of the game in JPEG compression. The format's defining attributes are its capacity to translate massive amounts of nuanced color information into a much smaller and manageable series of abstract digits. The key to understanding JPEG compression is that with it, a "photograph," in the traditional sense of the term, ceases to be a photograph because a JPEG "image" is in fact entirely made up of a series of numerical abstractions and computer algorithms. A JPEG is therefore no longer tied to a specific light-capturing medium, but instead a linear and numerical organization of color information that can be reduced to binary data.

JPEGs also employ a "lossy" method of data compression. This means its compression logic enforces the removal of "redundant" information, based on the sensitivity of a so-called standard human observer. Lossy compression is one of two standard methods for digital image compression. It is the most common, typically found with the majority of downloadable sound and image media. Lossy compression also involves a good deal of information loss, the space for and through which noise emerges. The MP3 format for instance uses psychoacoustic filtering to remove data deemed unnecessary to reproduce a normatively acceptable sound quality (again, defined by a so-called standard observer) with the goal of making the file smaller. At the same time, when MP3 files circulate online, they do so through "lossless" networks which is to say, the loss of data typically occurs when the file is originally created, not by way of network distribution.

The second core compression method is "lossless" compression, which, as its name suggests, involves negligible data loss. Because the accurate transmission and reception of data is fundamental to all networking, whether wire, radio, internet, or telephone, the majority of data compression is lossless, where zero data loss is routine. ZIP and DMG files are two examples of lossless compression. In both cases, all data are kept on file but there is a removal of redundant data upon encoding that is later restored upon decoding or, the decompression of the file at its end point (i.e., when you click on a zip file to open it).[45] Where lossy images are useful for saving time and space and for increasing processing speed or facilitating transmission and circulation on the internet, lossless images are more useful for high-end print reproduction where detail is required. Because the JPEG's lossy compression sequence is bare bones, it is much easier to tweak and degrade its rendering algorithms to produce visual "noise."

There are also different levels for rendering the quality of JPEGs. Photoshop, for instance, offers a range from one to twelve, with twelve being the least amount of compression for the file, retaining the most amount of information and producing a JPEG with the highest possible image quality. In contrast, a JPEG quality of "1" offers a version of the image that will be compressed into the smallest file size and is the most efficient choice for internet uploading, downloading, and circulation, but will also inevitably result in artifacts and pixilation. As noted, it was this most extreme form of JPEG compression that Ruff chose for the images in this series, successfully highlighting the most dramatic discontinuities between adjacent pixel blocks.[46]

In sum, the reductive logic of compression, outlined here, is central to Ruff's *jpegs* series. There is the exploitation of the codec and pixelated rendering already described. There is also a use of compression *language* to nominalize each image in the series. Many images are given titles that appear as codes: "ca02," "wl01," "ka01," "la01," "d01," and so on, themselves so compressed they are not even words anymore (like Shannon's definition of "Information" noted in chapter 1). The titles thus create additional conceptual noise that further complicates meaning and a viewer's ability to decode when or where the image is sourced from, let alone when it was taken.[47] This same logic of compression also extends to the artist's treatment of otherwise devastating international tragedies. This is not to be taken as a coldness, in the sense of a lack of concern or care for the well-being or tragedy of others, but rather, as a critical and mimetic performance of the impersonal nature under which the vast majority of us are increasingly exposed to images of war and international disaster. Many of us increasingly access the world through low-resolution newsfeeds and cell phone screens where what happened to whom and when is often unclear, save for the fact that something catastrophic occurred (again).

V. BEAUTY IN A BROKEN WORLD

Despite Ruff's cool style, appropriation of error, and detached mode of display, there is still some old-world beauty to be gleaned from his digitally distorted work. All of the images discussed in this chapter are still images, which is to say that they are frozen and static in time. By definition, they open a space for a pause and reflection. In this pause, Ruff's visual noise—for all its explicitness and exploitation— still manages to generate a peaceful moment of contemplation in our otherwise nonstop flow of information. In this space, beauty returns as the unresolved truth of seeing and being seen. Put differently, what is beautiful in these images is their strategic break with illusions of transparency so deeply entrenched in the history and rhetoric of Western culture and photography in particular. Photographic conventions have for decades laid claim to a crystal-clear, objective reality. In some ways, this is precisely what Ruff's early work sought to do but never seemed to drive home on a mass scale. This is undoubtedly not the case with his later work where noise is clearly unclear. His denial of objectivity and (illusions of) visual transparency render the invisible noise of our media environment on the very surface of the image, however frustrating their cognitive reception may be. In this way, his artificial noise is perhaps one of the most accurate reflections of how daily life is actually experienced in a media-saturated society: unclear, dismal, and exceedingly reductive.

At the same time, this is not to say that Ruff's work is overtly political, or even tacitly so. Rather, in allegorizing the conditions of visual and communicative failure, he subtly iterates what is already troubling in modern life and experience. Jodi Dean's concept of "communicative capitalism," introduced in chapter 3, is again useful for describing this condition as one marked by "noise" and a ubiquity of failed communications. Communication fails in global capital because it no longer functions in the sense of a "communicative bridge," as noted by John Durham Peters (chapter 1). That is, capitalism no longer communicates at all, but instead excels at broadcasting noise, while laying claim to the inverse. "What hinders communication" today, Dean explains, is "communicability itself."[48] Circa 1990, Luc Boltanski and Eve Chiapello identified a similar tendency in contemporary art, a failure running alongside the neutralization of critique. Their claims, albeit referring the post-1989 political situation, connect politics and art, wherein both have lost the possibility of generating meaning, returning us to the same contradiction between content and mode of expression.[49] Ruff's work shows us how the internet is a paradigmatic example of this gap and failure across art, politics, and cultural communications writ large. He does so elegantly and "honestly," which is to say, he makes poetry out of the sad fact that the more data we produce, the less meaning we find. He is also hardly alone in using glitch techniques to do so, as we have seen in the previous two chapters and will see again in the chapters that follow.

5

Chroma Glitch

Data as Style

*The digital image is too ordered and too rational—and not random enough.
In our experience of it, it lacks . . . "being."*

—JOHN BELTON, "PSYCHOLOGY OF THE PHOTOGRAPHIC, CINEMATIC,
TELEVISUAL, AND DIGITAL IMAGE"

I. DATA AS STYLE

Awash in platitudes of progress, transparency, and control, the innovation age also breeds an inversely proportionate dose of fragmentation and failure.[1] This much was established in the Introduction and chapter 1. Subsequent chapters have analyzed philosophical and aesthetic strategies for coping with this situation. This chapter builds on the discussion of color as noise in chapters 3 and 4, extending it to a threefold analysis of the formal attributes of "datamoshing."

Defined as the aesthetic manipulation of digital video compression codecs and decompression algorithms, datamoshing is decked in bold hyper colors and eye-popping animations. It is a subgenre of glitch art, which, as noted in the Introduction, can be found throughout the pop culture, art, and design industries.[2] Datamoshing's anti-communicative, chunky aesthetic presents a powerful antithesis to the ideology of signal processing, with its unspoken investments in radical compression. As a subgenre of glitch art, datamoshing has been subject to numerous and often disparate definitions. Priscilla Frank defines the genre as a "widespread net art trend in which images crumble into a colorful bath of pixels," a designation that seems to suggest more of a happy accident than anything deliberate or artful.[3] Alice Pfeiffer, however, writing for the *New York Times*, defines datamoshing as the "manipulation of compression frames" to produce "an overly pixellated appearance," identifying the crucial role of intentionality in the aesthetic.[4] "Appearance" is the keyword here. Artists-qua-programmers generate excessive pixilation to create a veneer of chaos and lack of control. This

FIGURE 22. Paul B. Davis and Jacob Ciocci, *Compression Study #1 (Untitled Data Mashup)* (2007), digital video, color, 2 minutes. This pioneering datamosh mixes Rihanna's smash hit *Umbrella* (2007) with the Cranberries' *Zombie* (1994).

FIGURE 23. Kanye West. *Welcome to Heartbreak* (2009). Directed by Nabil Elderkin, edited by Ryan Bartley at Ghost Town Media. Digital video, color, 4 minutes, 23 seconds.

out-of-control façade is definitive of the genre, one that first and foremost involves a controlled and strategic manipulation of digital media.

One pioneering example is Paul Davis and Jacob Ciocci's *Compression Study #1* (2007) for which they combined a clip from Rihanna's smash hit video *Umbrella* (2007) with a clip from the Cranberries' music video *Zombie* (1994), featuring vocalist Dolores O'Riordan, in addition to a selection of television clips and internet videos. The piece begins with an image of Rihanna singing which, a few seconds later, begins to break apart. Pixels formerly concealed in shimmering bronze flesh break into macroblocks, bleeding until the entirety of the image has morphed into an image of O'Riordan singing in the Cranberries' *Zombie*. The effect is both sudden and poetic, designed to mosh the image and sound simultaneously.

Similar examples of datamoshing in mass media and pop culture music videos include Chairlift's "Evident Utensil" (2008); Linkin Park's "New Divide" (2009); Kanye West's *Welcome to Heartbreak* (2009), directed by Nabil Elderkin and edited by Ryan Bartley at Ghost Town Media; and A$AP Mob's "Yamborghini High" (2016), edited and directed by Shomi Patwary of Illusive Media. Whether off-line or online, datamoshing draws from emerging trends in internet culture and the deliberate deterioration of high-resolution images into "colorful baths of pixels," as Frank puts it.[5]

The "moshing" of computer code marks one significant difference between glitch art (and by extension, datamoshing) and the more general forms of visual or conceptual noise found in the work of John Baldessari (Introduction), Ryan Trecartin (chapter 3), and Thomas Ruff (chapter 4). Where glitch art and datamoshing involve hacks into computer algorithms, they are unlike other techniques in visual noise, which could include anything from abstraction to loosely defined anti-communicative breaks from representational norms. At the same time, as a subgenre of glitch art, datamoshing embodies a slightly narrower definition than the more general category of glitch art. For example, the latter includes work from Rosa Menkman, Jon Cates, and Andrew Benson, which certainly involve programming-based interventions into computer processing, but is not to be confused with datamoshing because a good deal of their work does not involve specific interventions with video compression codecs (I provide a technical exegesis of video compression codecs below).

Minor genre distinctions aside, it is undeniable that the chunky digital artifacts of datamoshing and glitch art seem to say nothing and communicate even less. How then can we explain their popularity as a cultural style, from fine art to mass media? How did these formerly erroneous glitches manage to move from signifying an unwanted state to the essence of a pop culture fashion, whether as nightclub special effect or hip décor for *Bloomberg Businessweek*?[6] What is it about glitch art and datamoshing that provides added value, whether organic, trendy, superficial, counterhegemonic, or otherwise?

This chapter provides a preliminary set of responses by analyzing key examples of datamoshing in a threefold framework of the analog and the digital. I do not have in mind the physical technologies we are familiar with, but rather the analog and digital as *metaphors*; as aesthetic strategies connected to specific historical and material registers. My first conceptual framework for the analog and digital adopts the lens of colorism, which denotes the particular way an artist or designer uses color. For instance, saturated complementary colors typify the fauvist style, while strong blacks denote German expressionism, and primary hues embody cubism or

FIGURE 24. Rosa Menkman, *Demolish the eerie u25bcoid* (2010). Digital video, color, 1 minute. Menkman's work masterfully illustrates data as noise, while still conveying deeper meanings. Courtesy of Rosa Menkman.

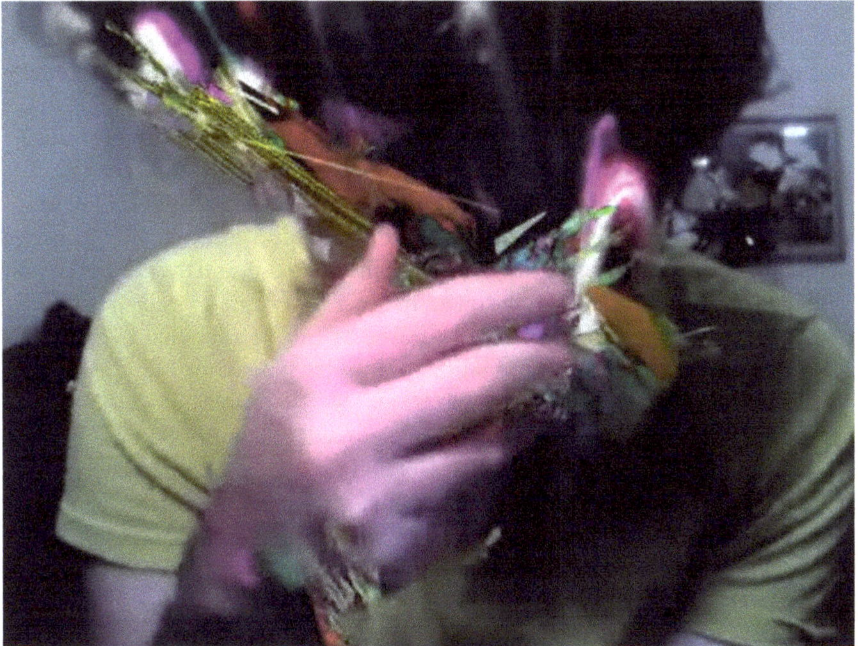

FIGURE 25. Andrew Benson. *Sparkle Face Test* (2011). Digital video, color, 40 seconds. Made with Max SP, a motion-tracking software, Benson uses his hand gestures to control the multicolored rays of glitch abstraction. Courtesy of Andrew Benson.

De Stijl.[7] My second framework considers compositional structure. I draw on Gilles Deleuze's theory of aesthetics, articulated in terms of analog and digital synthesizers. The third frame turns to Heinrich Wölfflin's account of the historical development of style from the High Renaissance to the baroque. The chapter concludes that the analog and digital, as metaphors removed from the technical systems they normatively signify, provide insight into the development of an aesthetic paradigm rooted in uncertainty, hyperactivity, and sensory overload; not coincidentally, the very same attributes definitive of the contemporary media environment.

II. COMPRESSION ECONOMIES

To be clear, the popularity of glitch aesthetics does not imply that the long-standing demand for media fidelity and crisp visual imagery has dissipated. To the contrary, the vast majority of consumers, producers, and users expect as much, especially from well-advertised "new media" products like HDTV, IMAX cinema, or Blu-ray Disc, all of which turn on the successful engineering of compression algorithms for digital formats. Such industry standards derive from a broader history of engineering, beginning with nineteenth-century research in psychophysics, through acoustical engineering conducted at research centers like Bell Telephone Laboratories, Xerox Parc in the mid twentieth century, and Tesla and Google Labs today.[8] In short, decisions for establishing which codecs to use in optimizing a signal are based on rigorous research into communicative efficiency and control.

A host of media theorists have critiqued our culture's relentless drive for smaller and more compact media, capable of delivering cleaner, faster, and more enriched content.[9] Vernacular digital formats like the GIF, MP3, MP4, JPEG, PDF, PNG, TIFF, or TARGA all have histories of radical data compression, straddling tensions between innovation and experimentation, on the one hand, and the need to comply with engineering standards, on the other. In order to become an industry standard at all, compression schemes must be approved by the International Organization for Standardization, an international standard-setting body for the internet, and the International Telecommunications Union (ITU), established in 1865 as the International Telegraph Union. According to media historian Sean Cubitt, the ITU is the "oldest intergovernmental treaty body still functioning today." Its tasks include safeguarding the "interoperability of telecom systems, pricing regimes for international calling, and infrastructures for audiovisual services," which includes "moving image encoding," or simply, "low bit-rate communications."[10] One result of this governance is an endless stream of faster and more efficient "universal" standards for global communication media. As consumers, we have been trained to expect this much, and more, at ever cheaper prices.

When new and improved technologies fail to deliver these cheaper and faster options, or reveal a brief stutter, dropped signal, or failure to load, one is immediately disappointed. What happened to all of these rigorous standards? We are more lenient with internet imagery, where the occasional glitch is tolerated, but too much interruption, static, or noise yields the same dissatisfied results, causing us to revert back to older media—the telephone, face-to-face visits—inquiring what "went wrong." In sum, global culture's hegemonic imperatives for technocratic progress ensure that innovation in compression engineering will continue to be big business in years to come. But consider now that the very thing that is unwanted in prosaic media experience is precisely what is sought after in glitch art. To better understand these seemingly unwanted glitches, we must set aside these otherwise normative cultural demands for high resolution, fidelity, and verisimilitude.

III. THREE APPROACHES TO STYLE

Analog Color versus Digital Colors

While my goal here is to depart from literal digital and analog systems, a cursory technical distinction is nonetheless in order. The analog is defined as a series of continuous wave forms and infinite gradations of data, as found on a vinyl record, in the sound waves exchanged in face-to-face conversation, or in analog electronic computers. Data operate through analogy. An analog computer, for example, takes a quantity from a physical source, like an electric current or sound, and abstracts it into a corresponding value that is directly representative of the input, such as a sound wave or X-ray. Data are then transferred from input to output in a continuous form, which a producer can control by "modulating" the single frequency between them.

Digital technology, on the other hand, is defined by a series of discrete units of information from which other formations can then derive. In a digital system, such as a digital computer, the basic language is arithmetic. A digital computer operates through a rigorous quantization of discrete numerical values, often in binary form, where each unit (0 or 1) is the baseline from which all other digital media derive. But digital technology is not exclusive to modern computing. Our two sets of five digits known as fingers are a digital system that has always been a part of human culture.

James Small has defined the difference between the analog and the digital by comparing them with the slide rule and the abacus, respectively:

> In the abacus, quantities are represented by a number of beads, thus the quantity being represented can only vary, up or down, by a minimum of one bead—there are no partial beads . . . . all operations are performed as a series of additions or subtractions. In contrast, the slide rule represents quantities as continuously varying magnitudes: in this case length. The granularity of the result is limited only by the coarseness of the scale used to perform the measurement.[11]

The British artist and color theorist David Batchelor makes a series of insightful claims about colorism in contemporary art based on the distinction between

TABLE 1. Analog and Digital as Cultural Technologies

Analog Technology	Digital Technology
• Analog technology is identified by its *continuous and uninterrupted* waveforms. Examples include vinyl records, audiocassette tapes, "wet" photography, and the human voice.	• Digital technology is defined by a series of *discrete* units of information. For example, binary digits consist of two integers, 0 and 1, which are the basic units of measure used to calculate and build all additional developments.

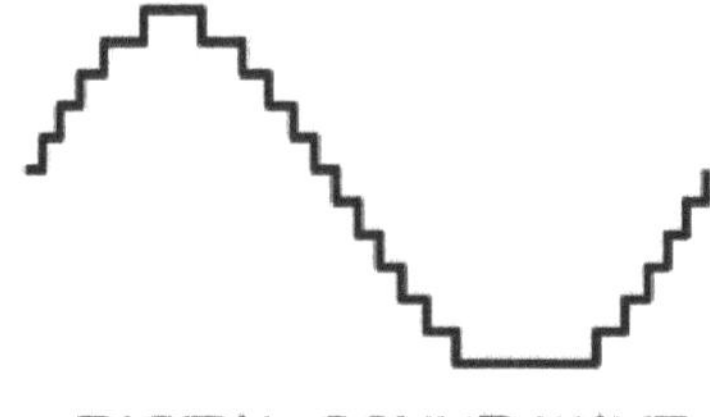

• If an "analogy" implies a general likeness or indexical relation between two things or concepts, analog technology likewise involves an equivalence between two sets of terms. With traditional "wet" photography, for instance, light is captured on a photosensitive substrate which, after processing in the darkroom, reveals an analogous imprint.	• Digital systems are not exclusive to computing, though this is where they are most commonly affiliated. Digital technologies also include the five digits on each hand, an abacus, or any other system where individual units are divided into discrete entities.

analog and digital. I ultimately take issue with his periodization of color styles, but they are worth exploring as a preamble to his more germane conceptual distinction between analog color and digital colors.

The widespread introduction of industrial-ordered color after World War II, Batchelor argues, led to an overall digitization of color, by which he has in mind a style, not a literal technology.[12] "Colour-chart colours" contributed to a "change in the use and understanding of colour. This might be called the digitalization of colour, whose opposite is analogical colour."[13] A number of artistic and industrial design examples support this claim, but many examples also contradict it. Table 2 provides an overview of the comparison between the analog and the digital as styles of color and composition.

In Batchelor's theoretical approach to the twin concepts, analog color denotes "the one" and digital colors connote "the many." As a singular phenomenon, analog color has no inner or outer divisions, formal limits, or intrinsic distinctions. It is conceptually and perceptually undifferentiated, regardless of discipline or medium. Analog color invokes the "magical splendor" of witnessing color phenomena mixing and melting in the sky, a moving image or a spinning wheel. Where analog color is a wheel, digital colors are the "infinite and infinitely thin

TABLE 2. Analog and Digital as Stylistic Modes

Colorism (color treatment)	**Analog Color**	**Digital Colors**
	• Continuous, undifferentiated color; no inside or outside; indivisible and indecipherable mixtures. Color "spreads flows bleeds stains floods soaks seeps merges. It does not segment or subdivide" (Batchelor, *Chromophobia*, 86).	• Discrete colors that can be divided or indexed within a larger system or organization (CIE lab, HTML, Pantone).
	• Gamut is often represented as a circle, allowing mixing and blending.	• Gamut is represented as a chart or table with distinct divisions between colors.
	• Nietzsche's Dionysian chaos	• Nietzsche's Apollonian individuation
	• Associations with romanticism, utopia, childlike innocence.	• Associations with nominalization, order, systems, and hierarchies.
	• Artistic illustration in Seurat, Rothko, Rist.	• Artistic illustration in Mondrian, Riley, Hirst, Bulloch.
Compositional Structure	**Analog Synthesizer**	**(Digital) Code**
	• Analogical compositions are "modular," involving fusions of difference.	• Less a diagram than a symbolic code.
	• Color is used to structure an analogic and continuous language.	• Units are grouped visually in terms of binary opposition.
	• Relation to the haptic; the "manual lines" of Jackson Pollock, having neither inside nor outside; an abysmal chaos deployed to the extreme.	• Colors are derivative of predetermined codes or machinic orders.
		• Piet Mondrian's "digital grids" create a "code" that is cerebral and lacks sensation.
	• Generative of a new creative order and rhythm to come, emerging from the ground of (haptic) sensation.	• Relation to classical perspective (see Deleuze, *Logique du sens* [Paris: Minuit, 1966]).

spokes inserted in the wheel."[14] Consider the effect of watching a spinning wheel, even a bicycle wheel, where the individual spokes (or colors) become indecipherable. In rapid movement, we do not experience one color in isolation but instead, an ineffable mixing of all the colors on the wheel, as a whole. In this way, analog color touches on holistic visions of a mystical cosmos, like Heraclitus's "All things are one,"[15] or Spinoza's "univocity of being" as interpreted by Gilles Deleuze. One could also align analog color with Galloway's recent work on François Laruelle, or Nietzsche's Dionysian "primal oneness," where analog color, like some conceptions of noise, act as a signifier of undifferentiated beings.

In the history of art and design, analog color can be identified in the amorphous, shape-shifting colors of an Olafur Eliasson or James Turrell installation; the melting, multilayered hues of a Marilyn Minter photograph; the soft and melting pigments in Terrence Malick's *Days of Heaven* (shot with cinematographer Néstor Almendros); or one of Mark Rothko's meditative color fields. To propose Ryan Trecartin's work as an example of analog color may be a stretch, though his strategies do involve the same kind of categorical blurring required for analog color's anti-individualism and lack of difference. And hence, in these pre- *and* postwar examples of analog colorism, we find an active mode of color use that is not specific to medium or exclusive to postwar periodization, as Batchelor indicates.[16]

To take this a step further, analog color—*as concept*—can retroactively be understood to play a vital role in the history of science and technology. Newton's optical experiments of 1666, for example, were initially analog. In his most famous experiment, also observed by Batchelor, Newton made a small hole about 1 cm in diameter in a window shutter in a dark room. He then placed a prism in front of the small hole, the only point where outside light could enter the otherwise black box. In studying the incoming daylight refracted through the prism, he observed what has become known as the seven spectral hues, which he at first referred to as a "kaleidoscopic promiscuity."[17] His choice of words captures the essence of analog color as an ineffable and mysterious mixture of scintillating visual displays, akin to the ephemeral noise framing the background of experience observed by Nietzsche, Attali, Kittler, and Virilio, as noted in the Introduction. At first, then, Newton's perceptual experience was analogic and continuous. He observed white light as "a confused aggregate" of colored rays.[18] Shortly thereafter, when he classified and divided these colors into seven discrete identities (red, orange, yellow, green, blue, indigo, and violet), he catapulted them into the digital terrain.[19] The distinction is key because it elucidates the difference between phenomenological experiences of color on the one hand (i.e., holistic, analogic, continuous, and, typically, poetic and romantic), and techno-rational models of classifying and controlling color on the other. And thus we arrive at digital colors.[20]

One must be careful not to be swept away into the poetic idealizations of analogic color. We cannot lose sight of the fact that, in order to use color at all, it is essential to create standards, so that multiple persons can use the same color with a shared understanding of the differences between it and other colors. In short, in order to use color in any practical or collective way, it is necessary to turn analog color into digital colors. CIE lab, HTML, Pantone, the 12-hue color circle, and hexadecimal color charts are all examples of digital color systems inasmuch as they all systematically divide color along a continuum, grid, matrix, chart, or index. Digital colors retain distinctions between inside and outside: where one color begins and where it ends, and what one color is and what it is not. Zoning, distinction, and separation are the catchwords of digital colors. If analog color is Dionysian in its maddening blurs, digital colors are Apollonian in their levelheaded individuation.[21] Artistic examples abound in modern architecture and design, which unequivocally privileges line, form, and order over shape-shifting color. In art, examples of digital colorism can be found in Robert Rauschenberg's black and white monochromes, Gerhard Richter's color chart paintings, Warhol's aggressive and jarring separations between screen-printed color and line, Peter Halley's cells and conduits, and most of Piet Mondrian's work. All of these artists engage digital colorism in unique ways, but not all of them use electronic digital computers to do so, again illustrating how analog color and digital colors are here construed as styles, not specific to medium or platform.[22]

To sum up thus far, the two modes of working with color—the analog and digital—are radically distinct but nonetheless play a pivotal role in producing aesthetic value and signified content. How and why an artist or designer makes certain choices with color is deeply meaningful, as is their treatment of compositional space.

The Analog and Digital as Compositional Logic

My second analytic framework adopts the lens of *compositional structure*. Key fragments selected from the late work of Gilles Deleuze, when braided back together, provide an account of his aesthetic theory of composition (see Table 2). In these fragments, Deleuze addresses cinema, painting, and color, theorized through analog and digital metaphors.[23] His initial approach follows Goethe's pivotal 1810 *Zur Farbenlehre* (*Theory of Colours*), where sensation is placed prior to interpretation and cognitive recognition.[24] Goethe's approach was in itself eccentric, radically reversing not only Newton's claims about color but also, art history's long-standing opposition between *colore* and *disegno*, which privileges the role of design, line, and structure over sensuous color. As can be expected, Goethe's theory of color only serves Deleuze as a starting point, after which he moves in an orthogonal direction.[25] While Deleuze's initial loyalty to Goethe lands him on the romantic side of analog style—versus the discrete logic of digital code—his recourse to synthesizers in articulating his theory, and his invocation of the "diagram," complicates any clear-cut classification. To reiterate, the following discussion of analog and digital synthesizers presents *metaphors* for creative compositional structures, not descriptions of physical media.

The creative process never begins with a blank slate, Deleuze argues; rather, an artist begins with a whole history of art and cultural clichés already written on the canvas or screen. The painter "has many things in his head, or around him, or in his studio . . . [and] everything he has in his head or around him is already in the canvas . . . before he begins his work."[26] Noise and color are implicit on a seemingly empty white canvas, as Rauschenberg's white monochromes suggest (see chapter 2). Before beginning a piece, one is required to intervene and clear the noisy clichés. This initial creative gesture is therefore destructive, it must unhinge, mobilize, and "deterritorialize" convention. Scraping, scratching, and clawing are all valid techniques for accomplishing this. From here, there are two possibilities for the composition: the analog and the digital.

The first kind of compositional structure is based on the analog synthesizer. This kind of composition is created by analogy, which is to say, using heterogeneous bits and fragments—scraps and leftovers from the destruction process—to establish an immediate or qualitatively new connection between them. If used successfully, one creates a diagram. In his theory of cinema, Deleuze identifies the need for free-floating, subjective affect (noise, color-as-color, abstract pixels) to be modulated through a synthesizer. Controlling such free-floating modulations allows one to construct a "diagram," a compositional system created from re-ordered units of raw sensation. Paul Cézanne, Deleuze notes, used basic geometry to develop analogies between line and color, elevating these relations into his own diagram, expressive of movement and unique sensation. Antonin Artaud's "signs, groans, whispers, [and] moans," and Francis Bacon's melting, torn, disfigured bodies also used raw sensation to reorder them in depicting "flesh versus meat"; a diagram of new color sensation versus clichés already tired and dead.[27] Destruction must occur, producing raw color affects, but it is then the job of the artist to re-order and control them. Noise, like color, "allow[s] itself to be heard" through specific modulations between order and disorder, like a "sieve whose mesh will transmute from point to point."[28]

Insofar as color / noise cannot be modulated, it sustains "hysteria." This is not yet a diagram, but it is the raw material for making one. In the case of Jackson Pollock, Deleuze argues, we find an artist who successfully clears the ground of cliché and convention, but then pushes his "manual lines" too far, producing only abysmal chaos with no inside or outside, failing to generate a synthesizer or active filtering mechanism to modulate color effects into a new rhythm and order that would form a diagram.[29]

If analog modulation deploys color affects to synthesize and *in*-form matter, color in digital code can only be applied to predetermined units in an a priori structure. Deleuze's notion of digital code is largely akin to "digital colorism." Both involve discrete systems of pre-divided units (individual colors or sections of a grid) for processing and determining in advance all future possible variations. To adopt digital code as the guiding rubric in a composition means generating only predetermined relations, a "limited set of simple, discrete forms" that are less diagrams or active machines than "symbolic codes."[30] Mondrian's compositions are such examples of digital code; his choices are always binary and cerebral, "lack[ing] sensation," but not so much that he eclipses spontaneity entirely. Mondrian does not reduce the entire composition to this code, Deleuze insists, he leaves open a few unpredictable steps for new moments and mixtures.[31] Like the abacus described above, the digital composition requires that all operations be "performed as a series of additions or subtractions" of the initial code.[32] This is why the digital synthesizer does not bear the same kind of spontaneous or creative capacity as the analog synthesizer, but is instead referred to by Deleuze as a kind of pre-sanctioned series or reiterations of what already exists. If we translate this model back into the datamoshing, we can reexamine issues of creative control as pivotal in determining the relative value of a work in the genre. To do this, a brief technical exegesis of digital video compression is first in order.

Digital Video Compression

A digital video frame is composed of mathematical codes and functions known as compression schemes or codecs, responsible for the transmission, storage, and distribution of information. Relative to the still image formats designed for the Internet or related media—GIF, JPEG, TIFF, TARGA, or PNG—digital video is one of the most challenging to compress because video files tend to be larger and informationally denser, due to their time-based nature, and demand to be seen at higher resolutions (HDTV). Because superfluous and repetitive information must be eliminated to keep the file size down, digital video compression codecs tend to rely on semi-autonomous modules known as "macroblocks," units of 4 × 4 or 16 × 16 pixels of video data, grouped together and averaged for their hue, saturation, and brightness values. Macroblocks are the chunky pixelated blocks that appear on screen, generally misrecognized as pixels. But these sequences are *not* individual pixels, they are groupings of similar bits of data, based on luminance and chrominance values. Macroblocks are not unique to video; they are also common in JPEG, H.261, and various MPEG formats, all of which use lossy compression.[33]

As noted in chapter 4, most digital video uses lossy compression. The lossy compression scheme reduces bits of data in a file by identifying unnecessary information and removing it, making it possible to distribute the image or sound files faster and more efficiently. The trade-off is that lossy compression produces a file with a lower quality than the original photograph, video, or sound material. Nonetheless, lossy compression formats like the MP3, GIF, or JPEG are ubiquitous, due to increasing demands for faster and more frequent transmission, coupled with a diminishing concern for image quality (at least on the internet).

The compression algorithms used to engineer these lossy formats further divide data into three different frame types: I-frame, P-frame, and B-frame. The I-frame (intra-coded picture) or *reference key* frame is the first frame inserted and used to indicate a significant change in content, like a change in scenery or sudden movement.[34] It is in a sense the most important key frame, the least compressed, and does not rely on other picture frames to decode its data. Contrarily, P-frames, "forward predicted frames," and B-frames, "bidirectional frames," are more compressed, used to maintain consistency in movement and data. The I-P-B-frame logic derives from the classic film animation technique known as interpolation, a technique that assumes that a patch of color will remain consistent for at least a few frames in a sequence, so redundant or repetitive data can be discarded. Interpolation is common in MPEG codecs, especially with the H.261 codec, underlying YouTube's proprietary .flv format.[35] One result of this compression scheme is a dramatic reduction in information relative to the original, which means much less color detail and nuance, but results that are nonetheless "economically satisfying," as Sean Cubitt puts it, at least for those who value smooth and speedy downloading over detail and subtlety.[36]

Because the I-frames are the most expensive frames—containing more data and instructions regarding movement, the most logical way to reduce overall file size is either to minimize movement in a video image from the start or to develop more sophisticated vector-prediction algorithms to eliminate movement perceived to be unnecessary. For Cubitt, this has led to a "self-fulfilled prophecy of YouTube videos" populated by immobile, "talking heads" and minimally changing animations.[37] Datamoshers exploit this logic by deleting key I-frames, the necessary signposts to signal a dramatic shift in the clip. What remains are only the "filler" P- and B-frames, which contain motion vectors that only note differences in the position of the macroblocks between the immediately surrounding frames.[38] As a result, the rendering algorithm does not understand how or when to properly shift to accommodate changes in content, so it simply moshes the content together, creating the liquid but chunky block effect definitive of the genre. The extent to which an artist has control over the I-frame deletions determines the potential for excellence in a work.

To be clear, all creative work should be controlled. Even techniques in chance and randomness require an artist to make explicit choices as to where and how a piece will begin and end. Artists should be able to master their tools and fluidly negotiate between chaos, accident, and chance, on the one hand, and a consciously desired outcome, on the other. The Los Angeles–based media artist Andrew Benson's *Sparkle Face Test* (2011) is an excellent example of such interaction between chaos and control. And while this work is not a datamosh in the strict sense I have defined, the piece offers a unique use of vector-based graphics to create a glitch aesthetic in time-based media. In this exuberant 40-second digital video, Benson programs Max SP, an interactive motion-tracking software to create the illusion that he is sculpting multicolored abstractions with his hands. The piece is tightly choreographed, leaving little room to misinterpret it as anything but extremely well measured (i.e., his modulated diagram), and yet, the communicated meaning is deliberately and precisely the opposite: a seemingly chaotic, "colorful bath of pixels" swimming in uncontrollable arrays. The tension between chaos and control is the wellspring from which his diagram is drawn.

In fact, the issue of control is so central to datamoshing, it may even be more vital than the pixelated "errors" that define its façade. Control over technological error is not only datamoshing's form of appearance, it is also its condition of possibility. Understanding the backend technical decisions for *Compression Study #1* (fig. 22), helps us to see its value as an early datamosh (2007). If the control process is to include both the hack and the sculpting of the final work (i.e.: the diagram), then a problem emerges midway through *Compression Study*. In the first Rihanna-Cranberries sequence of the piece, the artists' results were achieved by elegantly mixing two video sources together, resulting in the I-frames of one image appearing to pause on screen and then suddenly vaporize into the next image.[39] They also chose two music tracks whose melodies synchronized to achieve this fluid

FIGURE 26. Takeshi Murata. *Monster Movie* (2005). Digital video, color, 4 minutes, 30 seconds. An accidental error transformed into an elegant datamosh.

yet harmonized affect when mashed together in the remix. Because the sound is so evenly integrated, the pixels, while choppy, seem to fuse a little more smoothly. However, if a successful diagram requires control over the entire composition, then this mandate has only been achieved for the first two scenes, after which the careful balance between chaos and control dissolves and the rhythm is lost. Their diagram flops as the piece segues into a series of retrogressive montage cuts of children's television shows. The diagram is botched.

I end this chapter with a final example of a pioneering datamosh where the diagram is maintained throughout. Japanese American media artist Takeshi Murata's four-minute *Monster Movie* (2005), made two years prior to *Compression Study #1*, was developed from a "wild" error Murata encountered while downloading a movie file. He then isolated and repeated the error numerous times, creating this elaborate work, which dances between the analog and the digital.

Monster Movie opens with an amorphous mass of gray pixels, somewhat resembling the shape of a head rising from a pool of what appears to be ice water in an underground cave (the image is taken from the 1981 film *Caveman*). But as soon as the filmic image reveals portions of the monster's head, hair, and fangs, it disappears back into the soupy mix of monochromatic pixels. Edgy, pixilated colors undulate and flow in wave formations, smoothly animating the same monster head to ever so briefly reemerge, only to sink back down, again and again. Colors detach from the familiar, cognizable world, as in Bacon's paintings, where forms morph, merge, and bleed into each other through color mixing. But here the technique

FIGURE 27. Takeshi Murata. *Monster Movie* (2005). A "catastrophe of experience" (Deleuze, *Francis Bacon: The Logic of Sensation*, xix).

is more aggressive. Backgrounds fuse with foregrounds as foregrounds transcend themselves a hundred times over. The image's focal point counterintuitively generates infinite space and depth from within itself, destroying conventional notions of horizon, ground, or perspective. With no stable focal point, *Monster Movie* clears clichés of visual representation.[40]

After this clearing, a "catastrophe" emerges from which, in contrast to the Kantian sublime (discussed in chapters 6 and 7) reason does *not* achieve recuperation. Daniel Smith explains Deleuze's orthogonal interpretation of Kant's aesthetic sublime in appropriately colorful language: "My entire structure of perception . . . is in the process of exploding. . . . I can no longer apprehend the successive parts, I cannot reproduce the preceding parts as the following one arrives. . . . I can no longer recognize what the thing is. I can no longer qualify the object in general."[41] It is in this state of "incompossibility" that a clear-cut distinction can be made between Deleuze's aesthetic philosophy of the sublime on the one hand, and Kant's more traditional one, on the other.[42] For Kant, as I address in chapters 6 and 7, the aesthetic sublime denotes a dizzying state in which a subject is suspended in awe, but, and this is key, this catastrophic encounter introduces only a *temporary* gap in cognitive experience, from which the subject is ultimately rescued by the faculty of reason.[43] For Kant, the aesthetic sublime is merely a demonstration of the force and magnitude of reason to deal with situations that at first appear beyond it. As he puts it in the *Critique of Judgment*, "aesthetic judgment refers not merely, as a judgment of taste, to the beautiful, but also, as springing from a higher intellectual feeling, to the sublime."[44] In classical aesthetics, reason, and hence understanding, always trump the raw and deceptive realm of sensory affect (color, noise, glitch).

By contrast, for Deleuze, a subject voluntarily and intentionally enters this state, at first resembling a kind of (Freudian) trauma in experience. But, in opposition to Freud's normative trajectory of therapeutic resolve (and Kant's recuperation by the force of reason), Deleuze lingers in the hysteria.[45] The successful artist must land in a "purely aesthetic clinic" for hysterics and schizophrenics, he writes, where the noisy stopping and stuttering of chaos and chromatic profusion can be sustained long enough to transform black and white into an aesthetic more "related to green and red."[46] The multitude of colors, with avid juxtapositions and ceaseless contrasts of hue, allow visual noise to proliferate to an extreme, suggesting a lack of control and pure chaos akin to Jackson Pollock's lines or datamoshing's trademark visual signifiers. The power of color is movement from singular, linear, and rational frameworks into noise, nondistinction, and the deceptive but vital qualities of visual perception.

One cannot leave their colors or composition in this state, however, at least not if one wishes to make "art." The next step is to modulate the diagram or code. This returns us to the controlled catastrophe of *Monster Movie*. Accordingly, Murata instigates this crisis in knowledge and perception, but does not allow it to overtake the work. Rather, chaotic color is modulated to persist at his discretion and, through repetitive animations and editing, he establishes a new rhythmic order. Just as the moshed artifacts reach maximal color intensity and abstraction, they settle into a holding pattern, echoed through the half-identifiable yelps and groans heard throughout, mixed with the offbeat percussion track by Plate Tectonics. So while Murata modulates and develops errors, he also transforms them, bringing them back into the domain of aesthetic control. This is his diagram: a rhythmical composition balancing the tension between the jagged and rigid pixelated artifacts of the digital, on one hand, and their elegant, continuous animations, on the other.

A similar strategy is used in Murata's *Untitled (Pink Dot)* (2007), where pixelated digital video artifacts are fused with images of Sylvester Stallone from the 1982 film *Rambo: First Blood*. Throughout the piece, a large, pulsating fuchsia dot gently flickers off and on in the screen's center. The visual motif resembles glitches and noise effects in such classic video artworks as Steina and Woody Vasulka's *Noisefields* (1972) or Scott Bartlett's *Off /On* (1972), where the core pulse and rhythm of the work breaks with visual convention and depth perspective, reframing a noise-laden visual experience of chromatic, synthetic pulses. Here Murata's color and compositional techniques appear analog, resembling Bacon's blurs, where, Deleuze argues, figure and abstraction emerge through color, destroying form and creating a new, dynamic "monstration" or, synthesized motif as the seed and rhythm of a world to come.[47] At the same time, Murata's careful sculpting of polychromatic noise into tightly controlled color animations is far from an unstable becoming. Rather, he enforces a structure back into the wildness of the color affects that he initially unleashed in the composition. The artist's mastery over the medium, with its invisible yet pervasive attempts to shape content is rearticulated here through a balanced play between control and failure. In sum, glitch aesthetics and datamoshing in particular, with its still eccentric edge, provides us with a visual language derivative of, and suited for, the specific contours of the technologically mediated present. And this brings us to the third and final framework: historical contingency.

IV. HISTORICAL APPROACHES TO STYLE

What is edgy and new in one paradigm is cliché in another. One way to understand the transitions between an emergent cultural style and the obsolescence of an older one is to turn to periodization claims. In 1915, the German historian Heinrich Wölfflin provided an especially compelling account of the differences in the shift from the High Renaissance to the baroque in the sixteenth and seventeenth centuries. It is "for the sake of simplicity," he argued, that "we must speak of the sixteenth and seventeenth centuries as units of style," even though they do not signify a homogeneous mode of production and have features that appeared prior to 1600.[48] Wölfflin looked for general, overarching trends in a historical period, rather than narrow or directly causal chronologies.[49] An era's style is also indisputably linked to technology, material culture, and the ways in which creative practitioners adopt, or fail to adopt innovations. The popular use of saturated, synthetic colors in the 1960s, for example, unified an era through similar color choices in interior design, fashion garments, light shows, and posters. Scholars of historical periods from Wölfflin through Jonathan Crary have gone to great lengths to articulate how contrasting and contradictory forces coexist in a given culture's zeitgeist. To speak of a period style is thus a generalization, but also, largely accurate.

Wölfflin's analysis begins with an examination of the linear versus the painterly, followed by a consideration of distinctions between plane versus recession; closed versus open form; multiplicity versus unity; and absolute versus relative clarity. I focus here only on his first set of terms: the linear versus the painterly, proposed as synonyms for the digital and the analog, respectively. For Wölfflin, the linear is in line with the High Renaissance's striving to achieve an image of perfection. In such an image, all of the figures and forms will be clearly outlined, made distinct from each other, and clearly illuminated for the viewer.[50] In contrast, the painterly style, he proposes, conveys a sense of indeterminacy, accomplished through the play of color, light, and shadow, illustrated by a Giorgione or a Titian.[51]

The comparison between the linear and the painterly also reinforces age-old debates between *disegno* and *colore*, where *disegno* (the origin of the word "design") implies the use of clear line and a rational, formal, structure, and as such, is associated with honesty and moral rectitude. In contrast, *colore* is associated with luscious brush work, the instinctual and primitive, and all those "Other" things tied up in Western culture's chromophobia.[52] Understood through Wölfflin's pairing, *disegno* is analogous to the linear, with its canvas structured by lines used to create

TABLE 3. The Analog and Digital as Precursors to Modern Style

The "Painterly" Baroque Style (17th century)	The "Linear" High Renaissance Style (16th century)
• Non-planar approach to painting; objects may be shown from angles or slightly askew.	• Straightforward, planar approach and grid-like representation of objects, making them appear flat and parallel to the picture frame.
• Sensual forms, implicitly lush and celebratory of curves and contours.	• Implicit reliance on clear and well-defined lines to create volume.
• Unity is accomplished through subordination of all elements into a single theme or motif. Elements thus appear integrated and inseparable.	• Unity is accomplished through rationalized balance of component parts.
• Flow and movement created through color and the play of light (arguably connected to the origins of animation).	• Color is structured through a composition's more dominant lines.
	• Image appears static, studied, and balanced.
	• Objects appear separate and detachable from the whole, though contained within the frame.
	• Political and ideological correspondence with Western logos, claims to truth, knowledge, and the empirical sciences of the Enlightenment.
• Emphasis on becoming versus being.	• Emphasis on being versus becoming.
• Phenomenal representation of things as they appear.	• Claims to absolute clarity and the representation of things as they "actually are."
Examples:	Examples:
• Sandro Botticelli's "impetuous verve and animation";	• Lorenzo di Credi's "deliberate modeling and repose";
• Gian Lorenzo Bernini's "turbulent figures";	• Gerard ter Borchs's "peaceful, delicate little pictures" (Wölfflin argues his style is more linear than Bernini's).
• Jacob van Ruysdael's "grave style" of undulating outlines, "compacting the mass of foliage" into a "ponderous," somber whole.	• Meindert Hobbema's freer "bounding lines" that rise "airily" and gracefully in space

NOTE: Quotations are all from Heinrich Wölfflin's *Principles of Art History.*

a clear visual path to guide the eye. Elements and figures maintain distinction from each other, akin to the discrete logic of the digital. The painterly, in contrast, prioritizes color (*colore*) as the means and method of expressing form. Paint is handled loosely, forms are less defined, lines are less discrete, and edges tend to be blurred and less readily apparent than in the linear method. The more "limitless" and "colossal" baroque aesthetic of *colore* aspires to dissolve into the sublimity of the infinite, creating a feeling of opening and "play rather than proof, illusion rather than reality, effects rather than resemblance."[53] Thus the painterly qualities of the baroque are affiliated with the mixing and mystique of analog colorism, and, let us now suppose, the melting chunks of pixels in datamoshing.

On the one hand, then, datamoshing tends to the painterly. It prioritizes color (*colore*) with less defined shapes, layers, and blurs. It also finds affiliation with the baroque aesthetic in that it draws on ambiguous techniques to articulate changing relationships between the individual and the world. In this case, it is not an aspiration to the divine, but instead, a grasp to make sense of the many obfuscations engendered through high-tech. We can further identify stylistic affiliations between the baroque and datamoshing if we recall that the former sought to render new relationships between the individual and the world, in the same way that I have suggested glitch art and datamoshing struggle to articulate the challenges indigenous to a new world of rapidly changing technology. Andrew Benson's *Sparkle Face Test* (2011) and *Status Update, 2 AM* (2011) also illustrate this tension. In both works, we witness an unresolved struggle between man and machine. In *Status Update 2 AM*, the performer (Benson) is immersed in a hurried techno-sound space, overwhelmed, but keeping up by drawing colored lines in synch with the frantic pace, ostensibly working past 2 A.M., even though this human, relative to the machine, seems doomed to fail by virtue of being too slow and too human.

On the other hand, datamoshing falls under the linear, not deliberately, but by default. Insofar as it and many other forms of glitch art are produced through digital technology, where the conditions of possibility for creative production are always already limited to 8 × 8 macroblocks of pixels, numerically confined to unique locations on an invisible grid. As John Belton puts it, "the digital image is too ordered and too rational—and not random enough. In our experience of it, it lacks . . . 'being.'"[54] This may be so but what other option do we have for giving face to the human struggles in a digital culture? Additionally, one obvious difference between the baroque and datamoshing is that the former captured the angst of change while simultaneously remaining open to new aspirations and sublimity. In contrast, glitch art and datamoshing are from the start cynical of techno-optimism and faith in any expansive, transcendental register. This is amplified through the anxieties created by our dwindling control over our socioeconomic and political situations, making life in digital culture seem less connected to the limitlessness of the baroque era, and much more in tune with the "black box" framing discussed at the end of chapter 2. In sum, datamoshing accurately stages the particular anxieties and tensions of life in the twenty-first century. At the same time, and by way of the above, it perpetuates cultural fantasies of mastery and control. That is, it plays according to the rules of computational order, and its negotiated diagram is thus more code than sensuous spontaneity. And yet, again, this contradictory mix of breakdown and control in the genre is, precisely, an accurate rendering of our real relations to the high-tech world we live in.

Glitch Out

One could argue that glitch art succeeds in making the matter of digital technology immanent, by conflating content and its mode of expression. But it is also true that we always fail to attain this goal (if it is one). Each artist must master his or her data set and then reorder it in a cool and controlled fashion. It also goes without saying that the vast majority of cutting-edge effects make their way to the center stage of commercial media and as they do, lose whatever political edge they may have once had. The following concluding anecdote illustrates this point.

One morning in March 2009, less than two months before the opening of Paul B. Davis's second solo show at the Seventeen Gallery in London (in which *Compression Study #1* was to be included), he woke up to find a flood of emails, "telling me to look at some video on YouTube." On his computer a few seconds later, Davis "saw Kanye West strutting around in a field of digital glitches that looked exactly like my work. It fucked my show up . . . the very language I was using to critique pop content from the outside was now itself a mainstream cultural reference."[55] The field he alludes to is the mise-en-scène for Kanye West's 2009 *Welcome to Heartbreak* music video, directed by Nabil Elderkin. Elderkin's video displays West strutting on stage with Kid Cudi, immersed in chromatic glitch artifacts. In the video, colors dance across the visual field, echoing the psychological heartbreak denoted in the lyrics. Given the music video's widespread commercial success, *Welcome to Heartbreak* illustrates how the proliferation of datamoshing and glitch styles have little to do with challenging habits of visual consumption or sustained critique, but instead with the effective control and engineering of mass media entertainment.

Kim Cascone refers to this neutralization of an experimental edge as a new style paradigm of "competitive consumption" indigenous to a "post-digital" age.[56] Glitch and datamoshing's fate as a quickly appropriated mainstream special effect may then have more to do with recognizing this genre's failure as de facto in the way things work today; rapidly moving from so-called cutting-edge "innovation" to obsolescence as mainstream cliché. The cycles move so fast, one hardly has time to notice them. The appropriation of DIY effects into digestible forms of mass media is ubiquitous, intensified by the lightning speed of the internet and instantaneous digital processing. If we can slow down to take a closer look, as this chapter has done, we can catch a glimpse of the way in which these highly stylized digital artifacts have taken a thin slice of the process and temporarily abstracted it from clear channels of commerce and communication, giving us just enough time to catch it on the rebound and decode its broader value for understanding life as it is actually lived; strenuously and in eternal strife.

In Part III (chapters 6 and 7) and in the Postscript, I move away from an analysis of screen-based error to address phenomena in the culture and the environment that are failure-ridden as a result of high-tech industries. The material fallout resulting from the overproduction of so-called fast and efficient computational media has engendered inconceivable quantities of trash and e-waste, which, like noise and glitch, are unwanted but nonetheless necessary to consider if we wish to gain deeper insight into ourselves and likely futures.

Toxic Beauty

6

———

The X-Ray Sublime

The world is suffering for our success.
—EDWARD BURTYNSKY, *NO MAN'S LAND*

Whereas chapters 1 and 2 analyzed error and failure as constructs of human art and philosophy, and chapters 3 through 5 did so in digital aesthetics, this chapter and the next analyze man-made waste and environmental deterioration as a direct result of the high-tech industries.[1] In the same way that glitch and error are normatively concealed from view, only returning to the foreground of experience through actual failure or critique, contemporary images of man-made waste discussed in this chapter and the next foreground the trash otherwise hidden from, but directly generated by "us"— First World consumers. The trash of the so-called innovation age is our collective, shameful error.

The cultural failure to adequately care for the earth (and one another) appears in the images of Part III as a heady noise entangled in an even more disturbing visual beauty. This chapter focuses on framing man-made waste through the classic aesthetic concept of the sublime. It also draws on the landscape photography of the internationally renowned Canadian photographer Edward Burtynsky.[2] Contrary to numerous critics' suggestions that Burtynsky's work is pure spectacle, this chapter argues that it is indeed visually beautiful, while also driving a deeper critique. By exposing privileged audiences to previously undetected scenes of environmental destruction, Jennifer Peeples argues, Burtynsky opens the door for "social, cultural and/or political analysis, even if it simply prompts the question, 'Why haven't I known this exists?'"[3]

The chapter begins with a computer-animated example of trash characteristic of our culture's baleful yet deeply mythological relationship to the environment. This is shadowed by a brief introduction to Burtynsky, followed by a return to Peeples's work and a lengthy exegesis on classical and contemporary conceptions

129

of the Sublime, a concept central to this and the following chapter. In the last part of the chapter, Burtynsky's work is connected to what I call the "X-ray sublime," a twenty-first-century updating of the classical concept.[4] While breakdown and destruction are indigenous to any environment, this chapter inquires: What does it mean to make beautiful images of otherwise horrifying environmental conditions? What kind of aesthetic sublime do we encounter at the dawn of the twenty-first century, and how do ethical and cognitive failures shape its contours?

I. FUTURE TRASH

Beginning several hundred years into the future, the 2008 Pixar film *Wall•E* (directed by Andrew Stanton), opens with a shot of its protagonist, Wall•E, seen in the midst of his job activities, piling and compacting exceedingly high towers of human trash. Wall•E, whose name is an acronym for "Waste Allocation Load Lifter Earth," does not seem to mind the task, perhaps he even enjoys it. Regardless, he is acting in a frenzy, obsessively and compulsively, without pause or patience. The turmoil is not normal, the film implies, there is a glitch in his software making him act this way, the nature of which, Timothy Morton notes, remains unclear.[5] Some may identify with this militant fanaticism and relentless drive to clean up his home—the earth—by picking up garbage but, unfortunately, such a drive is alien to the majority of us. Consider too that Wall•E's obsessive compulsive drive to pick up heaps of trash is construed by the film as an *error*.

The film's opening scene thus invites reflection on the markedly human relationship between technological innovation and destruction. It is precisely this appeal to "humanness," Morton suggests, that Wall•E is searching for in a "discarded Rubix cube, a *Hello Dolly* video, or a tiny sprout in a flowerpot."[6] It is also likely that some viewers, like myself, sat in a dark theater pining for Wall•E to succeed in finding an advanced technological solution to ecological problems (and maybe even social and political injustices), thus letting us humans off the hook. Such fantasies of absolution point precisely to the ethical failures addressed in this chapter.

Towards an Ethical Ecology

We may take instruction from studies in ecology where "ecology" is understood as distinct from the environment or landscape. The German noun *Oecologie* (commonly spelled *Ökologie*) was coined by the zoologist Ernst Haeckel in the 1860s, combining the Greek root *oikos,* meaning household, or habitat, and *logos* (knowledge). The term was utilized as a way of describing not just a wild and unpopulated place called the environment, but also an environment that was just as much a "home" to humans, seemingly amending earlier associations with the notion of "environment" as a space of cultural non-existence.[7] In the same moment we began to see ourselves as separate from the world, Dominic Pettman argues, we

FIGURE 28. Pixar's *Wall•E* (2008). Stills. The film's robot protagonist looking to solve ecological problems.

began to see the world itself as an object of ownership. This proprietary ethos, he argues, has led to extensive manipulations and attempts to ravage and control the planet, evidence for which we can find everywhere around us.[8] And while I am in agreement with this, I also wish to shift this focus to how and what responsible ecological ownership might look like.

Responsibility implies care. Impressive man-made developments in industry, architecture, and public culture may dwarf individual agency, but if the earth is our collective household (whether we use the word "environment" or "ecology"), it is therefore also the home to which we all belong and share accountability for. Heidegger proposed this in his 1927 reconsideration of the Latin myth of *Cura,* noted in the Introduction. To briefly rehash: Cura is crossing a river, after which she pauses to mold some clay. While selecting a name for her creation, she is caught in a dispute between Heaven (Jupiter) and Earth (Gaia). Saturn, god of time, decides that Heaven will have the clay's spirit in death, and Earth will have it in life. Because Cura is the creator of the beings, she will keep them in her care while they live, with the name "human beings." Insofar as we are alive, we live in and through care. Care is intrinsic to being; a prerequisite for making peace with one's individual being (*Dasein*) in the world, a collective to which one also belongs in and with ("alongside"). *Collective* concern becomes the key to living well for one*self.* The paradox plays into Heidegger's larger ethical demand to question not only *that* one cares for a world that brought forth being, but also, *how.*[9]

The *how* determines the quality of care. How do we actually address the urgency of ecological toxicity and e-waste? To begin, we must understand humans and technology as coextensive, co-evolutionary systems. If high-tech industries are creating toxins and poisoning the air and water, they do so because *people* make decisions to operate in borderline conditions, to exploit workers without rights or unions, to use raw materials of poor quality and precarious origin, and dispose of by-products and toxins irresponsibly. The environment is not falling apart because plastic is evil. It is failing because we fail it, a cumulative outcome of each person's failure to question the consequences of their actions. On a daily basis, millions of individuals make seemingly negligible decisions regarding the environment. Every single gesture, Chris Jordan (chapter 7) points out, accumulates into a much larger collective liability.[10] I do not intend to exclusively scapegoat individuals—versus the corporate and government entities that fail to regulate such activities—I highlight this only because it is an immediate and accessible starting point. Moreover, it is also individual people who make up these corporate and government bodies. Burtynsky's work provides a set of visual materials to further assess this tension.

II. EDWARD BURTYNSKY

Born in Canada in 1955, as a child, Burtynsky was fascinated with industrial images. His father worked at the local General Motors factory and spent his leisure time painting and engaging in amateur photography. Not surprisingly, by the age of seven, Edward had found a love for painting landscapes.[11] At eleven years old, he received his first 35mm camera and access to a darkroom. By the age of twenty, he was taking night school courses in photography and studying graphic arts at college.[12] After enrolling in Ryerson University's esteemed photography program in Toronto, Burtynsky benefited from the instruction of Canadian photographer Robert Gooblar (1945–97). Gooblar introduced him to hybrid practical and conceptual experiments, a dynamic pedagogy that the Faculty of Communication and Design (FCAD) at Ryerson is known for. In one such experiment, Gooblar sat in the studio with a seashell in one hand with a light suspended above him. For an hour, he spoke about the seashell, its geometry, translucence, the kinds of images it conjured up for him, and the disparate ways in which one could approach even the simplest of objects. Also at Ryerson, Burtynsky learned to use a 4 × 5 medium format camera.[13] The apparatus "hit a direct chord in me," he explains, possibly due to its capacity to capture opulent detail in a medium typically associated with documentary and social realism, or perhaps it was the slow pace and patience required to work with it.[14]

During his studies, he also developed what has become his trademark X-ray-like capacity to detect the "negative spaces" in the world around him. In one illustrative example, he was assigned the task of photographing the "human presence in the landscape."[15] While examining the urban landscape of downtown Toronto

FIGURE 29. Edward Burtynsky, *China Recycling #8, Plastic Toy Parts Guiyu, Guangdong Province* (2004). © Edward Burtynsky, courtesy of Nicholas Metivier Gallery, Toronto.

that fuses with the Ryerson campus, Burtynsky took special note of the compact but large concrete and quartz architecture, especially the buildings serving the nearby financial district. In these structures he saw "negative spaces"—not large slabs of concrete protruding from the ground, but rather, images of absence. The negative space in an image is typically the "background" or empty space, but, as any design student will tell you, it is also an active space. All of the glass, sand, and raw materials used in these structures, he reasoned, arrived from somewhere else, another ecology that is depreciated yet ever so subtly implied in the striking presence of these hefty counterparts. Seemingly eschewing postmodern fashions of the time, Burtynsky henceforth adopted a retrogressive modernist agenda, questioning the linear history and ecological origins of the raw materials used to build the skyscrapers surrounding him. Because the stones "appear to have been taken out of a quarry one block at a time," he reasoned, somewhere there had to be an inverted complementary structure.[16] His inquiries sent him in search of evidence of this "reciprocal action on the environment," and in Vermont and rural Ontario he found it in the shape of what he calls "inverted skyscrapers"—multilevel, vertical excavations in the Earth's crust.[17] While this chapter does not focus on his photographs of these inverted architectures at length, they remain helpful in highlighting Burtynsky's early interests in the visual beauty of residual, leftover landscapes, compounded by a sensibility already tuned towards the inverted and negative. Further, we also see evidence of the artist's attunement to media archaeology, in both the theoretical (media studies) and practical (actual archaeology) sense. By translating the concept of negative space from graphic design to ecology, Burtynsky brought to light what was not visible in the landscape, but intrinsic to its material history.

Aside from his images of the Vermont and Ontario quarries, Burtynsky is also known for his photographs of global waste and the ruins of industrial and postindustrial cultures, including shipbreaking practices in Bangladesh, e-waste recovery in China, mineral-polluted lakes in Canada, oil-pollution in the Gulf of Mexico, and urban renewal projects and e-waste in Shanghai.[18] He typically uses a large-format (8 × 10) Hasselblad camera, which lends a visual richness to his work and confirms his preference for stylized surfaces with rich detail, color, and resolution. Although the resulting images—typically printed in extra-large format—are extremely beautiful, they have consistently been received as exploitive renderings of human trash and environmental destruction, leveraged for the sake of lavish spectacle. But why would Burtynsky want to glamorize waste and toxicity by beautifying these shameful sites? The answer lies in what I term the "X-Ray sublime," a series of aesthetic and philosophical contradictions that draw from the classical concept of the sublime, with its roots in a complex play between the beautiful and the horrific. In the next section, I provide a historical context for this philosophical legacy, allowing me to situate the X-ray sublime alongside Burtynsky's contemporary practice. Following this, I return to the socioeconomic factors leading to e-waste and the ways in which Burtynsky's images intersect with them.

III. THE SUBLIME

In aesthetic philosophy, the concept of the Sublime has traditionally implied a liminal space of uncertainty and confusion, whether between pleasure and pain, madness and reason, or chaos and control. Deriving from the Latin *sublimis*, the term denotes a "looking up from," which is to say it already signals a hierarchical tension between figure and ground. The Latin word *limen* connotes a threshold between conscious and unconscious where, as a result of many years of cultural practice, the former is privileged over the latter. This basic tension between the two forces has been preserved throughout the history of aesthetic philosophy, albeit in divergent ways. To elucidate how and why a contemporary offshoot like the "X-ray sublime" arrives at the tail end of this trajectory, I provide an exegesis of the concept from its early development in Plato and Longinus, through Enlightenment instantiations in Burke and Kant, to the present, when I reconnect it with Burtynsky's work.

The Proto-Sublime

Plato's *Ion* (380 B.C.E.) is the only one of Plato's dialogues devoted exclusively to art. It addresses the possession of an artist by god and theorizes this (divine) madness as immanent to the creative process. This occurs primarily through Socrates' arguments with Ion to determine that poets are unconscious and void of reason. The text proposes a model of creative activity wherein sublime creation is analogous to madness, yet it is still placed at the center of creative practice—even if it will later be dismantled by the rational mind. At the same time, creative madness is in no way glorified in the text. Plato draws a clear distinction between reason and creative madness: in order to create at all, an artist or poet must be mad: "there is no invention in him until he has been inspired and is *out of his senses,* and the *mind is no longer in him.*"[19] Elsewhere Plato reaffirms this same distinction between rational, scientific practice (*technē*), and the whims of *poiesis.*[20] Whereas the former involves a well-measured, logical relation between cause and effect, the latter is relegated to the mysteries of the soul (artistic practice) and deemed unstable in knowledge-formation.[21] The distinction is key because, as we will see, in the contemporary sublime, level-headed technical activities no longer retain their link to logic and reason. Instead, they become confusing and "out of their senses." That is, noisy and unstable.[22]

The relationship between reason and (creative) madness is taken up again by Longinus in the first century C.E. in *On the Sublime,* where he identifies five sources of sublimity: "great thoughts, strong emotions, certain figures of thought and speech, noble diction, and dignified word arrangement." For Longinus, the sublime was more than merely persuasive or madly inspired rhetoric, it was also inflicted with a sense of the impossible, connected to a "certain excellence, distinction, and expression" extending beyond the concrete or verifiable.[23] And even though the sublime is impossible to attain or master, he argued, it nonetheless draws from an "irresistible force" that many cannot resist.[24] Longinus invokes the image of a lightning bolt to illustrate the effect. A sudden flash of sublimity throws one into an immediate trance, scattering everything that came before and after it.[25] The sublime is thus proposed as an aesthetic concept with a not-so-visible transformative force at its center. In the same way, a flash of lightning can in an instant transform a dark landscape into an inverted image of light. In sum, for thousands of years, the sublime has been linked to a poetic sense of the world that is greater than, and beyond, scientific understanding.

The Classical Sublime

Jumping ahead several centuries, English philosopher Edmund Burke introduced a full-bodied theory of the sublime in his Gothic-inspired *Philosophical Enquiry into the Origin of Our Ideas of the Sublime and the Beautiful* (1757). Burke shed light on the ways in which combined feelings of terror and delight fuse in the sublime, typically when one confronts the powerful or threatening forces of Nature.[26]

Things like the roar of the ocean and poisonous snakes evoke astonishment and terror simultaneously.[27] All-powerful and external to oneself, Nature triggers "the drive for self-preservation."[28] Since a sublime object may evoke the overwhelming likelihood of death, it must be distinct from mere pain. Amanda Boetzkes quotes Burke: "The only difference between pain and terror is that things which cause pain operate on the mind, by the intervention of the body; whereas things that cause terror generally affect the bodily organs by the operation of the mind suggesting danger."[29] Sublime satisfaction derives from the exertion of the mind as it grapples with its palpable encounter with mortality. However, the fact that it will not actually result in death—one has merely come face to face with the *idea* of death—results in pleasure. The experience is nonetheless construed as transformative because, as the feeling of terror dissipates and the "burden of physical pain and threat"[30] is removed, the subject is suddenly liberated in the acknowledgement of recovery from this temporary loss of control.[31] In recognizing this process, a subject presumably transforms ("transcends") the limits of one's mental faculties, therein experiencing cognitive delight.[32]

We can now understand the sublime as an aesthetic condition ensuing between subject and object, an "atmosphere" as the Greeks proposed, in which nature or some state of it (art will later assume this role) invokes an experience of terror, acting to weaken the individual sense of autonomy and control, but is ultimately overcome by another human capacity for self-preservation. In this way, the sublime must be understood as distinct from classical aesthetic theories of the beautiful. Burke differentiated between the two as follows: beauty can be found in small objects, things that are smooth, delicate, clean, fair, mild in color, and excite "the passion of love." The sublime, in contrast, is typified by vastness, privation, difficulty, infinity, magnitude, and magnificence. If it is capable of evoking "terror" and the kind of destabilizing fears noted above, an object or phenomena can be a source of the sublime, even if it results in pleasure, as the beautiful must always do.[33]

Shortly after Burke, Immanuel Kant introduced another systematic inquiry into the sublime. His interventions catalyzed nothing short of a paradigm shift in modern philosophy. This cannot be overstated. In his work, subjectivity moved to the fore of the concept of the sublime because he refreshingly validated a *subject's experience,* limited only by the impossibility of knowing the essence of an external object or thing in-itself (such as Nature). Kant writes, "true sublimity must be sought only in the mind of the judging subject, and not in the object of nature that occasions this attitude by the estimate formed of it."[34] In short, he proposes a total inversion of classical thought.[35] By moving away from traditional "object-focused" considerations of the sublime to focus instead on *how* aesthetic experience occurs in the subject, Kant's approach might at first resemble Plato's concern with an artist's madness, but this is far from the case. Plato fundamentally distrusted the madness of the poet and his creative process, whereas Kant placed this disorientation at the heart of aesthetic experience.

Like Burke, Kant also distinguished between the beautiful and the sublime. In his 1790 *Critique of Judgment,* Kant argued that the beautiful is associated with "appearances," the smallness and brightness of ornamental things like color, décor, surface shine, and is "directly attended with a feeling of the furtherance of life."[36] However, while such surface phenomenon like color could support the category of the beautiful, in themselves they could only ever be secondary attributes; always already subordinate to "higher forms" of truth, meaning, and order (and here one does detect a trace of Platonism). Where the beautiful maintains clear boundaries between form and object,[37] the aesthetic sublime, in contrast, is connected to a temporary cognitive breakdown expressed as fear and terror. The aesthetic sublime, Kant writes, "contravene[s at] the ends of our power of judgement[,] . . . ill-adapted to our faculty of presentation, and to be, as it were, an outrage on the imagination, and yet it is judged all the more sublime on that account."[38] In short, it does not fit nicely into aesthetic experience at all, as the beautiful does so well, but is instead valued by its very incapacity to do so. Kant eventually accepted some forms of beauty into the sublime, though Burke did not. For the latter, beauty was merely pleasing but not capable of sublimity. In this chapter's analysis, the beautiful is taken as a surface aesthetic and as capable of integration with the sublime, especially in the X-ray sublime where, as we will see, it upstages the functioning of reason.

Kant's aesthetic, or "dynamic" sublime, as he referred to it, is central to understanding Burtynsky's work.[39] The concept, as explained above, articulates an experience where there is an apparent transgression of the limits of reason and dissolution of the boundaries between it and external phenomena, coupled with an intrinsic link to Nature's beauty and awe. In the sublime, Kant explains, "it is rather in its chaos, or in its wildest and most irregular disorder and desolation . . . that nature chiefly excites the ideas of the sublime."[40] A hurricane or, to cite Kant's examples, "mountain masses towering one above the other in wild disorder, with their pyramids of ice, or . . . the dark tempestuous ocean" invoke this dual force of fear and awe, but only insofar as one contemplates them through the imagination ("without any regard to their form, the mind abandons itself to the imagination"). Both fear and awe are necessarily constitutive of the concept, albeit void of any real danger. If imagination and reason work together to produce this sublime experience then, ultimately, the mind "feels itself elevated in its own estimate of itself."[41] That is to say, reason and understanding reconcile the imagination from having sought to exceed its own limits. If the sublime bears an implicit threat of fear, reason brings the mental faculties back into balance by distinguishing between simulated and real danger. The sublime experience necessarily involves reason's laboring to master the faculty of the imagination. It is crucial to recognize that, for Kant, it is the faulty of reason that rescues the subject from the mental overload experienced by the imagination's reach towards the infinite, a reach that engendered an initial state of cognitive oscillation, experienced as the threat of the sublime, but is eventually reigned back in by the faculty of reason. Put differently, the imagination reaches a limit that only reason can acknowledge, not to master or control it, but to acknowledge it and, as such, recognize its own drive for self-preservation as a form of self-congratulatory pleasure.[42]

To summarize, Kant's pivotal intervention in the history of the sublime was to reconceive it as a condition of subjective experience, existing in the mental faculties of the viewer, and not a condition of any so-called objective, external world. The Kantian sublime induces an unhinged state of mind in the subject, triggered by worldly representations that occupy the energies of both the imagination and reflective judgment, but are ultimately appeased by the latter.[43] Henceforth, when I refer to *images* as sublime, I am implicitly referring to this lineage, ending with Kant's reordering of aesthetic relations, and not a formal set of properties intrinsic to any object or work of art.[44]

When I use the term "X-ray sublime," I have in mind something else. Namely, an inverted, X-ray situation. Decades after Kant, aesthetic philosophers adhered to his views. Over the past half century, however, critical theorists (e.g., poststructuralists, deconstructionists, and postmodernists) have diverged from this orthodoxy. One of the key points of contention is the last step, where, according to Kant, the faculty of reason steps in to save the day, rescuing the imagination from attempting to move too far beyond the limits of understanding. For many intellectuals—the late Gilles Deleuze and myself included—this last step is too clean; too neat and tidy for a world of constant breakdown and uncertainty. Deleuze's late aesthetic theory, noted in the last chapter, is connected to my concept of the X-ray sublime as follows: drawing on Freud's theory of hysteria, Deleuze proposes that reason *fails* to recuperate the imagination. In Deleuze's reconceptualization of the sublime, Daniel W. Smith explains, one's "entire structure of perception . . . is in the process of exploding . . . [one] can no longer apprehend successive parts . . . no longer recognize what the thing is."[45] Rolf Tiedemann identifies a similar refusal of (dialectic) closure in his discussion of Walter Benjamin's "dialectics at a standstill."[46] The failure to provide resolution is also at the heart of my concept of the X-ray sublime, which turns on the inversion of classical and modern aesthetic pursuits for unification and cohesive symbolization. Put differently, the X-ray sublime does not overcome itself but instead lands in constant and perpetual chaos; the "incompossible" in Benjamin's work, as theorized by Judith Butler (see the Introduction); Ryan Trecartin's ambivalence; and here, our relationship to our own trash.

IV. BURTYNSKY'S X-RAY SUBLIME

From aggressive public and private advertising to the cheap and unethical overproduction of transitory commodities, waste figures prominently in psychic and social life. It goes without saying that landscapes did not always look like this. The history of landscape photography tells us as much beginning with classical depictions of wonder and awe, to "feats" of industrial progress. Chapter 7 addresses this history in more detail, including the work of Carleton Watkins, August Sander, Margaret Bourke-White, and Harold Edgerton. Unlike these precursors, however, Burtynsky's landscapes do not convey a modern ethos of power and triumph. Rather, he offers a more restrained, distant, and arguably balanced point of view. Both success and failure come into a complex conversation in his work, which depicts the waste and trash of the contemporary world in beautiful tones and textures.

Burtynsky was also acquainted early on with the images created by the well-known Brazilian photographer and economist Sebastião Salgado, who photographed shipbreaking in Bangladesh eleven years before him, after fleeing Brazil's politically repressive climate in 1969. Salgado's work focuses on issues of human labor, alienation, migration, and exploitation, evoking concern with the precariousness of human life. While these themes are also present in Burtynsky's work, they are secondary to his primary interest in capturing the patterns of oil, water, metal, or other objects moving through the landscape.[47] Three sets of Burtynsky's photographs are discussed here: his images of shipbreaking in Bangladesh; e-waste in China; and his more recent aerial photography in the *Water* series.

Shipbreaking Spectacles

The multi-billion-dollar shipbreaking industry thriving on the beaches of Pakistan and Bangladesh is simply not a part of the reality with which most First World residents are acquainted. For the shipbreaking industry, however, dismantling massive oil tankers has been both a booming success and a horror show. Up until the latter part of the twentieth century, dismantling ships tended to occur in the ports of developed countries like the United Kingdom and the United States, "where the disposal of ships [was] regulated to protect workers and the environment."[48] But things have changed. In 1965, a ferocious storm left a giant cargo ship beached on the pristine coast at Bhatiari, a city just to the west of Chittagong in Bangladesh.[49] Locals immediately began stripping the ship of anything they could use, recycle, or re-style. Moreover, since Bangladesh has no iron mines, the masses of steel that the ship was built from became invaluable to its economy.

Almost half a century later, the majority of the world's ships are dismantled on the shores of Bangladesh, India, China, and Pakistan, countries "subject to less control and inspection" and precarious if any enforcement of labor laws.[50] Here, tankers and other ships are run onto the beach and dismantled at low tide "without proper installations and equipment."[51] For many, such "beaching" has proven a lucrative industry, providing thousands of tons of steel for construction rebar at "rock-bottom prices,"[52] which impoverished countries like Bangladesh could not otherwise afford. A single tanker can yield up to 50,000 meters of copper cable, 35,000 kg of aluminum anodes, 20,000 kg of zinc, and tens of thousands of liters of lubricating hydraulic oil, used for fuel. Even the gummy residues left over in empty fuel tanks are mixed with sand and compressed into logs for use in cooking fires.[53]

FIGURE 30. Edward Burtynsky, *Shipbreaking #04* (2000). A breathtaking image of the highly precarious shipbreaking practices in Pakistan and India. © Edward Burtynsky, courtesy of Nicholas Metivier Gallery, Toronto.

In short, every bolt, bar, and bathtub is recycled. In the 2010s, over 80 percent of the iron and steel used in Bangladesh came from forty-five shipbreaking yards along the Chittagong coast.[54] According to Global Marketing Systems (GMS), Chittagong produces "around 1.3 million tons of finished rods" annually, all of which contribute to the country's development.[55]

As noted, the shipbreaking industry now extends well beyond Chittagong. Soon after Chittagong's lead in the late 1960s, ships began to be beached in Alang, in India, which is now, arguably, the "leading ship-recycling yard in the world, catering to nearly 90% of India's ship recycling activity."[56] Pakistan also got into the game early on, in the 1970s, and became a competitor to India by the beginning of the 1980s. On Gadani Beach in Pakistan, about thirty-five miles west of Karachi, old ships from around the world are beached, sometimes up to a hundred ships at a time. Once they arrive, workers are responsible for hauling them up onto the sand as far as they will go, until a team of workers arrives on board to dismantle and mine the hulk for usable parts. All of this also amounts to employment opportunities for citizens. Although numbers vary between sources, it is estimated that

FIGURE 31. Edward Burtynsky, *Shipbreaking #11* (2000). © Edward Burtynsky, courtesy of Nicholas Metivier Gallery, Toronto.

somewhere between 100,000 and 200,000 workers are involved in the Chittagong ship recycling industry, with similar numbers reported for India, and smaller but comparable figures for Pakistan and China.

Edward Burtynsky began photographing the shipbreaking practices in Pakistan and India in 2000, a year after international policies changed to reflect a more serious consideration of the disturbing effects of international oil spills. First there was the Exxon Valdez oil spill, one of the most devastating environmental disasters in human history. In 1989, the Exxon Valdez oil tanker destroyed 1,000 miles of shoreline in Alaska.[57] But it was not until 1999, after the twenty-five-year-old single-hull tanker, *Erika,* leaked 10,000 tons of heavy oil into 250 miles of the Brittany coastline of France that the International Maritime Organization mandated that tankers built prior to 1974 be removed from service by 2003.[58] In theory, 2,200 tankers would be scrapped by 2010. These ships can measure up to a thousand feet long, be twenty stories high, and weigh 25 million pounds.[59]

For those already in the industry, the new shipbreaking mandate was good news. One such beneficiary was the internationally respected Dr. Anil Sharma, president and CEO of Global Marketing Systems (GMS), based in Maryland, with offices in Dubai, Shanghai, and Singapore, with claims to being the "world's largest and only ISO 9001 (BV) certified cash buyer of ships for recycling."[60] Sharma launched GMS in 1992 and is responsible for determining where a number of large oil tankers will end up. The company's website outlines the advantages of choosing the country best suited for breaking up a ship based on the needs and goal. Sharma reports delivering more than three hundred ships in a single year.[61] The International Law and Policy Institute explains, "the shipping industry now faces tremendous financial challenges, and the risk that additional vessels will be sent to beaching has never been greater. Even Norwegian-listed companies made this choice in 2015."[62] Since steel and other salvaged materials fuel developments in Pakistan, India, and Bangladesh, it is abundantly clear that what is "waste" to some is a "natural resource" to others (akin to the arbitrariness of signal versus noise, discussed in chapters 1 and 3).[63]

Nonetheless, a number of problems simultaneously emerge. For one, a lot of this bulk material cannot be recycled at all. Second, an overwhelming number of unethical procedures are used to acquire ships and dismantle them, most notably the unethical treatment of the land and nonunionized, underrepresented workers involved. For example, each ship contains an average of 15,000 pounds of asbestos and ten to a hundred tons of lead paint, all of which end up on Asian coasts, where they have caused a significant degree of environmental damage to marine life, beaches, and fishing villages.[64] Asbestos and lead waste have also negatively affected many of the children who go to work on these ships barefoot or wearing flip-flops and are expected to use hammers to break apart the asbestos in the ship (which they then shovel into bags, carry outside, and dump in the sand).[65]

One of the most neglected areas in existing environmental critiques of this industry is the treatment of human life as waste. Environmental scholars have traditionally construed waste and trash as something other than human, as noted in the Introduction, but Michelle Yates has recently disclaimed this legacy, demonstrating instead that in capitalism, the human is also utilized as a form of waste.[66] This is in and of itself tragic, aside from the toxic materials people are asked to work with. Shipbreakers are expected to travel to remote locations to pursue whatever relatively minimal economic gain is available there and live in huts made of shipbreaking leftovers. At the turn of the millennium, India, Pakistan, and Bangladesh were home to 80 percent of the world's dirtiest and most dangerous jobs.[67] The International Federation for Human Rights (FIDH) reported in 2009 that 25 percent of the workers on the beaches of Chittagong were children, often between the ages of 10 and 13, who worked twelve hours a day, seven days a week for wages under U.S.$0.32 an hour. "Instead of raising wages or paying the proper overtime premium, yard management always holds back five days' wages—up to 1,200 taka ($17.40) to 'bond' the laborers to the yard. The fact that workers can be 'bonded' and held in the yard for just $17.40 is an indication of how desperately poor and on the edge these workers are."[68]

It is also estimated between one and two thousand workers have been killed in Bangladesh's shipbreaking yards over the past thirty years. On average, a worker is seriously injured every day and one worker is killed every three to four weeks.[69] Sometimes the number is higher. In November 2016, the BBC reported the death of eleven people in an explosion at a shipbreaking yard in southwestern Pakistan, while fifty-nine other workers were badly burned.[70] "If there is a hell on earth, this is it," Charles Kernaghan says, executive director of the Institute for Global Labour and Human Rights.[71] Nevertheless, workers continue to arrive by the dozen, motivated by pay. A migrant farmer from northern Bangladesh can earn at least triple on the beach what he could back on the farm, making it worth the risk.[72]

Burtynsky's unusually large-scale images of these shipbreaking practices, and those in related Chinese factories and e-waste sites, address these scenarios. In Burtynsky's *China* series, for example, many images seduce the viewer, despite an implicit, unavoidable cynicism in what the images depict. In one image from the series, workers are clad in identical pink and blue uniforms at the Deda Chicken Processing Plant in Dehui City, Jilin Province China (2005), revealing endlessly repeating shapes and colors by virtue of their sheer number. In one of the closing scenes of Jennifer Baichwal's 2006 documentary *Manufactured Landscapes*, in which the *China* series is discussed, we similarly see rows and rows of the workers identically clad in yellow and black lining up outside the Cankun Factory in Zhangzhou, Fujian Province, after work. The patterns created by their uniforms, echoing those of the buildings behind them, somehow render the image aesthetically pleasing. The uniformity and repetition make the images easy to understand graphically, but, as critics have suggested, is this enough to leverage a commentary on the exploitation of labor, life, and the environment?

Similar questions emerge in Burtynsky's *Oil* (1997–2009) series, a project that involved the artist's driving around the United States documenting automobile culture.[73] In some of the images printed in the catalogue for the series, one finds a myriad of full-page, large-scale printed images, with beautiful colors and magnificent detail, but little context and no captions. The text and essays are located in the back of the book, as is also the case with his monographs *Water* (2009–13) and *Quarries* (2007, with photographs from the early 1990s), and portions of volumes published by independent galleries like Robert Koch in San Francisco and Sundaram Tagore in Los Angeles. Leafing through the first hundred pages of these exquisitely produced catalogues, and without knowing much about the background of any given project, one is forced to view the images unfairly, purely in terms of their surface aesthetic. As patterns and colors dazzle, they supersede any notion of fear or discomfort, gradually moving questions of context into the background of consciousness. This is also why, when first encountering Burtynsky's work, his photographs seem to fit in conventional "art photography" rubrics: an exclusive concern with primary and secondary light sources, composition, cropping, color, patterns, and abstraction, and indeed, he diligently and conscientiously

FIGURE 32. Edward Burtynsky, *Manufacturing #17, Deda Chicken Processing Plant, Dehui City, Jilin Province, China* (2005). Digital chromogenic color print. © Edward Burtynsky, courtesy of Nicholas Metivier Gallery, Toronto

FIGURE 33. Godfrey Reggio, still from the film *Koyaanisqatsi* (1982), 35mm and 16mm film, 86 minutes. The colors of consumption are chaotic and organized.

works with his large-format camera to achieve an uncompromising quality for each image.

Other documentary photographers have used similar approaches for depicting international crises across global landscapes. In cinema, the ecologically attuned yet highly stylized films of Godfrey Reggio or Ron Fricke invoke economic, political, and social turmoil portrayed through spectacularly phenomenal cinematographic art. Reggio is best known for his Qatsi trilogy, which includes the films *Koyaanisqatsi* (1982), *Powaqqatsi* (1988), and *Naqoyqatsi* ("Life as War," 2002), while Fricke is known for *Baraka* (1992), *Chronos,* (1985), and *Sacred Site* (1986), as well as for his innovative use of time-lapse photography and role as director of *Koyaanisqatsi.* What Reggio and Fricke do in cinema, Burtynsky's work does in art photography.

In the long tradition of landscape painting, artists have also developed approaches to the sublime by depicting tensions between beauty and waste. Thomas Cole's *Course of Empire* series (1836), Boetzkes points out, "traces the emergence and demise of an imagined city,"[74] while J. W. Turner depicted beautifully dark, coal-polluted landscapes. Photographs documenting the atom bomb explosion in the Nevada desert and the somber beauty of blazing oil refineries at night also invoke this tension between visual beauty and environmental destruction. Arguably, this double-edged sword of beauty and terror cuts to one of the most persistent and pressing concerns of our time.[75]

We can now appreciate why critics have responded to Burtynsky's work as decontextualized modern art or mere spectacle. "But dang it's lovely," former *Washington Post* columnist David Segal concludes, while still conceding that Burtynsky's images of Bangladeshi shipbreakers may document the most dangerous worksite in the world.[76] Gerda Cammaer likewise argues that Burtynsky creates "art," not social commentary. He "destabilizes the very ontological character of the photograph," she writes, "deflating the evidential real in favor of aesthetic value." For her, the triumph of the aesthetic ultimately deprives the work of "any other reading, be it an ecological, social or cultural."[77] Concluding her review of Burtynsky's 2002 show at the Charles Cowles Gallery, *New York Times* critic Margarett Loke writes "Mr. Burtynsky's pictures have a way of looking wonderful despite man's most determined tampering."[78] And lastly, Meghan Bissonnette, in her assessment of Burtynsky's work, alongside J. Henry Fair's and David Maisel's, she writes, the "photographs provide an aestheticized and detached view of destruction." Burtynsky's manufactured landscapes, she continues, are "hauntingly beautiful. Despite their desire to raise awareness for environmental issues," they "evoke the detached gaze of contemporary ruin porn."[79]

To be fair, Burtynsky unequivocally prioritizes the lush surface. At the same time, it would be hasty to conclude that his work is entirely void of criticality. Yes, he relies on classic techniques in symmetry, line, and the repetition of form first and foremost. Works like "Densified Oil Filters, #1, Hamilton, Ontario," depict hundreds of neatly crushed oil filters tossed on a pile at random angles, each reflecting light from the rusted, silvery metal, but the harshness of the industrial context is still preserved. Jennifer Peeples makes comparisons between Burtynsky's work and Jackson Pollock's paintings, "with their abstraction of shapes and colors."[80] Burtynsky's bright dots and colors punctuate the landscape in the way Pollock's black, white, red, yellow, and sometimes blue abstractions do, but in Burtynsky's work we can still identify the oil filters *as* oil filters. The same cannot be said of Pollock's total abstractions. Burtynsky's strategy plays with the ostensibly apolitical, but at the end of the day, it is undeniably rooted in the social and political sphere, not in its transcendental elimination.

In this way, notwithstanding the criticisms noted above, Burtynsky's work consistently and deliberately manufactures tensions that require us to rethink how we see what we see, whether consciously or not. According to Lori Pauli, Burtynsky is "cautious about applying the term 'beautiful' to his photographs." What interests him is "getting beyond the automatic response that equates manufacturing with ugliness and pollution."[81] His aim is to invite people into the piece, to make it an "immersion experience where people say, 'I'm in here but I shouldn't like it.' I want to create that tension, have them attracted yet repulsed, to show them the dilemma we're in."[82] No conclusion or solution is reached, and this is precisely the point: he leaves the viewer in a precarious standstill, akin to the stopping of the X-ray sublime outlined above.[83]

To return to Peeples' point, by granting affluent audiences access to previously unseen sites of environmental destruction and trash retrieval, he opens the door for a new form of self-reflection.[84] How our waste accumulates and circulates is an issue of local and global concern. Heidegger once wrote, the "question concerning technology is never technological," rather, it is the questioning itself that matters. Questioning builds consciousness, a human consciousness that sees any "what" about machines and their waste as intrinsically connected to the how. In sum, to remain on the surface of the work—however beautiful it may be—is a disservice to it and the history and culture that shaped it. Burtynsky's images of metal and mine tailings, densified oil filters, scrap metal, and rebar production are beautiful, but they are far from the naïve "landscape aesthetic of wilderness appreciation," as Joan Schwartz puts it.[85]

VI. CHINA'S E-WASTE

Burtynsky's e-waste series, which began in China in 2002, further explores this ambiguous tension between light and dark, and beauty and terror. Like the Chittagong images, they seduce the eye with rich color, pattern, and detail while they are simultaneously haunted by a darker subtext.

In the first decade of the twentieth century, growth in the Chinese economy placed it on the international stage. The country thundered ahead in manufacturing,

FIGURE 34. Edward Burtynsky, *China Recycling #07* (2004). Wire Yard, Wenxi, Zhejiang Province, China. Chromogenic print. The eye is drawn to the colored wires, seeking an organizing principle. © Edward Burtynsky, courtesy of Nicholas Metivier Gallery, Toronto.

recycling, shipbuilding, urban renewal, and in particular, the development of the Three Gorges Dam, one of the world's largest hydroelectric power projects. Burtynsky's China images address multiple aspects of the country's developments during this time. I focus here only on those depicting e-waste and related forms of high-tech recycling.[86]

Electronic waste ("e-waste") is one of the largest sources of toxic heavy metals in municipal and global dumps.[87] In 2018, almost fifty million metric tons of e-waste were estimated to be generated worldwide.[88] Researchers at Carnegie Mellon concur, reporting that the amount of e-waste is growing three times faster than ordinary household trash. Even outdated statistics astound. In 1999, the National Safety Council predicted that between 1997 and 2007, more than 500 million computers would become obsolete in the United States alone, approximately 136,000 per day. The problem of e-waste disposal also remains acute, especially if the materials cannot be resold for profit. Burning them is sometimes proposed, but this has not yet been proven practical or safe. Open burning, for example, can create acid baths and toxic land dumps, exposing people to the poisons in the water and air,

FIGURE 35. Edward Burtynsky, *China Recycling #05* (2004). *Phone Dials, Zeguo, Zhejiang Province* (2004). © Edward Burtynsky, courtesy of Nicholas Metivier Gallery, Toronto.

including dioxins and furans.[89] The use of "scrubbers and screens," Elizabeth Royte argues, could hypothetically catch many of these toxic emissions, but "scientists consider even minute quantities, once airborne, to be dangerous."[90] The next best option appears to be recycling, but this can be done economically with only a portion of these materials.[91] The remaining items are smashed up by laborers and the debris frequently accumulates in pools of toxic sludge, which itself finds its way into groundwater (tests on the soil and water in regions where this is done have revealed levels of lead, chromium, and barium a hundred times higher than those allowed by the U.S. and European environmental health standards).[92]

Like the shipbreakers in Bangladesh, many Chinese workers engage in dangerous activity without any protective gear, policy, or law. In 2002, researchers from Silicon Valley Toxics Coalition (SVTC) and the Basel Action Network (BAN) investigated and videotaped unprotected "men, women, and children" in the rural Chinese village of Guiyu "extracting copper yolks from monitors with chisels and hammers." Investigators observed the workers moving through a *Wall•E*-type landscape, maneuvering "swirling mixtures of hydrochloric and nitric acid" (a caustic, highly poisonous chemical) in open vats.[93] Further research into ethical policies are urgently required, yet the United States, a leading producer of e-waste, has been exceedingly negligent about taking significant steps. "Rather than having to face the problem squarely," SVTC and BAN explain, "the United States and other rich economies that use most of the world's electronic products and generate most of the e-waste, have made use of a convenient, and until now, hidden escape valve—exporting the e-waste crisis to the developing countries of Asia."[94]

Any visual document of e-waste, therefore, cannot help but dissolve myths of unfettered technological progress, efficiency, and glistening utopias. But how does one do this elegantly and carefully without horrifying or shocking viewers or merely sensationalizing the surface qualities of a colorful image? Burtynsky's *China Recycling #7, Wire Yard, Wenxi, Zhejiang Province* (2004), is one example as it carefully depicts plastic wires in multiple colors. The eye is first drawn to the red heap in the center of the composition, which casually merges with some yellows, and eventually blue and green plastic wires in the foreground, where seemingly arbitrarily colored wires are strewn across the earth. After a slightly prolonged viewing, the order becomes clear: a highly systematic, methodical process of recycling the e-waste is under way, reinforced as the eye wanders to the secondary and tertiary piles of bronze copper wires to the right and the silver-metallic and black piles of wires in the upper left and lower right. The same technique is used in other images in the series, including *China Recycling #5, Phone Dials, Zeguo, Zhejiang Province* (2004) and *China Recycling #8, Plastic Toy Parts Guiyu, Guangdong Province* (2004). In *China Recycling #5*, one sees hundreds, possibly thousands, of black and silver circular metallic plates with little donut holes cut through the center. All of the pieces are exactly identical but through their seemingly random distribution throughout the pile, their pattern of difference and repetition offers the mind a pleasing sense of rhythm and coordination (again, the most basic form of optical delight). And then there is a double take: all of these many pieces of metal are from the interiors of rotary telephones, objects one will likely never encounter in the West again, but which pile up here as heaps of trash.

Similarly, in *China Recycling #8 Plastic Toy Parts, Guiyu* (Guangdong Province, China, 2004) heaps of scrap plastic and metals are at first beautiful on a graphic level, gently accented with pink, red, yellow, and blue in a sea of silver, black, and grey. And then one notices the metallic fragments spilling into the nearby groundwater. As artifacts of a mechanical era almost forgotten by the developed world, these defunct, "dead" media return to haunt a one-sided historical consciousness. This leaves an unresolved tension between the visual beauty of the abstract color and the harsh global realities of the e-waste recycling it is sampled from. Likeminded images in the series include *China Recycling # 18, 20,* and *24,* all of *Cankun Aluminum, Xiamen City, Fujian Province,* and *# 12* from *Ewaste Sorting, Zeguo, Zhejiang Province,* 2004. As with Burtynsky's shipbreaking images, environmental toxins and rampant air pollution simultaneously appear as dark and beautiful. His images consistently straddle this dialectic between pleasing visual

FIGURE 36. Edward Burtynsky, *Ford's Highland Park Plant #2* (2008). Assembly line corridor in a factory in Detroit, Michigan. Industrial ruins aestheticized to appear precious yet abandoned. © Edward Burtynsky, courtesy of Nicholas Metivier Gallery, Toronto.

pattern and the more disturbing context of e-waste and consumer excess, without offering any easy answers.

Burtynsky's 2008 Detroit images offer a variation on this dialectic between horror and awe. The series features the interiors and exteriors of abandoned automobile factories and warehouses in the city, speaking to the devastating economic downturn in the United States after 2007, especially as it hit hard in cities like in Detroit. The Detroit images romanticize ruin, a claim only marginally applicable to the China and India images. Here, however, images transform industrial and urban failure into visual spectacle.[95] And thus the question returns: Is Burtynsky using nostalgic beauty, as critics suggest, to alleviate guilt and shame at having failed to take responsibility for these industrial wastelands? Or, can such disturbing realities only ever be understood indirectly and partially, as Nietzsche famously argued, through metaphor and poetry?[96] My opinion has already been divulged in the Introduction: beauty and dazzling surfaces (color, and color as noise) are required to digest otherwise uncomfortable truths. Furthermore, because the X-ray sublime leaves the final steps of aesthetic experience unresolved,

FIGURE 37. Jennifer Baichwal and Edward Burtynsky, *Watermark* (2013), 100 minutes. Documentary still. The aerial perspective stylizes the industrial landscape through abstraction and brilliant color.

a work becomes that much more susceptible to criticism as nonsensical fluff. A slew of critics have purported as much. Catherine Zuromskis, for one, argues that Burtynsky's images capture a "static beauty . . . [a] landscape that simply cannot work: paralyzed, impossible."[97] Likewise, Jill Gatlin concludes that the tension between anxiety and pleasure in Burtynsky's images of toxic and high-tech waste is so intense that it halts (and problematizes) direct political action. "The toxic sublime," she writes, "disturbs . . . viewers' aesthetic sensibilities, not their identities as consumers, polluters, or political agents."[98] While I agree with these observations to the extent that Burtynsky's images halt the assumed teleology of classical aesthetic experience, I do not concede that the work is apolitical, even if the politics are covert. Burtynsky's failure to resolve the tension in the juxtaposition between a number of contrasting realities—the imagination and the understanding; beauty and ugliness; magnitude and insignificance; the known and the unknown—are a sign of the X-ray sublime's *success*.[99] Left without easy answers or a prefabricated conclusion, the images stare back at us, like Brecht's direct gaze. Their impossibility implicates *us,* not just "them." The beautiful pictures ask us: Can you look at this peacefully, undisturbed? And even if the answer is yes, then the image has at least done the work of raising the question.

FIGURE 38. Edward Burtynsky, *Benidorm #1, Spain, 2010*. Still from Jennifer Baichwal and Edward Burtynsky, *Watermark* (2013).

VII. AERIAL PERSPECTIVES ON THE X-RAY SUBLIME

In the 1930s, the French photographer Henri Cartier-Bresson complained about conventional landscape photography. "The world is going to pieces," he exclaimed, "and people like [Ansel] Adams and [Edward] Weston are photographing rocks!"[100] Taking a stab at their ostensibly irrelevant, apolitical, and non-technological "Nature" aesthetic, which persists across historical eras, Cartier-Bresson was drawn instead to the modern consciousness made possible through new tools and techniques. Like-minded photographers concurred, even August Sander and Carleton Watkins, who had been imaging landscapes since the nineteenth century, had begun to eschew the idealized nature aesthetic. It is not surprising that both Sander's and Watkins's innovative works were largely influential to Burtynsky. When first encountering Sander's *Quarry Pit* (1925–35) at the National Gallery of Canada in 1982, an image of a gigantic hollow cavity inside of a rock quarry, Burtynsky recalls a delightful confusion, "I stared at it for a minute before I could figure out what I was looking at."[101] He was similarly riveted when he first encountered a Watkins print at the Metropolitan Museum in New York in the early 1980s. Unlike traditional approaches to landscape, Watkins's work hovered over a mythical, archetypal world from an oddly elevated perspective, intentionally distancing itself from its depicted object.[102] Since 2008, Burtynsky has used emergent media (helicopters, digital lighting and photographic equipment) to create aerial images that continue to abstract from conventional approaches to the landscape. *Anthropocene: The Human Epoch* (2018) and *Water* (2013), illustrate these methods as the artist images the earth from thousands of feet above, widening the already precarious gap between human and world.[103]

This chapter has only scratched the surface of the many crises of e-waste. Egypt's "Garbage City" and the Long Island Fresh Kills landfill both evoke a horror and beauty akin to the X-ray sublime, with nothing of the transcendental or divine to speak of, a sobering moment of realization that forces a reconnection to the body, earth, and world. This waste is our waste. Paul Virilio once suggested adopting a "Gray Ecology" where "aesthetic pollution . . . doesn't mean that it's ugly, or that it's beautiful. It means that it interferes."[104] The troubled beauty of the X-ray sublime does just this—like noise and abstract color—by shattering delusions of transparency and unfettered success.

In the next chapter I draw on Kant's notion of the mathematical sublime to further explore how computer-generated images of trash and waste figure in depictions of ecological breakdown.

7

———

Landscape as Data

From the Classical to the Consumer-Mathematical

I. COLD CARE

According to garbologists William Rathje and Cullen Murphy, the cliché "Out of sight, out of mind" rings true when it comes to garbage. Its inverse, however, is not.[1] Even when spotlighted, garbage somehow manages to escape notice, let alone anyone taking responsibility for it. Perhaps this is because waste is normally concealed from the everyday lives of privileged, "First World" citizens, whether under the kitchen sink, outside a city's limits, or on a barge on its way to international waters. On occasions when garbage and consumer waste is seen—on the news, the internet, or occasionally, in an art gallery—it elicits destabilizing responses ranging from discomfort to fleeting terror or, in the case of Burtynsky's art photography, a chilling beautification. But the environment is in crisis and these realities, no matter how disturbing, can no longer remain out of mind.

What better way to analyze these beatified "art world" images of unfathomable crisis then through the polarized forces of shock-and-awe intrinsic to the sublime? At least this has been the trend in recent years, from my analysis in the previous chapter to recent scholarship from Jill Gatlin, Catherine Zuromskis, Finis Dunaway, and Jennifer Peeples, all of whom explore the distraught relationship between visual beauty and its role in photographs of disturbing toxicity and waste. The crux of this debate was addressed in the previous chapter. Yet another problem arises when artists turn to big data and numerical visualizations of global waste. This chapter examines this dilemma through a genealogical argument about the evolution of landscape imaging in art photography. The middle sections discuss the work of German photographer Andreas Gursky, whose cool images of industrial

154

landscapes echo the anonymity of postindustrial global capital. The last part of the chapter turns to photographs and computer-generated images from Al Gore and Seattle-based eco-artist Chris Jordan (1963–) to discuss the way in which they convey complex forms of failure and breakdown. Building on chapter 6's analysis of the aesthetic sublime, this chapter discusses the twin concept of the mathematical sublime. I argue that adopting numbers and statistics to depict environmental waste engenders a twofold structure of failure related to (a) the literal depiction of trash and waste and (b) a failure in visual communications. Because the latter is only brought to light after an exegesis of the history of landscape photography, the chapter first provides this history, from the late nineteenth century to the beginning of the twenty-first. In charting a shift from classical "Nature" aesthetics to industrial and, eventually, postindustrial, mathematical techniques of data visualization, I establish an aesthetic archaeology of "waste landscapes," on the basis of which Jordan's and Gore's works can then be discussed.

II. TWO SUBLIMES

The above noted scholars are loosely affiliated with what Jennifer Peeples calls the "toxic sublime," a genre of contemporary fine art photography depicting waste and ruin, often as a result of the high-tech industries.[2] Some images in this genre highlight beauty (as in Burtynsky's work), while others prioritize political and activist issues (e.g.: Chris Jordan's and Al Gore's works). The divide has prompted a number of critics to question the efficacy of either one: do slick and expensive, large-scale "art house" photographs of toxic waste divert attention from environmental concerns or, to the contrary, does beauty allow us to accept otherwise horrifying realities? Concurring with the former, Gatlin argues that sublime images of waste present an "improbable catalyst" for political mobilization.[3] Unlike chapter 6, this chapter concurs with Gatlin insofar as sublime images of toxicity and environmental breakdown nullify political action when treated *mathematically*. As abstract statistics, I argue here, they engender yet another crisis in human perception and corresponding failure-qua-fascination with the transcendent capacities of the human mind.

The theoretical and epistemological failures at stake in this chapter are akin to the critical failure of the romantic sublime that precedes it. To briefly rehash from chapter 6, in the aesthetic sublime, an individual is exposed to an awe-inspiring scene or object, like a massive mountain range or a powerful thunderstorm that generates a series of complex negotiations between the imagination and the faculties of reason and understanding. This begins with a failure to grasp this breadth and a sense of fear and diminishment that this has occurred at all, followed by a questioning of identity. It concludes with a final recuperation by the faculty of reason. But given that we are discussing images of toxic waste, not pristine mountain ranges, this final state of recuperation is again precarious. And indeed, this is what I argued in chapter 6. The toxic sublime, and what I theorized as the "X-ray sublime" in the previous chapter, unlike the classical aesthetic sublime, only finds an irresolvable standstill in the perpetual oscillation between two ambivalent forces. After acknowledging one's lack of control and inability to provide a quick fix or remedy, a subject is void of resolution and in this way, fails again.[4]

When these toxic images are pictured through mathematics and numerical abstraction, this too leads to another kind of failure, qualified by an entirely distinct set of conditions. Where both the aesthetic and mathematical sublimes, according to Kant, involve measuring size and related feelings of superiority in relation to "something great,"[5] it is only the mathematical sublime that requires a basic apprehension of numerical quanta in such a way that, strangely, relieves the subject of the need to resolve the sublime experience as something fully comprehended or even understood.[6] In the mathematical sublime, greater and greater numbers increasingly challenge the faculty of understanding. As the size of an object or phenomenon continues to grow, the faculty of reason demonstrates its capacity to reach by stretching to apprehend what is being shown or represented, and yet, Kant argues, because there is no limit in the "mathematical estimation of magnitude," all that is needed is a mere acknowledgment of quantity.[7]

The word "apprehension" derives from the Latin *prehendere,* meaning "to seize," denoting only a surface awareness of something. One "seizes" or recognizes a state of the world but does not, and cannot, judge or assess if it is true or false, ethical or unethical, and so forth. Apprehension, Kant writes, is "prior to any concept."[8] Consider Kant's own distinction between apprehension and comprehension: in judging a person's height, he explains, an assessment is made relative to the average magnitude of other people known to us.[9] This estimation of size is something we do every day, intuitively, and without much need to calculate it. This is comprehension, a basic ingredient for aesthetic experience. In contrast, in the mathematical sublime, one can attribute a precise numerical quantity to an object without "comprehending" it at all. Here, a person's height is not simply an eyeball guess or intuitive concept, but rather, quantitatively determined "by means of [external] numerical concepts."[10] In short, in the mathematical sublime, failure on the level of integrated understanding is not only acceptable, it is prescribed.[11]

In this way, the mathematical sublime becomes a suitable lens for analyzing our relationship to large quantities of computational data that surpass human understanding. In science and engineering, massive sets of numbers are manipulated by computers. In visual art and media, however, we are discussing images made *for* humans, *by* humans, which is to say, integrated understanding and hermeneutic breadth are the benchmarks of success. After the next section's archaeology of landscape photography, I return to this polemic in my analysis of Chris Jordan's and Al Gore's use of mathematical abstraction to depict the toxic sublime.

III. LANDSCAPES: FROM THE CLASSICAL TO THE INDUSTRIAL

It is not by accident that the landscape genre evolved alongside Western capitalism, from agrarian industries to mechanized production and electronic information technologies. Some of the strongest evidence of this trajectory is provided in the American and, to some degree, German landscape traditions.[12] We must first consider these non-mathematical precursors before turning to more recent, mathematically inspired landscapes.

Classical Landscape Photography

Prior to the industrial era, the landscape tradition tended largely to romanticism. Classically lush paintings of the pristine American wilderness and European hinterlands emerged on the heels of Burke's and Kant's doctrines. And even though photography (introduced in 1839) only became commonplace by the second half of the nineteenth century, in the landscape genre, it did so at first as an instrumental device—not quite the "fine art" photography that it has since been construed as.[13] At the same time, it did not take long for the first generation of photographic practitioners to test the poetic limits in the medium. Such pioneers included Eadweard Muybridge, Darius Kinsey, Carleton Watkins, Timothy O'Sullivan, and William Henry Jackson, initially hired to document the American West and its unexplored "wilderness" for government surveys. In these pursuits, they simultaneously found creative new ways to photograph the landscape.

This first generation of landscape photographers is also renowned for aiding pioneers as they trailblazed new routes across the then-wild frontiers of the United States. Carleton Watkins's massive plate work in Yosemite National Park, California (1861–65), for example, began as a set of commissions documenting a quicksilver mine for courtroom evidence,[14] while Timothy O'Sullivan's landscape images (1890–1940) were later used by the U.S. Senate in establishing the National Park Service.[15] Darius Kinsey's photographs were instrumental in documenting the logging industry's environmental effects on the Pacific Northwest from the turn of the century to the 1940s. Almost all of these photographers also had vested interests in supporting one political issue or another, albeit often inadvertently, and as a result, this body of work foreshadows both activist strategies and landscape aesthetics.

Despite the persistent encroachment of industry and Western-moving settlements, photographers and environmentalists like Ansel Adams, Minor White, August Sander, and Edward Weston perpetuated iconic images of a pristine, untouched "wild" West well into the middle of the twentieth century. Adams produced striking black-and-white landscapes showing very little evidence of human presence.[16] Even as this once-wild terrain began to disappear into the "well-traversed frontier of cultural development" that much of it has now become, such romantic images maintained a hold on the imagination of many Americans.[17]

Industrial Sublime

As the century progressed, however, clinging to mythologies of utopian purity became increasingly challenging. A second generation of landscape photographers had had enough of the deluded myths of an untainted wilderness and turned instead to industry and man-made accomplishments. August Sander, Berenice Abbott, Charles Sheeler, and Margaret Bourke-White, among others, helped to transform the naivety of the American psyche through their industrial-based landscape aesthetic. Some worked independently, while others were commissioned to document the triumphant new world of man-made concrete, iron, glass, and steel. Their work resonated with the simplicity of pure shape and form, characteristic of purist painting, related minimalist techniques, and architecture's International Style.

In 1927, Sheeler was commissioned by N. W. Ayer & Son to photograph the Ford Motor Company's new River Rouge plant in Dearborn, Michigan. He produced a series of clean, modernist images of the plant's natural architecture, emphasizing the beauty of its hard lines and geometrical "bisections" and the way they formalized a pattern of repeating lines.[18] Bourke-White's influential work featured equally bold industrial shapes and forms, most notably her *Plow Blades, Oliver Chilled Plow Company* (1930); her upward-looking views of the Chrysler Building (1930); and her remarkable images of a DC-4 flying over Manhattan in 1939, presumably shot from the upper stories of the Empire State Building. Bourke-White's *Diversion Tunnels, Fort Peck Dam* (1936) are also spectacular in their stark depiction of gargantuan steel structures used to manage water in the Fort Peck dam. In the foreground one sees enormous sections of the pipes waiting to be installed in the Missouri River.[19] In some images from the series, people stand in the foreground, their relative size dwarfed by the gigantic pipe sections they face. In other images from the series, the metal edifices are featured in the foreground with an overcast sky and a small range of hills barely detectable in the background. The contrast, again, retroactively intensifies the magnificence and dominating presence of the man-made structures.[20] The land that once impressed classical landscape artists here becomes the mere backdrop for a new generation of nature-defying machines.

Sheeler's and Bourke-White's work reinforce David Nye's concept of the "Technological Sublime." According to Nye, the concept of the sublime transformed from the "natural sublime" to a "technological" one with the advent of industrialization and mechanical reproduction. The massive changes to culture and society resulted in such "incomprehension" and "astonishment," industrial culture readily supplanted their earlier fascinations with nature for the grandeurs of man-made achievements.[21] Examples abound, from New York City's Times Square spectacle to early skyscrapers or, Peeples suggests, to watching Neil Armstrong walk on the moon.[22] A century of such achievements has replaced the God of Nature with symbols of humanity's omnipotence. Hence Nietzsche's dictum that "God is dead" because he has been replaced by modern science and industry. Nye's notion of a technological sublime also invokes a Promethean pride in humanity's endeavors. But recall from chapter 1 that Prometheus *stole* fire from the gods to make amends for his brother's error. Furthermore, according to this origin myth, technology is not only a prosthetic, supplementing what we do not have and cannot accomplish without it but also, a mark of eternal dependence. This side of the myth is of course largely absent in the work of this generation of landscape photographers. Industrial materials like metals and ores may not be stolen from the gods, but they are mined from the earth in ways that are often reckless and without care. I return to this in my concluding discussion of Jordan's work. Here, such environmental concerns are still a distant reality, if at all.

IV. POSTINDUSTRIAL HABITATS

The "New Topographic" Landscape

As noted in chapter 4, one 1975 exhibition is accredited for single-handedly pioneering a shift in contemporary aesthetics.[23] *New Topographics: Photographs of a Man-Altered Landscape*, shown at the George Eastman House, included work by Robert Adams, Lewis Baltz, Bernd and Hilla Becher, Joe Deal, Frank Gohlke, Stephen Shore, and Henry Wessel Jr., all of whom depicted flat and vernacular landscapes, in stark contrast to the Promethean visions noted above. The artists in the show chose generic, man-made landscapes like tract houses, suburbia, strip malls, industrial parks, trailer parks, roadside hotels, and generic cars and apartment buildings, and photographed them in a deadpan, prosaic fashion.[24] Writing for the *New York Times*, Vicki Goldberg claims this turn to the vernacular christened culture's second nature, one more authentic than the God-given first one.[25] The exhibition's curator, William Jenkins, called it "anthropological rather than critical, scientific rather than artistic,"[26] marking a growing pessimism towards so-called triumphant machines and their implicit links to social and cultural progress. This generation of artists worked in the postwar boom of the 1960s, which is to say, during a time when most people sought and found comfort in the stable and familiar. But the *New Topographics* artists (in conjunction with the German School, as discussed in chapter 4) rejected this, turning the mundane into a too-cool aesthetic, which, for better or worse, went largely unnoticed.[27] Their key move, Catherine Zuromskis argues, was to consider the landscape as a "cultural formation" versus "simply what is out there." The landscape was taken as a complex system where politics, ideology, mythology, and economics all played vital roles constructing who we are and how we experience the world.[28] These photographers moved away from naturalism and the modernist mythology of unfettered progress to embrace instead a prosaic intimacy with everyday material life, ironically in touch with the culture's broader tendency to prioritize economic advancement over collective, social, or environmental good.

Artists like Lee Friedlander, Robert Adams, David Hanson, David Maisel, Alan Berger, Peter Goin, Emmet Gowin, and German photographer Andreas Gursky continued to work in this vein for the next few decades. Friedlander's work, for example, while not included in the 1975 exhibition, accurately reflects a nascent consciousness of postwar consumerism. He made his name by renting a car and driving around the country, using black-and-white photography to document the highways, motels, and strip malls of Cold War America. From this, he produced his best-known series, *America by Car* (1995–2009), depicting the new Fordist landscape of automation and convenience from the inside and out. On the surface, Friedlander's images speak to the cliché postwar American psyche, with its expectations of comfort and convenience. On a deeper level, his images confront a subtle play between cultural nostalgia and destitution more familiar to the present. Likewise, Robert Adams's *Santa Ana Wash, Next to Norton Air Force Base, San Bernardino County, California* (1978) depicts a desert landscape with shrubs and trees. Barely detectable in the distance is an airplane. Its bareness illustrates how the image is blatantly unconcerned with glamorizing nature or paying tribute to industry's greatness. In fact, it actively eschews such precursors, apropos of the new school of landscape cool, favoring the flat and banal, the "here and now," as Britt Salvesen puts it. In sum, what we see here, and in other images from this landscape genre are the "mundane qualia" saturating the contours of postwar life.[29]

Andreas Gursky's Consumer Landscapes

On the other side of the Atlantic, German photographer Andreas Gursky blazed a similar trail towards man-made landscapes. Before discussing Gursky's work, it should be noted that while some of the concerns of the American photographers noted above may be shared with the German School, they also have acute distinctions and should not be treated analogously.[30]

Gursky's primary connection to the New Topographics was through the exhibition, which included the work of his teachers Bernd and Hilla Becher (see chapter 4).[31] My inclusion of figures from the Becher-led Düsseldorf school in an analysis otherwise focused on American landscape photography further elucidates historical and aesthetic connections between the two countries and the ways in which they have both operated as industrial power houses.[32]

Gursky is known for an elegant series of "eye-zapping" images that, according to Chris Jordan, depict our commodity-patterned world.[33] Synthetic and industrial colors are normalized as vernacular facets of our second nature, characterized by post-Fordist office spaces and global communication networks. Like others in his generation, Gursky's work is shot in color, but his hues, like Stephen Shore's, evoke neither the bright, hypersaturated colors of William Eggleston nor the supernatural hues of Eliot Porter.[34] Rather, his palette is washed out and dulled, corresponding

FIGURE 39. Andreas Gursky, *Tokyo Stock Exchange* (1990). Gursky photographed crowd scenes in the 1990s and 2000s, illustrating a key shift in the distribution of objects and bodies in space. © Andreas Gursky / SOCAN (2019).

with the energy level of the workers he depicts who spend thousands of hours toiling under electronic lights and screens. For example, Gursky's *Düsseldorf, Airport, Sunday Walkers* (1985) depicts a small group of people who have "either walked or biked to the airport." The image is composed from behind, Michael Fried points out, suggesting that what is to be seen is…nothing! That is, we see the same banal reality that the people in the image see. No magnificent airplane is taking off nor is there an awe-inspiring landscape in the background. Rather, the image documents banal sightseeing on a boring "overcast" Sunday afternoon.[35]

In the 1990s, Gursky began digitally manipulating his images, producing what are now considered his capstone works: *Tokyo Stock Exchange* (1990), *Paris, Montparnasse* (1993), *Prada I* (1996), *Atlanta* (1996), *Untitled V* (1997), *Chicago Board of Trade* (1997), *Times Square* (1997), and *Rhine II* (1999). Taken together, Fried suggests, they evoke an ontological and spiritual void. *Singapore Stock Exchange* (1997) and *Hong Kong Stock Exchange* (1994) portray extremely geometric images of a large number of Asian workers assembled around their computer stations.[36] As both Peter Galassi and Fried argue, the photographs depict many people, but no individuals per se; they are portraits without subjectivity. For one,

FIGURE 40. Andreas Gursky, *99 Cent* (2001). Spectral colors pop and compete for a viewer's attention. None of nature's subtle charms remain. © Andreas Gursky / SOCAN (2019).

the images are not composed from a particular viewer's perspective, suggesting instead a new landscape of rational and homogenized indifference.[37] *Tokyo Stock Exchange* (1990) is somewhat less rigid in its geometric organization, but comparable in its absence of any single focus, perspective, or horizon line. The image depicts stock market traders' "somewhat fervent absorption in their transactions," Fried writes, conveying a collective human-economic system, while still lacking specificity or personal expression.[38] This machine-like "all-overness," captures a slice of the pervasive postindustrial landscape, sadly void of a graspable whole.[39]

Lastly, more recent but related work by Gursky includes *Dortmund* (2009), an image of a massive crowd wearing yellow at a soccer match, and *99 Cent* (2001), a view of the aisles in a grocery store with various synthetically colored candy wrappers and processed food items, deploying seriality and repetition to create a playful and purely graphical visual interest. Like the human workers depicted in the preceding images, the candy bars are equally void of individual identity or presence. Both humans and machines are treated as anonymous nodes in much larger systems of command and control. Such is the paradox of global infrastructures: the more sophisticated they become, the less we can see or relate to them.[40] In sum, Gursky's work offers a preliminary set of strategies for visualizing how excessive technology in an age of global capital operates in relation to human experience. His images take a slice of the rapid movement of people and data and freezes them; making them static in movement and momentum, but already beyond any one single, human vantage point. There is no longer room for individual experience, let alone social ideals. Specific tasks, personalities, or unique psychologies become obsolete in this ominous landscape of network flows and invisible, but seemingly omniscient, imaging mechanisms.

V. CHRIS JORDAN'S MATHEMATICAL LANDSCAPES

Ecology in every way has to do with "love, loss, despair, and compassion," ecologist Timothy Morton argues, suggesting ecological images necessarily integrate physical and metaphysical registers, especially those displaying breakdown and ruin. And yet, how can any single image of ecological waste convey anything else, with 260,000 gallons of gasoline burned in motor vehicles in the United States every minute, not to speak of fifteen million sheets of office paper used up in five minutes, and 426,000 cell phones retired every day?[41] Moreover, when asked to "think green" in all of our activities and affairs, where and how does one seemingly insignificant person begin? Consider too, the preceding statistics are almost two decades old, taken from studies in 2000. In 2015, the *New York Times* alluded to the "1980 consultants for AT&T [who] projected that 900,000 cellphones might be sold by 2000. In fact, there were 109 million sold by then."[42] By the end of 2018, GSMA Intelligence reports, "5.1 billion people around the world subscribed to mobile services," with 700 million more projected to subscribe by 2025.[43] Yes, the numbers are big, and the difference significant, but in terms of grasping just how much and why, do we not fall short every time? Do recent trends in computational analysis and numerical abstraction help us to get a better grasp on these stark realities? Or, given our inability to absorb such large numbers (as outlined in the above discussion of Kant's mathematical sublime), do they not instead perpetuate blind and hysterical responses to what has become the fastest-growing and most toxic portion of waste in American society: e-waste?

Alongside a number of media activists, San Francisco-born photographer Chris Jordan has been seeking solutions to these questions by turning to computer simulation and big data. Such strategies seem to provide an appropriate response to the massive overhauls in global, infrastructural, and aesthetic registers, but in less obvious ways, they fail. This section analyzes Jordan's mathematically inspired strategies for illustrating mass consumption and corresponding forms of e-waste and garbage accumulating across the globe, presented as a provocative and not unproblematic turn in twenty-first century landscape imaging.

Jordan's giant images (some 6 to 12 ft tall and up to 5 ft wide) are not unlike Edward Burtynsky's phantasmatic large-scale images of toxic and industrial waste.[44] Many of Jordan's images are also printed in limited editions, for exclusive display in galleries or museums. Unlike Burtynsky, however, Jordan draws on and prioritizes mathematics—statistics and big data gleaned from internet research— to visually convey difficult and challenging "truths" about the global landscape's rapid environmental breakdown.[45]

Before turning to photography, Jordan was an attorney engaged in corporate litigation but eventually found the work "soul-draining."[46] In 2003, he tore up his law degree and turned to photography full-time. He has since made a number of portraits and series depicting global waste, high-tech trash, ecological breakdown, and the effects of mass consumption that, in his words, examine American culture "through the austere lens of statistics,"[47] resulting in a series of contentious images contrasting visual beauty with the ecological horror show of the consumer practices in which we are all complicit. His early work depicts numerically derived images of global landscapes in critical condition. More recently, he has turned from troubled landscapes to equally harrowing issues such as elephant poaching in Africa and the aftermath of disasters like Hurricane Katrina.[48] Below, I consider images from Jordan's series *Intolerable Beauty: Portraits of American Mass Consumption* (2005) and *Running the Numbers: An American Self-Portrait* (2007) to assess their efficacy in conveying environmental failure as a result of the high-tech industries.

Running the Numbers

Running the Numbers consists of a series of "intricately detailed prints assembled from thousands of smaller photographs," each one illustrating specific quantities of various products consumed in the United States during given periods.[49] *Plastic Bags* (2007), depicts 60,000 plastic bags, the number used every five seconds, while *Car Keys* (2011) presents an image of 260,000 car keys, equal to the number of gallons of gasoline burned in motor vehicles every minute. Similarly, *Cell Phones* (2007) illustrates 426,000 cell phones, the number retired every day circa 2000;[50] and *Plastic Cups* (2008) depicts a million plastic cups, the number used on airline flights every six hours.[51]

Running the Numbers began in 2005 as an "experiment with Jeep Liberty" (an SUV produced by Jeep from 2002 to 2012).[52] The artist's goal for the series was to repeat a set of images until they embodied his chosen statistic to reflect this facet of American culture. How, he asks, could he produce a "different effect than the raw numbers" did, and as we also encounter daily in books, magazines, and the news; "statistics [that] can feel abstract and anesthetizing."[53] The *Running the Numbers* images joined statistics with images to produce an alternative aesthetic that aimed to transform everyday manufactured objects into existential questions.[54] Images in the series also allude to iconic examples of landscape art, which, unlike his work, are intrinsically linked to norms of classical beauty. *Impressionism (Cans Seurat,* 2007), for example, is based on the well-known painting by Georges Seurat, *A Sunday Afternoon on the Island of La Grande Jatte* (1884). Seurat's image consists of dots or points of color in what has since become known as pointillism, and Jordan's image is similarly constructed out of 106,000 variously colored aluminum cans, the number used in the United States every thirty seconds.[55] When viewed on the artist's website or as documented during his appearance on *The Colbert Report,*

FIGURE 41. Chris Jordan, *Cell Phones* (2007). Jordan "stood on a ladder, gazing down at 3,000 or so used cellphones in a pile on the warehouse floor. His 8×10 view camera was perched even higher, on a tripod 12 feet above them" (Gefter, "Great Big Beautiful Pile of Junk"). Courtesy of Chris Jordan.

FIGURE 42. Chris Jordan, *Cans Seurat,* on *The Colbert Report,* October 11, 2007. Composite image of 106,000 soda cans—the number used in the United States every thirty seconds. The audience gasped when the camera zoomed in on the image to reveal cans with corporate logos used as the building blocks for the image.

the two-fold dynamic is illustrated as the camera zooms in to view the details of each soda can used as a "point" to make up the larger image.[56]

The juxtaposition between a more distant "whole" and close-up "parts" is one solution to the challenge of dealing with large quantities. But, again, the aim is not visual beauty as traditionally defined but the capacity to convey the breadth of such gargantuan numerical data. Put differently, Jordan's perceptual field is not constituted through light and color, but by quanta. The repetition of simple shapes and forms are used to draw a viewer into a social and environmental "territory they might otherwise be reluctant to enter," the artist explains, "inviting the viewer in close, to stay a while."[57] Granted the realities he points to are urgent and demand attention, one cannot help but wonder if the way he portrays them is effective. Substituting metal cans for colored dots or, for pixels in the world of computer graphics, is in essence a simulation. That is, it is further removed and abstracted, not only from landscape, but also from concrete experience. This is not a value judgment but an observation on the capacity of a digital image to speak to us. By depicting quantities of e-waste and high-tech trash resembling what very few people have ever seen or experienced firsthand—a reality not even seen in the image itself, but only pointed to through the caption—simulated image-worlds become a discursive exercise that attempts to relate to everyone about no-actual-thing in particular.[58]

Plastic Bottles (2006–7) raises the same issue. Jordan began this piece by taking a photograph of a few hundred plastic bottles assembled in his driveway. He then rearranged the bottles numerous times, photographing each new arrangement.[59] The images were then imported into Photoshop and reassembled into a single image, representative of the two million bottles opened in the United States every five minutes. The results were printed onto large-scale limited edition papers, 60″ × 120″ prints, using an Epson UltraChrome process. The method is efficient, given the large numbers with which Jordan is dealing, but ultimately, he was visually simulating a non-existent physical space.

Philip Gefter's 2005 *New York Times* article on Jordan's work discusses the artist's strategies for representing quantity. In one instance, Gefter reports, Jordan "stood on a ladder, gazing down at 3,000 or so used cellphones in a pile on the warehouse floor. His 8×10 view camera was perched even higher, on a tripod 12 feet above them." Jordan was photographing discarded cell phones at CollectiveGood in the suburbs of Atlanta, one of the few U.S.-based electronics recycling sites. He wanted to portray 130 million cell phones in one image, to represent the number of cell phones discarded annually. However, in order to do this, CollectiveGood informed him, he would have to "reproduce the picture he was now getting ready to take about 43,000 times, creating a panorama that would stretch 61 miles if the photos were laid side by side."[60] This presented an obvious logistical problem, especially given Jordan's goal to "give a concrete sense of our consumption" practices. In this way, his digitally simulated collages seem to be a viable solution.

Jordan's *Paper Bags* (60″ × 80″), *Cell Phones* (60″ × 100″), and *Denali Denial* (60″ × 75″) all use this technique to represent vast quantities of objects, standing in for equally gross patterns of consumption.

Recall that in the mathematical sublime, numerical abstraction only requires a basic "apprehension," which is always already "beyond understanding."[61] Perhaps then we do not require any further explanation for these data-driven simulations? In this way, Jordan's work employs the basic precondition of the mathematical sublime: to deploy numbers and abstraction (caption and simulated visual re-pre-sentation) to evoke a lack of comprehension or failure to fully grasp on the level of understanding.[62] Jordan's images then simultaneously undermine the integrity of the "landscape" genre as a realistic or contingent rendering of the world as it actually is, introducing a new form of digitally simulated landscapes by expand-ing the terrain of conventional data visualization. The role of the caption in rela-tion to the image arguably resolves this tension. Their integration in *Running the Numbers,* Jordan explains, produces a "translation, from the deadening language of statistics into a more *universal visual language* that might allow for more feel-ing."[63] In this way, his digital collages are antithetical to the landscape genre, offer-ing instead a proto-form of data visualization that, I submit, has begun the hard climb of moving a visual image away from the attributes of sense perception. If this is true, then can this work be included in the landscape lineage at all? The lineage I have charted in this chapter allows us to see how Jordan's work can indeed be positioned at the end of this legacy, a move that, in turn, reveals the limits of the now-older visual episteme. This lineage also sheds light on a progressive aesthetic tendency towards anonymous and numeric-based abstraction, lacking indexical relation to lived experience.

Recall too that Jordan is less concerned with the surface aesthetic than with an image's implied meaning. He has even gone so far as to note a dissatisfaction with viewers who associate his images with notions of beauty. Subsequently, he has attempted to eviscerate any possibility of "beautiful" interpretations of his work. His eccentric focus on activism over aesthetics (at least within the world of large-scale art photography) also explains his tendency to discuss his work in terms of the ecological facts driving the images, rather than the images themselves. Furthermore, rather than throw the baby out with the bathwater by reframing Jordan's use of abstract numbers within the legacy of landscape photography, we might reconsider the role of the mathematical sublime in contemporary land-scapes, especially ones addressing global relations and, by extrapolation, the increasingly prominent role of big data in them.

The mathematical sublime is a transcendent realm beyond the need of compre-hension; it needs only a basic, immediate apprehension, which makes it an obvi-ous choice for analyzing realities and phenomena that have already moved too far beyond human grasp or magnitude (computation being the primary candidate here). Put differently, and as noted in the chapter's introduction, the mathematical sublime presents a condition of "absolute greatness *not* inhibited with ideas of limitation";[64] it does not require comprehension, which is fine for indicating truth, but insufficient as a hermeneutic or for any humanities-based interpretation, which, arguably, the arts serve. In reaching the limits of the two-dimensional visual image in the globally connected infrastructures of the twenty-first century, the use of numerical abstraction in data visualization seems a promising solution, ostensibly without limit, as Kant proposed, but in terms of meaning, a whole host of other problems emerge.[65]

VI. BIG DATA'S FAILURES

Like Jordan's visualizations, David Guggenheim's documentary film *An Inconvenient Truth* (2006) employs numbers and computational data to represent environmental breakdown and global warming. The film focusses on former U.S. vice president Al Gore's efforts to educate people about global warming and it has been affiliated with great successes, including an Academy Award, being a co-recipient on the Climate Change panel of the 2007 Nobel Peace Prize, and underpinning Gore's "phoenix-like rebirth" as a global warming "rock star."[66] After viewing the film, critics noted "just how entertaining and enthralling" they found it. One critic noted his surprise when he assumed he was going to be watching a film on "the most boring of all subjects. . . . But I promise, you will be captivated and then riveted and then scared out of your wits." Another critic noted the film to be "full of surprises," offering viewers an "emotionally rich [and] visually entertaining story."[67] Unlike the vast majority of environmental media campaigns, Finis Dunaway writes, Gore's film challenged media conventions by articulating the "accretive crisis of climate change," global warming, and toxic waste over time, establishing a "bond" between historical, scientific, and emotional registers.[68]

At the same time, as the film employs statistics and cutting-edge computer simulation techniques to render future scenarios of dystopia and apocalypse, a concerning pathos takes hold. Scenes of environmental breakdown and global warming resembling Hollywood spectacle are a far cry from level-headed solutions or actual activist reform. For example, the film overwhelms audiences with data on environmental breakdown and global warming. Gore and Guggenheim make a "surprisingly captivating" use of a graph, Dunaway explains, with a "jagged red line" moving in an upward direction from the bottom left corner to the upper right of the image, representing the change in the amount of carbon dioxide in earth's atmosphere over the past 650,000 years on earth. A pale blue line indicating temperature runs along the horizontal X-axis (indicating time), just under the red line. When the blue line spikes, the red line does too. The X-axis is steady until the last section of the graph, indicating the present and immediate future, when the red line skyrockets to immeasurable levels. The message is clear: as the amount of CO_2 in the atmosphere rises, global temperature will dramatically rise in tandem.[69]

Unsurprisingly, the film's staggering statistics evoke intense emotional responses from the audience. "I can't think of another movie in which the display of a graph elicited a gasp of horror," *New York Times*'s A. O. Scott writes. "when the red lines showing the increasing rates of carbon dioxide emissions and the corresponding rise and temperatures come on screen, the effect is jolting and chilling."[70] The scene incites a heightened, horror movie-like pathos— but to what end? To my mind, this kind of shock effect through mass abstraction and extrapolation creates paralysis and an incapacity to respond. I do not seek to detract from the ethical or political importance of Jordan's or Gore's work, but it is nonetheless crucial to remain critical about the precarious ways in which the global landscape's changing conditions are represented through the visual arts and mass media. In short, Guggenheim and Gore's film, like Jordan's imagery, zero in on apocalyptic doomsday scenarios by leveraging inverted modern mythologies of human grandeur.

Asides from shocking privileged viewers in locations often far from the most critical sites of climate change, the film also marginalizes those who actually endure these environmental catastrophes. To unpack this claim, let's consider the film from a slightly different perspective: cuteness. Dunaway offers the example of Guggenheim's animated polar bear, which viewers watch "repeatedly but unsuccessfully" in its attempt to "climb on to chunks of melting ice."[71] The iconic polar bear's cuteness trumps reality. Another cute bear adorned the April 2006 cover of *Time Magazine*, Dunaway continues, a "lone polar bear" is seen "perched on floating ice, gazing uncertainly at the surrounding sea. The byline reads: "Be worried. Be very worried."[72] But the bear seems aloof. At the very least, Dunaway argues, the images made the polar bear a national icon of sensationalized environmental issues.

Around a year later, in the spring of 2007, the famed portrait photographer Annie Leibovitz photographed "Hollywood heartthrob" Leonardo DiCaprio for the next annual green issue of *Vanity Fair*. This would be the magazine's third such issue; the first one in 2005 featured Julia Roberts, and the second, Madonna in 2008. In Leibovitz's portrait of him, DiCaprio is perched on a glacier beside a "digitally added image of Knut, a popular polar bear cub from the Berlin zoo."[73] Such Hollywood mash-ups may help incite emotional responses to the long-term effects of global warming, but they do so through seduction and distorted visualization.

These kind of sensationalizing images can also be seen in the more recent collaboration between V Magazine and Oliver Peoples. In their short music video, *Heatwave* (2019), directed by Grant Greenberg and produced by Derby for V Magazine, the directors attempt to make "recycling fashionable." The video was shot at the Sims Municipal Recycling Center in Brooklyn and features dancers and fashionably-clad models prancing around stacks of plastic primed for recycling.[74] While the video may in fact increase the trendiness of recycling, it simultaneously perpetuates the production of waste by esteeming plastic and synthetic textiles in the form of wearable fashions (viscose, polyesters, and the various other plastic-based makeup and dyes that the dancers are wearing). Such materials not only produce more toxins and waste during their "off-shore" production but also, additional waste through "fast fashion" cycles of planned obsolescence. (This is discussed at length in the book's postscript.)

There is of course nothing wrong with invoking our intrinsic human need for affection, or our tendency to seduce through glamor and cuteness in order to connect, but the way in which this appeal is made in these magazines, videos, and animations either placates or exacerbates anxiety. The titillating sex appeal of movie stars and hip new fashions pander to aesthetic modes often divorced from the underlying issues. For example, as Dunaway explains of *An Inconvenient Truth*, it foregrounds a cute bear but "completely ignores the plight of Arctic indigenous peoples whose cultures and landscapes are facing profound changes produced by melting polar ice."[75]

Is manipulation through cuteness, fashion, or sex appeal any worse than manipulation through numbers? For one, cuteness and sex appeal can operate in a similar way to numerical abstraction, distancing a viewer from the complexities of a viewed subject, which, in turn, effectively soothes potentially panicked responses.[76] Aesthetic cuteness, as Sianne Ngai argues, is a political category rooted in dominant and submissive power relations.[77] The aesthetic category of "cuteness" seldom receives serious academic consideration, she notes, and, since Kant, has been marginalized—along with color—from the upper echelons of aesthetic judgment and truth.[78] Ngai's goal is to redeem this aesthetic category as worthy of serious consideration. For her, the surface-cuteness seen in a bear or animated character holds a much deeper significance, connected to an implicit and often unconscious violence or aggression on the part of the spectator. Participating in the cultural practices of cuteness, she suggests, implies one is also, perhaps unknowingly, enacting deeper fantasies of control and domination.[79] In "apprehending" something cute, a beholder or viewer does not have to cognize or make meaning, in essence, a watered-down equivalent to the low-level engagement intrinsic to Kant's mathematical sublime. That is, a failed attempt to gain control fit for an age where we all have less and less of it. The inability to grasp the magnitude of numbers in the mathematical sublime of Gore and Jordan, now ubiquitous in so many depictions of global waste, breakdown, and crises, is quickly replaced, not by an acknowledgment of difficulty or challenge, but instead by the quick and cheap apprehension of affect, whether as cuteness, fear, or both.[80]

In sum, any single image from Gore or Jordan, or others using data visualization strategies, removes reality from its "holistic lifeworld," as the phenomenologists referred to it. Abstraction by definition denies the nuances and subtleties of context. And yet, by abstracting signals into numerical representations, they become a kind of free-floating noise, up for grabs for any interest or re-signification, ripe for re-territorialized "capture" as Deleuze and Guattari put it.[81] But what other option is there? If information-intensive landscapes and data visualization have become the primary lens through which we access the world, then further consideration of the ways in which numbers fail to communicate is required. First, we must consider how data-simulated images fail worldly contexts, followed by their impressive but impenetrable capacity to exceed human comprehension. The task is not simple. As Paul Edwards notes, we may never know more about global warming trends because our constantly shifting standards have lost a consistent baseline to calculate deviations from.[82] Herein lies the perversity of bearing witness to our own destruction while erasing the very means necessary to track it.

This chapter has used landscape photography to map the historical trajectory behind this predicament, from its origins through the advent of consumer culture, drawing on the works of Ansel Adams, Andreas Gursky, Chris Jordan, and Al Gore as benchmarks in the process. In conjunction with the previous chapter, it charted the difficulties, failures, and successes in depicting waste and trash. Where Burtynsky's work introduced us to an environmental magnitude comparable to Kant's aesthetic sublime, and Gursky's to one apropos of the consumer environment, in Jordan's we face the limits of these strategies, but, in turn, a new set of imaging techniques that speak to the more immediate failures of communication in a global landscape.

Postscript

Miraculous Plastic's Retrograde Sublime

High-Tech Trash: Glitch, Noise, and Aesthetic Failure analyzes how artists and theorists have placed glitch, error, and noise at the center of their scholarly and creative practices, and second, how this allows for critical reflection on a broader ethos and aesthetic of breakdown. The many case studies and chapters in the book also analyze glitch, noise, error, and failure as an emergent visual rhetoric in media art and culture. Before closing, however, there is one last meaningful heap of high-tech trash to discuss, this time from a more distant historical perspective. That is, how strategies of planned obsolescence have shaped the social and political birth and afterlife of plastic. Given plastic's status as an older media (relative to digital technology), it offers a more comprehensive view of the broad trajectory from new to old (dead) media, which, in turn, can then be used to shed comparatively light on commodity production and material consumption in the information age.

I. DISPOSABLES

Marie Kondo, author of the best-selling book *The Life-Changing Magic of Tidying Up* (2017), is celebrated for her pioneering minimalism and decluttering trends. Kondo preaches a "ruthless" tidiness and a merciless "purge all." Her dream is to "organize the world," Taffy Brodesser-Akner reports for the *New York Times Magazine*.[1] Kondo's ethos comes across as an appropriate refusal of consumer excesses and yet, her practice also seems to endorse models of planned obsolescence, by virtue of encouraging people to throw things out. It would be incorrect to scapegoat Kondo as a driving force behind consumer waste, but it is undeniable that her ethos of radical discard contributes to the growing cycles of waste in consumer culture. Writing for *Esquire*, David Sax further critiques her fashionable brand of de-cluttering as catering to virtual fantasies longing for the "power to make a big chunk of our possessions just disappear."[2] The mythology appeals to many of us, six million in fact, who purchased Kondo's book. As Sax notes, the trend is merely the latest instantiation of a long-standing cultural dream for pure, noise-free worlds, transcendent of dirt and matter.

Planned Obsolescence

Of course, Kondo is not single-handedly responsible for perpetuating such fantasies. Strategies to efficiently get rid of stuff date back to the seventeenth century's introduction of planned obsolescence, a managerial strategy implemented in order to preemptively curtail the expected lifespan of a consumer object and promote its early replacement. The technique was first developed to encourage the unnecessary consumption and "wearing-out" of new commodities.[3] "Fashion," Nicholas Barbon wrote in his 1690 *Discourse on Trade,* "is a great Promoter of Trade, because it occasions the Expence of Cloaths, before the Old ones are worn out: It is the Spirit and Life of Trade; It makes a Circulation . . . to all sorts of Commodities; keeps the great Body of Trade in Motion; . . . as if [man] lived in a perpetual Spring."[4] Barbon had in mind raw materials, buildings, and anything else that would support "the great Advantage and Profit that Trade brings to a Nation."[5]

Over three centuries later, planned obsolescence has become a formal strategy in a number of commercial industries. In the 1920s, it was leveraged to help end the Great Depression in North America by promoting recurrent patterns of use and consumption. The approach is reiterated in American real-estate broker Bernard London's 1932 diatribe *Ending the Depression through Planned Obsolescence.* In some ways, London's pamphlet accurately voices the concerns of a society of production slowly segueing into a culture of consumption. The "essential economic problem," he argues, "has become one of organizing buyers rather than of stimulating producers." London also proposed the formation of a "government agency" to oversee and determine the legal lifespan of each manufactured object. He proposed that consumers who disobeyed such "law[s]" by keeping old stuff around, "using their old cars, their old tires, their old radios and their old clothing much longer than statisticians had expected," should be taxed for such continued use of what was legally considered "dead." In his view, criminality and the failure to keep up with cycles of consumption could be conflated as one and the same. The failure to buy was the failure to be a good citizen. One should feel obligated, in this view, to support the nation's industry through needless consumption. And while we do not have rigid laws restricting the use of objects, we do have the pressures of social convention and "conspicuous consumption," as Thorstein Veblen theorized it, to make us acutely aware when our clothing, gadgets, and other objects are embarrassingly out of fashion.[6]

A second benchmark in the development of planned obsolescence occurred in the postwar era. Around 1954, designer and tastemaker Brooks Stevens encouraged consumers to "own something a little newer, a little better, a little sooner than is necessary."[7] Marketing consultant Victor Lebow likewise advocated rapid waste. In a 1955 issue of the *Journal of Retailing*, Lebow argued that in order to keep businesses and retailers afloat, "We require not only 'forced draft' consumption," but also, "expensive consumption . . . We need things consumed, burned up, worn out, replaced, and discarded at an ever increasing pace."[8] His overarching goal was to "make consumption [a] way of life," and ensure consumers could find "spiritual satisfactions . . . in consumption." Nothing in the world is more terrifying than the proposition that "corporations have a soul," Gilles Deleuze asserted in 1990,[9] but the notion that superfluous shopping is the source of national pride, let alone our spiritual destiny, takes the cake.

When the ancient Greeks proposed a rigorous pursuit of the "good life," the acquisition of things and stuff could not be further from what they had in mind. And still, we have made a culture of consumption synonymous with "bettering" one's self, family, and country at large. Spiritual or not, it is what we do and work for. Micah White concurs. In pursuit of the "good life," he writes, we "constantly replace the objects in our daily life," which in turn, keep "us locked into our overworked, over stimulated and under paid daily grind. We work to buy things that are built to die so that we must work to buy more things that will break."[10] From Veblen's 1899 critique of conspicuous consumption to Barbara Kruger's 1987 work *Untitled (I shop therefore I am)*, artists and scholars have excoriated excessive consumption, yet the belly of the beast expands with each new consumer report.[11]

E-Tech Obsolescence

In electronics, planned obsolescence has resulted in unfathomable quantities of e-waste, as discussed in chapters 6 and 7. Speaking for the United Nations University (UNU), International Telecommunication Union (ITU), and International Solid Waste Association (ISWA), Cornelis Baldé et al. define e-waste as "electrical and electronic equipment (EEE) and its parts that have been discarded by its owner as waste without the intent of re-use."[12] The problem is not merely the growing quantities of e-waste, however, but the fact that many electronic products are developed with *the key aim of failing faster* (thus ensuring more accelerated replacement). A key example, as noted in the Introduction, is Apple's attempt to slow down the speed of its iPhone to enhance sales of newer models. Furthermore, Apple's iPods, iPhones, and iPads are now manufactured with no serviceable parts inside, including their batteries. The devices are often glued together, making discarding them and buying a new model a user's only option.

Apple's obsolescence strategy is further enhanced by the company's decisions to use cheap, short-lived materials. The lithium-polymer batteries in many Apple devices die after only three years of use. Preemptive consumption is also promoted from the retail end by devising marketing strategies that make "new" models with relatively the same features as the older ones. The average lifespan of computers in developed countries dropped from six years in 1997 to just two years in 2005.[13] With 44.7 million metric tons of e-waste generated in 2016, the UNU reported in 2017 that we can expect to foresee a 17 percent increase to 52.2 million metric tons of e-waste by 2021.[14] If we thought the manufacturing and information industries grew at a rapid rate, they pale in comparison to the unfathomable acceleration of e-waste accumulation, "the fastest growing part of the world's domestic waste stream."[15] Darren Blum of Pentagram Design remarks, "We joke that we design landfills."[16]

Further attention to the afterlife of retired high-tech objects is required. As an offshoot of media archaeology, zombie media provides one such method. Like the works analyzed in the previous chapters, zombie media submits that media never die, but, after being discarded or deemed obsolete, they assume afterlives in the media environment.[17] From a zombie media perspective, what comes to matter most in digital environments is the stuff we don't see (see chapters 6 and 7). Accordingly, this Postscript continues and completes the book's study of error-ridden and seemingly "dead," valueless digital media with an archaeology of plastic, a much older, but once just as magical new media. Beginning with a brief history of the early twentieth-century origins of plastic as a utopian substance, I follow it through its afterlife in this century, contaminating the world's oceans and killing marine mammals and sea life. One day, electronic media will also become old and dead. Awareness of what has and is happening with dead plastic may in turn help reroute the seemingly sad destiny of our quickly dying electronics.

II. MIRACULOUS PLASTIC!

Plastics . . . A Way to a Better More Carefree Life.
—"THIS YEAR REDISCOVER PLASTICS," *HOUSE BEAUTIFUL*, 1947

Plastic, Roland Barthes wrote circa 1954, is "the first magical substance that consents to be prosaic."[18] Indeed, many of the conveniences and major feats of modern culture would not exist without it. Found in such diverse objects as toothbrushes, water bottles, doorknobs, chewing gum, cellophane, electronic and computer parts, acrylic paint, vinyl, Formica, and the pervasive polyurethane plastic bags once received every time we bought anything, plastic has become so universal, we fail to recognize just how radically it has reconfigured the everyday. Plastics have also had enormous medical and technological benefits, insulating electronic wires to allow electricity to flow quickly and safely, making blood transfusions safe and common through vinyl blood bags, and transforming dentistry's use of hard rubber plates with lightweight plastic ones. Plastics are flexible, easy to produce, versatile, and few modern or natural substances can compete with them in all of these areas at once. Plastics were developed over the twentieth century into an extended family of amazing objects with thousands of different uses and applications. They were hailed from the start as a modern panacea; a man-made alchemical wizardry transforming nature through rational chemistry. And yet, it is no secret that in recent years, plastic has come under the gun of environmental, biological, and health concerns. Let us now consider how this turn of events came about.

The fashion for plastic evolved with the bourgeoisie in the second half of the nineteenth century.[19] By 1880, George Eastman was manufacturing photographic film from celluloid, developed by John Wesley Hyatt in 1870. By 1909, the New York–based chemist Leo Baekeland was using heat and compression to mix carbolic acid (phenol) with formaldehyde, producing the insoluble, non-conductive material called "Bakelite." Bakelite could be molded into almost any desired shape or form and henceforth newer, cheaper plastic facsimiles began replacing rare materials like ivory (used in billiard balls), tortoiseshell (used in hairbrushes), diamonds, silk, and furs.[20] Unlike many organic and pre-synthetic materials, plastics are stable, transformable, easy to work with, and capable of being mass-produced with economic benefit.

When the United States blazed a trail through the golden era of entrepreneurship in the early twentieth century, plastics were there to fulfill the ambitious dreams and visions of the zeitgeist.[21] Plastic was the most conducive "vehicle to express men's soaring imagination," Thelma Newman writes, "strongly reflect[ing] its own era."[22] The pivotal role of plastic in the construction of Hollywood glamour in the 1920s and 1930s is unsurprising. Used in film stock and on film sets, plastic products provided a repertoire of new materials and metaphors in mirrors, shiny surfaces, lighting effects, smoke screens, and synthetic auras. Plastic glamour was disposable glamour, as Judith Brown puts it, delivering its media fix quickly and easily.[23] The military also requisitioned the production of new plastic items at the outset of World War II, to replace metal and rubber items like standard-issue GI combs, mortar fuses, parachutes, turrets used on planes for gunners, and bugles.[24] Earl Tupper, inventor of Tupperware, argues that though plastics had proven themselves during the war, "like all young vets returning from the war," they did not yet have "civilian adult experience."[25]

Postwar Prosaic Shine

If landscape photography celebrated the feats of industrial modernism in the early twentieth century (chapter 7), with plastic, this heyday arrived in the 1940s. People were so enthralled with plastic, "cellophane" was designated the "third most beautiful [word] in English language, after mother and memory."[26] Plastic was by and large celebrated as the pinnacle of change and innovation, even though contenders had already begun to emerge.

In the late 1950s and early 1960s, plastic became feasible in art making and a significant number of visual artists gravitated to it.[27] Water-soluble acrylic paints

FIGURE 43. DuPont advertisement, *Saturday Evening Post*, ca. 1947. Cellophane is marketed as safe and miraculous, even for children!

(also derived from plastic by-products) appeared on the commercial market in 1955, making possible the thin and definitive edges in many ways definitive of modern art. Genres like op art would not have been possible using longer-to-cure or less controllable oil paints.[28] The new genre tended to a slick, shiny aesthetic,

FIGURE 44. DuPont advertisement, *Saturday Evening Post,* ca. 1947.

foreshadowing the cool, clean styles of postwar pop.[29] Meanwhile, Thelma Newman's *Metamorphosis of a Human* (1961) and *Surrogate Mother* (ca. 1961) depicted another side of plastic. Less machinelike in form, her work explored the manifold possibilities for the shape-shifting new medium to simulate amorphous glass and crystal. Other artists turned to plastic to draw on unexplored possibilities

FIGURE 45. Cover of *Mobilia* no. 145 (August 1967). Verner Panton / Louis Schnakenburg, Copenhagen, plastic chairs. The more plastic, the more modern.

with the new repertoire of synthetic multi-polymers, fiberglass, polyester, cellulose, and the use of deep glaze effects accomplished by spraying polyurethane.[30]

Museums of modern art responded with major exhibitions devoted to plastic, highlighting the then fashionable tensions between art and industry. For younger architects, designers, and artists, plastics had become a future-forward medium, popping up in sleek designs for living spaces, inspired in part by the space race. Colored plastic pneumatics carved a space for itself as an aesthetic medium of the future-now. From Buckminster Fuller-esque plastic dome habitats to space suits and helmets, plastic was the midcentury new medium de rigueur.

And yet, as indicated above, not everyone jumped on the celebratory plastic bandwagon. In his *New York Times* review of the 1966 Whitney annual exhibition,

Hilton Kramer simultaneously trashed and lauded the present "condition of sculpture in this country." On the one hand, he found "youth in the saddle [full of] energies and aspirations that are cheerfully and militantly in pursuit of a new modes of sensibility." On the other hand, he was appalled by the "superficial glitter of oversized plastic toys and ersatz geometric monuments passing for serious sculptural statements."[31] A similar ambivalence colors his 1968 review of the Museum of Contemporary Crafts' *Plastic as Plastic* exhibition.[32] Faced with a slew of plastic accessories, architectural components, industrial designs, kitchenware, clothes, jewelry, and sundry items, Kramer questions whether the exhibition was even, "strictly speaking, an art exhibition." Had art become the forearm of commerce? (*Had it ever not been?*) Plastics introduced a "Faustian freedom," Kramer concludes, the "answer to an artist's dream," but only if the artist was willing to pay the high price of "sharing the mechanism of creation with technical processes not always susceptible to the artist's will."[33]

Concerns about plastic grew beyond the art world. When industry began producing "schlocky kinds of things"[34] like pink flamingos for lawns, or DuPont's synthetic leather in the 1960s, plastic lost its cutting edge. Links were made to environmental and health hazards. Once hailed as a miracle development in vinyl blood bags, a 1970s experiment revealed rat livers wrapped in plastic had developed tumors. Other researchers observed that chemicals from the vinyl blood bags (called DEHP plasticizers) leached into the fluids taken into the rat bodies—and so too in the medical patients who had received treatment with the plastic bags.[35] Further investigations revealed people who had not even been medical patients retained trace levels of plasticizers (for example, by using plastic hoses in the garden). It was concluded at the time that these levels were "not harmful." Plastics were "fine for human health," except under "very, very particular and rare circumstances."[36] By the late 1960s, viewing plastic as a utopian substance had become a joke, as illustrated in a punch line in one scene of Mike Nichols's film *The Graduate* (1967). Playing the young Benjamin Braddock, Dustin Hoffman is told by an elder at a cocktail party, "I just want to say one word to you. Just one word . . . Plastic . . . There's a great future in plastics." In the film, this advice is framed as odd, spoken by an "old" person out of touch with culture's growing awareness of plastic's dark side.[37]

Plastic's Retrograde Sublime

Controversy about toxins, environmental damage, disease, and death related to plastic continues, but there is enough evidence to merit concern. The Toxic Substances Control Act (TSCA), passed by the U.S. Congress in 1976 and administered by the U.S. Environmental Protection Agency (EPA), ostensibly regulates the chemical industry, but it treats chemicals as safe until proven dangerous. Moreover, because manufacturers in the United States do not have to volunteer information about chemical development, the EPA is left without much-needed information.[38] One current problematic plastic is polyethylene terephthalate (PET), used in soda and water bottles. Studies show PET leaches a compound that stimulates and alters estrogenic activity, though specific impacts on health remain inconclusive.[39] Another controversial plastic is bisphenol A (BPA), used in numerous consumer products including medical supplies, safety equipment, audiovisual parts, and food packaging. Meanwhile, levels of plastic production accelerate at alarming rates. Over the past sixty years, the use of plastic has increased almost twentyfold, with an annual production reaching 280 million tons in 2011.[40] In 2008, a million plastic bags were being used every minute, the United States alone went through a hundred billion plastic shopping bags annually.[41] Recently there has been raised awareness of such plastic bags, and in particular, the question of where all this plastic goes.

Garbage Patch Plastic

Many plastics do not biodegrade (polyurethane takes a thousand years to break down) and their toxic debris contaminate the earth's soil and water, harming ocean life among other things. An area of the Pacific Ocean strewn with floating plastic called the Great Garbage Patch is twice the size of Texas. According to Laura Parker writing for *National Geographic* in 2018, "18 billion pounds of plastic waste [continue to] flow into the oceans every year."[42] Ocean life and marine vertebrae, including birds, dolphins, fish, and turtles, often misinterpret colorful plastic debris (lighters, toothbrushes) as food or prey. Prolonged or repeated ingestion can result in obstruction and malfunction of the digestive track and/or entanglement in plastics (called "ghost nests"). Both cause starvation and eventual death. Each year, approximately a billion seabirds and mammals die from eating plastic bags, a horrifying outcome that screams for attention.[43]

Chris Jordan's *Midway: Message from the Gyre* project began in 2009. It focuses on Midway Atoll, a cluster of islands in the Great Garbage Patch more than two thousand miles from the nearest continent. *Midway* documents how the plastic detritus of consumer culture surfaces here inside the stomachs of thousands of dead baby albatrosses. Parents feed their baby chicks lethal quantities of plastic, having mistaken the floating trash for food while foraging.[44] To record these activities, activists like Jordan collect digested plastic parts found on the beach, and in one case, he laid them out on the sand according to color and consumer class. As a photographic document, their variegated, synthetic hues create a bizarre tension between graphic order and environmental breakdown.

Before closing, I cite two last noteworthy zombie media projects. The first of these, according to Jennifer Gabrys, is an anonymously created "humanoid" sculpture representing the average amount of high-tech trash the average British citizen would generate over a lifetime. Built in London in 2005, and intended to "loom seven meters above the River Thames," the structure weighed in at three tons and incorporated 550 appliances and devices, including "refrigerators and computer

FIGURE 46. Chris Jordan, *Midway: Message from the Gyre* (2009). Birds mistake colored plastic for food and feed it to their chicks. Video still. Courtesy of Chris Jordan.

mice, mobile phones and microwave ovens, computer monitors and washing machines."[45] A second example is Canadian artist Kelly Jazvac's *Plastiglomerat.* This piece involved the artist traveling to Kamilo Beach in southern Hawaii with geologist Patricia Corcoran to study a series of new composite formations, consisting of "molten plastic debris and beach sediment, including sand, wood, and rock," and sometimes, "fishing nets, piping, bottle caps, and rubber tires." Her team termed the new species, "plastiglomerates," invoking the way they were born from "molten" plastic or other man-made materials binding with a "basalt flow" from nearby volcanic activity. The "time span" of the plastiglomerates, they argue, mark the "time span" of "human interaction with Earth's biophysical system."[46] Works by Zoe Beloff, Paul DeMarinis, Masaki Fujihata, Benjamin Gaulon, Garnet Hertz, Perry Hoberman, Aleksander Kolkowski, David Link, Bernie Lubell, Julien Maire, Catherine Russell, and Gebhard Sengmüller likewise draw on zombie media and media archaeology methods. By reviving obsolete or marginalized forms, these artists explore multiple nonlinear temporalities. The aesthetic of failure is rendered on the surface of their work, as a crucial reminder of the past we continue to create in the present.

· · ·

As glitch, noise, error, and trash continue to accumulate in culture and society, so too do creative appropriation practices in relation to them. The chapters of this book have discussed these strategies in a number of twentieth- and twenty-first-century contexts. In media studies, this has resulted in the growth of "media archaeology," defined in the Introduction. As media archaeology grows in intellectual, artistic, and academic breadth, it does so alongside industrial design trends towards more disposable, miniaturized "black boxes," which, of course, do not appear on the shelf as literal black boxes but as translucent, multicolored plastic ones. The work of media archaeology and critical aesthetic theory is to shed light on the darker sides of these multicolored forms, whether in the environment or as glitch and noise, disturbing myths of transparency undergirding computational culture.

A future generation of artists can still take heed from László Moholy-Nagy, who argued three-quarters of a century ago that artists "working with plastics inevitably have to take up scientific studies or else wait decades until knowledge about plastics becomes commonplace."[47] The same goes for silicon, precious metals, and the e-waste contaminating rural areas in places many privileged, First World consumers will never see or travel to. We no longer have to wait decades though, because, as this postscript and the last two chapters have shown, the baleful effects of our high-tech trash are already all too evident.

In closing, I briefly turn to Alexander Galloway's 2013 essay "The Poverty of Philosophy: Realism and Post-Fordism," in which he invokes Catherine Malabou's inquiry into the current stakes of human consciousness, given capitalism's prevailing expansions. His proposal, by way of Malabou, is *plasticity*: reworking the problematic conflation of contemporary "ontological systems and the structure of the most highly evolved technologies of post-Fordist capitalism."[48] Or, in Malabou's terms, finding new "flexible" ways to separate received accounts of life and being from those prefabricated and "molded" by the contemporary "spirit of capitalism." We must form ourselves anew, she argues, "be able to fold oneself, to take the fold, not to give it."[49] Granted Malabou and Galloway do not have actual consumer plastic in mind, their metaphors nonetheless invoke the malleable essence of the substance. In the context of this book, their proposals for existential plasticity could, in turn, allow for a future human-machine ontology that also defies sublimation to ideologies of transparency and efficiency so dear to current intellectual fashions in Western culture and the high-tech industries. May the brilliant colors of dead plastic and defunct pixels become a life lesson.

INTRODUCTION

1. The title of this Introduction is adapted from Adam Davidson's "Welcome to the Failure Age."

2. Donahue, "Fail Fast"; Von Kaenel, "Failure."

3. Zero-sum scenarios were introduced at the RAND corporation in the 1950s by the U.S. military strategist Herman Kahn.

4. General Electric, "What Is Six Sigma?"

5. Fidler, "Anarchy or Regulation."

6. "Sweden's Museum of Failure."

7. Fisher, "Why Most Innovations Are Great Big Failures."

8. Foucault, "Introduction," 22; Heidegger, *Being and Time*, 242.

9. See also Berlant, *Cruel Optimism*.

10. See Gamson, *Claims to Fame: Celebrity in Contemporary America*.

11. Anonymous entrepreneur quoted in Asghar, "Why Silicon Valley's 'Fail Fast' Mantra Is Just Hype."

12. Davidson, "Welcome to the Failure Age!"

13. Such strategic obsolescence is discussed further in the Postscript.

14. Toh, Geier, and Kottasová, "Global Backlash."

15. Al, "The Strip," 5.

16. Likely at the request of the marketing team. This process is further addressed in the Postscript as "planned e-obsolescence."

17. Le Feuvre, *Failure*, 14.

18. Solomon-Godeau, "Rightness of Wrong"; Le Feuvre, *Failure*, 52.

19. Bridle, "Something Is Wrong on the Internet." See also his 2018 book *New Dark Age*.

20. Bridle suggests such hacks are not deliberate. In this discussion I assume some are.

21. Stokel-Walker, "Algorithms."

22. See "The Algorithmic Lifeworld," in Kane, *Chromatic Algorithms*.

23. More specifically, chapter 2 charts a genealogy of glitch art through the avant-garde, while chapter 7 proposes that landscape photography cannot persist without addressing the overproduction and overconsumption of industrial and electronic devices.

24. There are of course exceptions, such as J. D. Peters, Friedrich Kittler, and a number of other scholars noted in this section.

25. Foucault, *Archaeology of Knowledge*, 62; Nietzsche Essay I, Section 13 in *On the Genealogy*, 45.

26. Ibid. The flash, in his account, is also a pun on the Enlightenment conflation of visibility and knowledge.

27. Zielinski, *Deep Time*, 1–4.

28. I thank Jessica Law at the University of British Columbia for bringing my attention to Alberti's book *On Painting*. Kemp, *Science of* Art; Masheck, "Alberti's 'Window.'"

29. Kelly, "Best Technology."

30. Wollen, "Godard and Counter Cinema." Wollen's invocation of the term "foregrounding" is applicable to critiques of transparency in digital glitch art, as the following chapters delineate.

31. Ibid. Wollen goes on to theorize other tenets of Godard's cinema, including "narrative intransitivity, estrangement, multiple diegesis, aperture, unpleasure, [and] reality."

32. Simondon, "On Techno-Aesthetics," 2. Also see Fuller, "Simondon and Techno-Aesthetics."

33. Simondon, "On Techno-Aesthetics," 2.

34. This is also the title of his 2012–2013 seminar taught at the University of Chicago.

35. Jackson, "Rethinking Repair," 452.

36. See Benjamin, *The Arcades Project*; Crary, *24/7*; Doane "Information, Crisis, Catastrophe"; and Kracauer, *The Mass Ornament*.

37. Larkin, "Degraded Images," 291; Lotringer and Virilio, *Accident of Art*.

38. Serres, *Genesis*, 6–7, *Parasite*, 126.

39. Serres, *Genesis*, 79.

40. Thompson, *Soundscape of Modernity*.

41. Virilio, "Primal Accident," 212.

42. Barthes, *Responsibility*, 245.

43. To make a tenuous analogy: Heidegger distinguishes between the "present at hand" and "ready to hand." The former sticks out as a dysfunctional tool or technology (making a noticeable "noise" in experience), while the latter goes unnoticed, blending into the nuances of the immersive life world (Heidegger, *Being and Time*, 265–68).

44. Barthes, "Grain," 188.

45. The same logic underscores Barthes's theory of color and his theory of the "punctum."

46. Barthes, "Grain," 189. The pheno-text, described earlier in the essay, borrows from Julia Kristeva. It is contrasted with the geno-text to denote the cultural-historical register including "all features which belong to the structure of the language . . . the rules of the genre, the coded form of the melisma, the composer's idiolect." In contrast, the geno-text denotes a kind of base matter, the space "where significations germinate 'from within language and in its very materiality'; [forming a] signifying play having nothing to do with communication, representation (of feelings), expression; . . . the voluptuousness of sounds-signifiers" ("Grain," 182).

47. Goddard, Halligan, and Hegarty, *Reverberations*. Similarly, Jacques Rancière defines the "distribution of the sensible" as a "delimitation of spaces and times, of the visible and the invisible, of speech and noise, that simultaneously determines the places and the stakes of politics as a form of experience" (Rancière, *Politics*, 1).

48. Noise is a "signal that interferes with the reception of a message by a receiver, even if the interfering signal itself has a meaning for that receiver" (Attali, *Noise*, 6, 26–27; see also Cox, *Audio Culture*, 6–9).

49. Brassier, "Against an Aesthetics of Noise."

50. See Krapp, *Noise Channels*; Menkman *Glitch Moment(um)*; Nunes, ed., *Error*; Hegarty, *Noise/Music*; Hainge, *Noise Matters*; Kahn, *Noise, Water, Meat*; and Paulson, *Noise of Culture*. Less relevant titles include Munster, *Aesthesia of Networks*; Kwastek et al., *Aesthetics of Interaction in Digital Art*; Halberstam, *Queer Art*; and Wiley, *Noise Matters*.

51. L. G. Cox, "Birth."

52. Cascone in *Designing Imperfection*, 17.

53. Goriunova and Shulgin, "Glitch," 114.

54. Moradi in Gilmore et al., eds., *Designing Imperfection*; R. Jackson, "Glitch Aesthetic," 41.

55. Ibid.; R. Jackson, "Glitch Aesthetic," 57.

56. Goriunova and Alexei Shulgin, "Glitch," 111.

57. Deleuze and Guattari, *Thousand Plateaus*.

58. Battles, "But It Moves."

59. There are of course exceptions, such as Rosa Menkman's excellent publications.

60. Other recent examples include Chairlift's *Evident Utensil* (2009); the video game *Kane and Lynch 2: Dog Days* (2009); and numerous audio and video plug-ins (iZotope's "warp" function for audio, the "BadTV4" plugin for AfterFx, which replicates the effects of bad TV interference, and Hipstamatic, which imitates analog imperfections using faux vintage lens flares and lomographic discolorations).

61. Attali, *Noise*, 26–27.

62. Derrida, "Typewriter Ribbon" (1998) and "A Certain Impossible." In this case, Derrida's notion is most applicable, despite other philosophers who have theorized the Event quite differently (Badiou's *Being and Event*, Deleuze's *Difference and Repetition* in 1968).

63. Kittler's one-sided media-fundamentalism has received criticism in recent years, but in this context, its militancy allows for a rigorous reconceptualization of noise as not merely benign but active and potentially disturbing. For more on this, see Hoffmann and Schickore, "Secondary Matters."

64. The so-called sharing economy, for example, has long lost its "innocuous veneer," revealing its bottom-line profit ambitions (Institute for Networked Cultures, "Failing Better").

65. Lynch, *Wasting Away*, 208–9.

66. See http://laplazacultural.com. Nin Garcia started the garden on what was then one of the East Village's many vacant lots.

67. Lynch, *Wasting Away*, 208.

68. Yates, "Human-as-Waste," 1688.

69. Ibid., 1680.

70. Yates, "Human-as-Waste," 1681.

71. See the discussion of "democratic color" in chapter 4 of Kane, *Chromatic Algorithms*.

72. Judith Butler, talk given at Brown University, October 15, 2014. Also see Butler, *Parting Ways*, 86.

CHAPTER 1. COLORS OF ERROR: INNOVATION AND FAILURE FROM PLATO TO DIGITAL SIGNAL PROCESSING

1. Lagadec paraphrasing Meyers, in Lagadec, *States of Emergency*: 4.

2. Meyers citing Geneen, ibid.; see also Stiegler, *Technics and Time 2*, 142.

3. This section does not purport to offer a philosophical exposé, but rather, an interdisciplinary approach that draws from epistemology, the philosophy of technology, and cultural and economic critiques of the development of failure-qua-innovation.

4. This section's summary is drawn from both Plato and Stiegler's account of the myth. And, as Stiegler points out, this version is markedly distinct from the story of Epimetheus in Hesiod.

5. Vernant, "Pratiques culinaires," 192.

6. Stiegler, *Technics and Time, 1*; Beardsworth, ibid., 280; Stiegler, *Technics and Time 2*, 214–17; 188.

7. Heidegger, *Being and Time*, 277.

8. Heidegger, "On the Essence of Truth," 133.

9. Meyers cited in Lagadec, *States of Emergency*, 4.

10. Peters, *Speaking*, 16.

11. Kissinger, *White House Years* 17, 938.

12. Peters, *Speaking*, 16.

13. It has since been noted that Tukey used the term in a distinct way.

14. Shannon, "Mathematical Theory"; Ballard, *Out of Order*, 85.

15. Shannon, "Mathematical Theory"; Ballard, "Information, Noise, et al."

16. Shannon, "Information Theory" 216; Ballard, "Information, Noise, et al."; Hayles, *Chaos Bound*, 52, 192; Hayles, *How We Became Posthuman*; and Paulson, *Noise of Culture*, 19.

17. I am referring to Hito Steyerl's notion of the "poor image" in *The Wretched of the Screen*.

18. Accomplished through encoding and decoding algorithms. Mackenzie, "Codecs," 50–52, and "Every Thing Thinks," 3.

19. Nyquist, "Certain Topics," 280–305.

20. Moles, *Information Theory*, 78.

21. Gjære, "Human Errors." I thank Elizabeth Churchill for bringing my attention to this concept.

22. Rescher, *Error*, 88–89.

23. For instance, the work of John Cage and related techniques with chance, accident, and error. See chapter 2 for further discussion. Rescher, *Error*, 88–89.

24. Exceptions can be found in the work of Nietzsche through Heidegger, Deleuze, and Derrida.

25. Rescher, *Error*, 89–90.

26. Roberts, *Necessity of Errors*, 28.

27. Rescher, *Error*, 89–90.

28. Roberts, *Necessity of Errors*, 27.

29. See Nietzsche, *Birth of Tragedy*; Heidegger, *Platons Lehre von der Wahrheit*, 228; Inwood, *Heidegger Dictionary*, 13–14.

30. Aristotle, *Poetics,* 4.48b; 6–9; 34; also see Lichtenstein, *Eloquence of Color,* 59.

31. Aquinas, *Summa Theologiae,* I, q. 39, a. 8., quoted by Jacques Maritain in *Art et scolastique.*

32. Roberts, *Necessity of Errors,* 34–35; St. Augustine, *On Free Choice of the Will.*

33. Rescher, *Error,* 90.

34. A different view was taken by Nicholas of Cusa (1401–64), who maintained that what we deem knowledge is actually erroneous conjecture (Rescher, *Error,* 91).

35. Descartes, "Discourse on Method," 54, in *Descartes: Meditations;* also cited in Roberts, *Necessity of Errors,* 35.

36. Roberts, *Necessity of Errors,* 34–35.

37. Ibid.; also see Bates, *Enlightenment Aberrations,* vii.

38. Bates, *Enlightenment Aberrations,* ix; 24.

39. Hobbes, *Leviathan;* Bates, *Enlightenment Aberrations,* 45.

40. Rescher, *Error,* 92. See also Spinoza, *Ethics,* book 2, prop. 35.

41. Rescher, *Error,* 91–92.

42. Bates, *Enlightenment Aberrations,* 34, 50; also see Locke, *Essay Concerning Human Understanding* (1689).

43. Bates, *Enlightenment Aberrations* 37.

44. Roberts, *Necessity of Errors,* 9.

45. Condorcet, *Esquisse d'un tableau historique,* 26–27, 37, 87.

46. Bates, *Enlightenment Aberrations* 31–32.

47. Ibid., 38.

48. This is a mixture of two citations, ibid., 35, 38.

49. Bates, *Enlightenment Aberrations,* 35; Roberts, *Necessity of Errors,* 8.

50. Bates, *Enlightenment Aberrations* 35.

51. Roberts, *Necessity of Errors,* 35-37.

52. Kant, "Of Transcendental Illusory Appearance," in *Critique of Pure Reason,* A 293. Emphasis added.

53. Ibid.

54. Roberts, *Necessity of Errors,* 10.

55. Ibid., 42–44.

56. Ibid., 8, 11.

57. Roberts contends that reason is impure for Hegel—unlike for Plato or Descartes, for whom it is pure. Roberts, *Necessity of Errors,* 8.

58. Hegel, *Phenomenology of the Spirit,* 274.

59. Roberts, *Necessity of Errors,* 44.

60. Ibid., 42–44.

61. I am not suggesting that readers will henceforth find a Hegelian analysis of error in the history of technology, but simply that his work has been pivotal in shifting the way we think about error in relation to human life and world history.

62. Davidson, "Welcome to the Failure Age!"

63. Beniger, *Control Revolution,* 7–8.

64. Davidson, "Welcome to the Failure Age!"

65. Ibid.

66. Ibid.

67. Taylor, *Scientific Management,* 47; Beniger, *Control Revolution,* 7–8, 294; Nunes, *Error,* 6.

68. Najafi, Serlin, and Sandage, "Invention of Failure."

69. For instance, we use such phrases as "I'm broke" and she's "good for nothing" (ibid.).

70. See, e.g., Durkheim, *Division of Labor,* 369–70; Bell, *Coming of Post-Industrial Society,* 29–30.

71. This continues today in the form of data surveillance, cookies, RFID tags, data "sharing," etc.

72. Freud, "Errors," in *Psychopathology,* 249–50.

73. Ibid., 253.

74. Nietzsche, *Birth of Tragedy,* 142.

75. *Dasein* (existence, being, presence) is literally "there-being," a stand-in for the (Western) subject; Heidegger, "On the Essence of Truth," in *Basic Writings,* 135–36.

76. Foucault, *Normal and Pathological,* 22. Stiegler's take on this is noted earlier in this chapter.

77. Foucault, *Normal and Pathological,* 22. Bernard Stiegler, for his part, worked and revised classical theories of error from the *Protagoras.* Working alongside a generation of media archaeologists, he provided new entry points to understand historical development through existential philosophy.

78. Daston and Galison, *Objectivity,* 273; Watson, "On the Errancy of Dasein," 49; Heidegger, "On the Essence of Truth," 133, 135–36.

79. Davidson, "Welcome to the Failure Age!"

80. Davidson, "Welcome to the Failure Age!"

81. For more on this, see chapter 4 of Kane, *Chromatic Algorithms.*

82. Harvey, *Condition of Postmodernity,* 150–53; 158–59, 163–64. Harvey notes four major increases in corporate business trends during the postmodern era: (1) mergers; (2) corporate diversification; (3) self-employment; and (4) outsourcing (158).

83. Turner, "Arts at Facebook," 56, also see: Bluestone and Harrison, *Deindustrialization;* also cited in Turner.

84. Davidson, "Welcome to the Failure Age!"

85. Up to the first quarter of the twentieth century: photography and telegraphy (1830s), rotary power printing (1840s), the typewriter (1860s), transatlantic cable (1866), telephone (1876), motion pictures (1894), wireless telegraphy (1895), magnetic tape recording (1899), radio (1906), and television (1923).

86. For more on this, see the work of Georg Simmel, Lewis Mumford, and Harold Innis.

87. Davidson, "Welcome to the Failure Age!"

88. Planet Money, "Will Your Job Be Done by a Machine?"

89. Uber operates on a model of extreme economic efficiency, doubling and tripling prices when it can, based on supply and demand, making it terrifying from the consumer's point of view.

90. Harvey, *Condition of Postmodernity;* Davidson, "Welcome to the Failure Age!"

91. Davidson, "Welcome to the Failure Age!"

92. Cf. Scott Sandage, *Born Losers: A History of Failure in America* (2005).

93. Marx, "Does Improved Technology Mean Progress?"

94. From this emerged what David Nye coins the "technological sublime," discussed in chapter 6.

95. Marx, "Does Improved Technology Mean Progress?"

96. Berlant, *Cruel Optimism*, 3.

97. Beckett, *Worstward Ho.*

CHAPTER 2. AVANT-GARDE GLITCH: RED NOISE, PURPLE HAZE, BLACK BOX

1. Roberts, *Necessity of Errors.* This has indisputably been the case in modern art and experimental music from dada and Duchamp on. For more, see the work of John Berger and Rosalind Krauss.

2. Steyerl, *Wretched*, 32.

3. I thank Artie Vierkant for our discussion on digital glitches and their precursors.

4. I thank Dan Kim at Brown University for his insight on this issue.

5. Granted the eye is more "receptive" to green-yellow hues, red travels through space faster and in longer wavelengths and thus has a more powerful effect. Certain species of monkeys develop red noses to communicate their dominance to other monkeys; some red berries convey a distinct message (i.e., as either poison or nutrient) relative to the greenery they grow on; and a "red sky at night," as the adage goes, "is a sailor's delight." I thank my talented research assistant Rachel Palen for pointing me to this information.

6. For a full analysis of infrared in media culture see Kane, *Chromatic Algorithms*, chapter 6.

7. Lotringer and Virilio, *Accident of Art*, 15. Virilio's correlations between art and war are in fact not fully supported by historic evidence. By 1909, after abandoning a brighter fauvist palette in 1908, Braque had already turned to the muted and less colorful fragmented forms at cubism's base. Moreover, during his service in the war, Braque experienced a serious head wound that left him temporarily blind. When he resumed painting in 1916, he seemed to adopt *more* color, not less, as is characteristic of the somber palette of German Expressionism.

8. For a more nuanced definition, see Harrison, *1910: The Emancipation of Dissonance.*

9. Cf. Ludwig Meidner's "Apocalyptic Landscapes" paintings (1912—13) or the work of Wassily Kandinsky or Franz Marc.

10. Harrison, *1910: The Emancipation of Dissonance*, 49.

11. Ibid.; Schoenberg, *Style and Idea*, 258–64.

12. Harrison, *1910: The Emancipation of Dissonance*, 18, 49, 63.

13. Harrison, *1910: The Emancipation of Dissonance*, 53.

14. Kandinsky, "On the Spiritual in Art," 161, 162, 195; Cheetham, *Rhetoric of Purity*, 76—77; Boehmer, *Schönberg and Kandinsky*, 17.

15. He then, paradoxically, bridges these elements in a "unified harmony of discord." Kandinsky, "On the Question of Form," 235–57.

16. Worringer, *Abstraction and Empathy*, 15; Waite, "Worringer's Abstraction," 210.

17. My focus is on the Italian Futurists, but noteworthy cases include the Russian avant-garde, who drew heavily on Russolo's work, as demonstrated in Arseny Avraamov's 1923

Symphony of the Sirens and by the citizens of the Soviet city of Baku in their celebration of the revolution using factory hooters, ships horns, and steam whistles.

18. Russolo, *Art of Noises,* 7.

19. The film benefitted from cinematographic input from Man Ray and a score by American composer George Antheil.

20. Similar dynamic "innervation" occurs in early cinema (e.g., Charlie Chaplin, Busby Berkeley). See also Léger, *Functions of Painting,* 52, and "Machine Aesthetic," 55. (Benjamin, "Work of Art," 113).

21. Breton, *Nadja:* "Beauty will be convulsive or will not be at all" (160).

22. Cf. also Tachisme, *art informel,* and the literary art group Oulipo in Europe and Allen Kaprow and early conceptual art in the United States. Franz Erhard Walther's experiments with *art informel* in the 1960s utilized error and chance occurrences as generative tools. Even Jackson Pollock's work could be construed as a series of happenstance visual abstractions, if not accidents. See Linger, "From Being to Seeing"; Barker in Nunes, ed., 45.

23. See Hertz and Parikka, "Zombie Media."

24. Grunenberg, ed., *Summer of Love* 33; Gawthrop, "Thunder and Lightning," 175.

25. Richter et al., Gerhard *Richter,* 33.

26. John Horton takes this one step further by painting images that emulate the distortion of corrupt digital files.

27. Cox, "Birth and Rebirth," 16. Warhol's *Kitchen* (1966), too, among other of his works, disrupt the narrative convention by having dialogue rendered silent by the seemingly unending noise of grinding coffee. For more on Warhol, see Crimp and Gawthrop, 171.

28. Other noteworthy films include Hollis Frampton's *(nostalgia)* (1971), where the filmmaker burns a series of photographs on a hotplate; Jeff Keene's frantic stop-frame animation and mixed media collage *Marvo Movie* (1967); Tony Conrad's *The Flicker* (1966), which investigates perception through the use of color stroboscopic effects (alternating black and white frames) at various frequencies; and a number of Paul Sharits's films, including *Epileptic Seizure Comparison* (1976) and *Piece Mandala* (1966), where colors are introduced in stroboscopic high-frequency patterns. Works by the experimental filmmakers Stan Brakhage, George Landow, Ken Jacobs, Ernie Gehr, Joyce Wieland, Stan VanDerBeek, and Michael Snow can also all be cited, since they collectively developed a material cinematic aesthetic by foregrounding the role of the medium in the production of vision. More recent work in this tradition includes Bill Morrison's film *Decasia* (2002), which presents found film footage that has deteriorated; parts of Gustav Deutsch's *Film ist* (1998); and Peggy Ahwesh's 16mm *The Color of Love,* which features various forms of celluloid degradation and breakdown. Thanks to Seth Waters for passing these references along.

29. Gawthrop, "Thunder and Lightning," 174.

30. Still other noteworthy examples include La Monte Young's *Poem for Tables Chairs Benches Etc.* (1960), which require the tables to be dragged across the floor, and his *Arabic Numeral (Any Integer) To H.F.* (1960), which requires a performer to play an unspecified sound, or group of sounds every 1 to 2 seconds. Malcolm Le Grice's *Little Dog for Roger* (1967), originally shot on the now obsolete 9.5mm film, bears the unique visual identifier of sprocket holes in the middle of the frame, rather than on the side (though the *simulation* of these sprocket holes is often used in contemporary image sequences to signify a nostalgic memory sequence). Le Grice used the actual holes. He transferred the original 9.5mm film

onto larger 16mm film, using an optical printer to shift the images forward and back and side to side, exposing the full shape of the frame. Halter, "Matter," 70.

31. Russolo argued in 1913 that industrial noises could be used as valid elements in a musical composition. Only a few decades later, John Cage argued that *all* sounds could be construed as music. Fineberg, *Art since 1940,* 174. Cf. also the computer artist Hiroshi Kawano, the painter François Rouan, the experimental composer Iannis Xenakis, and the graphic artist Jamie Reid.

32. Kostelanetz, *Conversing with John Cage,* 70; Fineberg, *Art since,* 178–79; Kahn, *Noise, Water.*

33. Annie Albers, Josef's wife, painted fractal search patterns before they were discovered. Future research on her work could thus introduce another set of intriguing precursors for glitch and computer art in general.

34. Fineberg, *Art since,* 178–79.

35. Roberts, *Necessity of Errors,* 238.

36. 60 Hz is a utility frequency standard in the United States and parts of Asia. It results in AC-powered appliances emitting a characteristic hum, produced by a motor and transformers vibrating with the magnetic field.

37. Roberts, *Necessity of Errors,* 237, 239. Also see Turner, "Arts at Facebook."

38. Manon and Temkin, "Notes on Glitch." Today, instead of short-circuiting a *Speak & Spell* toy to bring about disconcerting robotic noises, or "accidentally" breaking a glass and placing it in a museum (Duchamp), software-based approaches to glitch art involve coding strategies like opening an image file in a text editor and randomly or intentionally adding or deleting data to short circuit more sophisticated digital systems.

39. The term "noise rock" denotes the post-punk scene emerging in the wake of 1970s punk.

40. In 1966, The Who displayed Gustav Metzger's psychedelic crystal-destruction projections (Grunenberg, ed., *Summer of Love,* 32).

41. Sangild, "Aesthetics of Noise," 6, 10.

42. See Kane, *Chromatic Algorithms,* chap. 2.

43. Segments of Paik's other works, like his contribution to *The Medium Is the Medium* (1968), are also appropriate for this prehistory, but must be explored in detail elsewhere. (Fineberg, *Art since,* 354; Kane, "The Electric.")

44. Yalkut was formerly a filmmaker for the countercultural collective USCO.

45. Baig-Clifford, *Vasulka Lab.*

46. Electronic Arts Intermix, "Organic Honey's Vertical Roll."

47. For more of this kind of work by female video artists, see Phelan et al., *Rist,* or my analysis of Pipilotti Rist in Kane, "The Synthetic Color Sense."

48. For more on this, see Kane, *Chromatic Algorithms,* chap. 3.

49. At the same time, some but not all of the glitchy net art aesthetic associated with this early generation was due to technological limitation.

50. A number of other artworks could be used to illustrate my point. These examples were selected because they best support the chapter's claims.

51. Tilman, ed., *Install.exe/JODI,* 115.

52. Bosma, "JODI and the Cargo Cult," 92.

53. JODI in conversation with Niels van Tomme.

54. Connor, *JODI,* 10.

55. Hayles, *How We Became Posthuman.*

56. Simondon, "On Techno-Aesthetics," 2.

57. Kittler in Adrian Mackenzie, *Cutting Code,* 25.

58. See Kane, *Chromatic Algorithms,* chap. 6; Manovich, *Language of New Media;* and Mackenzie, *Cutting Code,* 25.

59. For more, see Paul, *Digital Art.*

60. GLI.TC/H began in 2010, and continues to "bring together glitchers from across the globe" (Briz, "New Ecology").

61. Ibid.

62. For more on "the algorithmic life world," see Kane, *Chromatic Algorithms,* chap. 6.

CHAPTER 3. COLOR AS SIGNAL/NOISE

1. The title of Part II is an allusion to Public Enemy's 1994 raucous-inspiring song by the same name. Cwelich, "Ryan Trecartin."

2. Koestenbaum, "Situation Hacker," 279.

3. Cotter, "Video Art Thinks Big."

4. Plato, *Republic,* 599d as trans. in Lichtenstein, *Eloquence,* 54.

5. Deitch, "Post" in Trecartin et al., *Any Ever,* 7.

6. Norden, "When the Rainbow" in Trecartin et al., *Any Ever,* 11.

7. I wish to thank Zeina Koreiteim and her Fall 2018 students at the Harvard Graduate School of Design, whose insightful comments helped shape this chapter.

8. It was also during this time that his work was assessed in terms of queer theory (see Trecartin and Podesva, "When the Time Comes"; Zulueta, *Queer Art*; Koestenbaum, "Situation Hacker"). In contrast, this chapter addresses his work from the perspective of a material history of color and media, not identity politics (including race, class, or gender theory). If one were to pursue an analysis of his work through the joint lens of aesthetics of queer theory, I recommend turning to the work of Kenneth Anger, John Watters, and George Kuchar. I wish to thank Jason Mittel for discussing this point with me and the sharp graduate students in Stanford University's 2018 Digital Aesthetics Workshop.

9. Kane, *Chromatic Algorithms,* chap. 1.

10. There is much to be said about the many ways in which colors change their appearance based on their surrounding colors. For more on this I again refer readers to chapter 1 of *Chromatic Algorithms.*

11. Albers, *Interaction of Color,* 3.

12. Plato, *Republic* 599d.

13. Plato as cited in Lichtenstein, *Eloquence,* 54. Also see Detienne and Vernant, *Ruses de l'intelligence,* 47–48.

14. For Plato, painting was "three removes from nature," imitating what was already a pale imitation of the essence of things. Lichtenstein, *Eloquence of Color,* 44; Kant, *Critique of Judgment,* 14; p. 55. Kant continues later in the section: "The colours which give brilliancy to the sketch are part of the charm. They may no doubt, in their own way, enliven the object for sensation, but make it really worth looking at and beautiful they cannot" (ibid., p. 56).

15. To offer another example, Melville writes, colors "are subtle deceits, not actually inherent in substances, but only laid on from without" (*Moby Dick,* chapter 42, 26).

16. Batchelor, *Chromophobia*, 22.

17. Lichtenstein, *Eloquence of Color*, 3, 62.

18. For more, see Kane "Broken Color"

19. In the late 1960s, the neo-Marxist Louis Althusser dubbed this process "interpellation," denoting the way in which bodies and subjects are "hailed" to undertake actions and ideas, such as the command: "STOP!"

20. Deitch, "Post," in Trecartin et al., *Any Ever*, 7.

21. Gioni in Kennedy, "His Nonlinear Reality."

22. Smith, "Like Living,"; Cooper, "A Family Finds Entertainment"; Zulueta, *Queer Art*, 159.

23. McGarry, "Ryan Trecartin"; also cited in Zulueta, *Queer Art*, 159.

24. McGarry, "Ryan Trecartin"; Zulueta, *Queer Art*, 163.

25. Zulueta, *Queer Art*, 134.

26. Ibid., 133–35; McGarry, "Lizzie Fitch / Ryan Trecartin."

27. Trecartin in conversation with Sherman, in Trecartin et al., *Any Ever*, 143.

28. Tiling is an effect where the same image is repeated on a screen or a desktop.

29. Lehrer-Graiwer, "In the Studio." Also in Zulueta, *Queer Art*, 243.

30. Trecartin refers to the technique as "substitution," by which we can infer a substitution of one class or kind of thing for an entirely different one. Trecartin and Ulbrist, "Ryan Trecartin in Conversation."

31. "The trick is to maintain a word long enough to let it lodge without depleting its creative potential," Linda Norden writes ("When the Rainbow" in Trecartin et al., *Any Ever*, 12).

32. Trecartin in conversation with Sherman, in Trecartin et al., *Any Ever*, 144.

33. Norden, "When the Rainbow," in Trecartin et al., *Any Ever*, 12.

34. Dean, "Communicative Capitalism."

35. Steyerl, *Wretched of the Screen*, 43.

36. Falconer, "What Is the Perfect Color Worth?" I thank Jessica Mudry for forwarding me this article.

37. Trecartin in conversation with Sherman, Trecartin et al., *Any Ever*, 145. Ingmar Bergman also did this sometimes, notably with the child actors in his 1982 film *Fannie and Alexander*.

38. Zulueta suggests that Snow White Girl is a dream sequence. This provides yet another interesting interpretation of the plot.

39. The effect is reiterated through the two other characters in this sequence: Linda (Lizzie Fitch) and Phalangena/Coughdrop (Alison Powell). Linda appears in a bold black-and-white patterned dress with matching bold black-and-white makeup—face paint rather—with red lipstick to match her red cardigan, an eyebrow painted in the shape of the top half of a triangle, intersecting with a large feather drawn outwards from the corner of her eye. Phalangena, for her part, wears shiny green eyeshadow extending from the circumference of her eye to her eyebrow, down to her upper cheek bone and out towards her hairline, comically alluding to what eyeshadow "should" *not* look like.

40. Granted some room must be left for spontaneous, intuitive choices. I thank the faculty and students at Stanford University for their insightful comments and questions during my visit to the school for one of the 2018 Digital Aesthetics Workshops.

41. Cf. Judith Butler's pivotal observation that while gender is performed, it is also "congealed" through life-long repetition. Much of Trecartin's work takes stabs at this now classic theory, or rather, at the many ways it has been misinterpreted as equating gender identity with mere performance.

42. Trecartin, *(Tommy Chat Just E-mailed Me.)*.

43. Trecartin, *K-CoreaINC. K (section a)*.

44. McGarry, "Lizzie Fitch / Ryan Trecartin."

45. EAI, "K-CoreaINC. K (section a)."

46. McGarry, "Lizzie Fitch / Ryan Trecartin."

47. Ibid.; Ngai, *Our Aesthetic Categories*, 12.

48. Ngai also offers less common examples, including Hugo Ball's Dada cabaret and Crazy Eddie commercials; see Ngai, *Our Aesthetic Categories*, 14–15, 182.

49. Ibid., 14–15.

50. Ibid., 174; Porte, "Zany."

51. Porte, "Zany"; Ngai, *Our Aesthetic Categories*, 9, 182.

52. Despite Trecartin's own working-class origins, it would be unfair to argue that his work is a classist mockery of so-called low culture, since his comic critiques attack everything from the "gauche" tastes of the working class to the solipsistic narcissism of millennial bourgeoisie. I thank Fred Turner for discussing this point with me.

53. McGarry, "Lizzie Fitch / Ryan Trecartin."

54. Ibid.

55. Two other chapters in the book perform similar work: chapter 1 adopts the phrase "colors of error" as a loose metaphor for the disparate formulations of error in the history of Western philosophy and industrial culture; chapter 5 theorizes color as an aesthetic category and compositional strategy in digital culture.

56. Deitch, "Post" in Trecartin et al., *Any Ever*, 7.

57. McGarry, "Worlds Apart," in *Any Ever*, 109.

CHAPTER 4. VISUAL NOISE IN THE NEW PHOTOGRAPHY

1. According to Belcove, Ruff, Struth, and Gursky, the Bechers' three well-known male students are jokingly referred to as the "Struffsky troika" ("Ruff Cut," 78).

2. Fried, *Why Photography Matters*, 26.

3. Herzog, "Subjective Propaganda," 28–35; Gronert, "Photographic Emancipation," 15; Grosenick and Seelig, *Photo Art*, 485.

4. Belcove, "Ruff Cut," 78.

5. Birnbaum, "Thomas Ruff," 93.

6. Ruff in *Thomas Ruff: Nudes*, 5.

7. Birnbaum, "Thomas Ruff," 93.

8. "He avoids all involvement, creating an air of extreme matter-of-factness" (Birnbaum, "Thomas Ruff," 93).

9. His work has been exhibited in France, Switzerland, Canada, Holland, the United States, Italy, Belgium, England, Scandinavia, Spain, Japan, and Israel, among other countries. Winzen, "Credible Invention," 131.

10. Hoelzl and Marie, "CODEC," 80.

11. Ibid.

12. Birnbaum, "Thomas Ruff," 93.

13. Fried, *Why Photography Matters*, x; Chevrier, "Adventures," where *tableau* is translated as "picture." See also Wall, "'Marks of Indifference,'" 266.

14. Jenkins, *New Topographics*.

15. "It is about using the tableau form to reactivate a thinking based on fragments, openness and contradiction, not the utopia of a comprehensive systematic order" (Chevrier, "Adventures," 28). Also cited in Fried, *Why Photography Matters*.

16. "Every series investigates an 'idea' of a specific generic photograph, yet this idea only exists in the forms of its different and multiple material manifestations" (Maimon, "Precarious Marks," 176).

17. "I'm not much interested in 'straight' photography anymore," Ruff explains; it has been "practiced for more than 150 years, and most of it is too conventional. I've always wanted to go beyond the limits" (Ruff in Famighetti, "Thomas Ruff: Photograms," 84–87).

18. Ruff in "Thomas Ruff in Conversation with Hans Ulrich Obrist," 5–6.

19. Ibid., 6.

20. For a more substantial discussion, I refer readers to the pioneering work of Linda Williams and recent issues of *Porn Studies*.

21. Hainge, *Noise Matters*, 214.

22. Winzen, "Credible Invention of Reality," 214.

23. Fried, *Why Photography Matters*, 154.

24. Ruff, Gagosian Gallery Press Release, 2012.

25. Hainge, *Noise Matters*, 222

26. Ibid., 215.

27. Ibid.

28. In color correction industries, "noise" is a term used to describe undesired static in certain parts of the image, typically as a result of weak resolution or low lighting situations. Some related experimental media work embraces this effect in a way that resembles Ruff's work. Examples include E. Elias Merhige's *Begotten* (1990), Daniel Myrick and Eduardo Sánchez's *The Blair Witch Project* (1999), and David Lynch's *Inland Empire* (2006). In all of these cases, a consistent use of hazy, cinematic noise doubles as an allegory for uncertainty in the hermeneutic of the image.

29. Hainge *Noise Matters*, 215.

30. Ibid.

31. Ibid.

32. Meanwhile, the *jpeg* series, Fried argues, bears affiliation with analytic cubism. Fried, *Why Photography Matters*, 154.

33. Basilico and Liebermann, *Paul Pfeiffer*, 67.

34. Also in Hainge, *Noise Matters*.

35. Jenkins, *New Topographics*.

36. Ruff in "Thomas Ruff in Conversation with Hans Ulrich Obrist," 7.

37. Ruff in Lane, "Thomas Ruff: Space Explorer."

38. Werneburg in Hoelzl and Marie, "CODEC," 81.

39. Hoelzl and Marie, "CODEC," 85. The International Telecommunication Union (ITU) is a United Nations agency that develops international standards for information and communication technologies (ICTs).

40. Euclid introduced the algorithm in 300 BC, though it remained marginal as a form of calculation until the introduction of computers as algorithmic machines. For more on the history of compression as the history of communications technology see Sterne, *MP3*.

41. Galloway, "Talk"; Galloway and LaRivière, "Compression in Philosophy."

42. Agre, "Surveillance"; Stiegler, *Technics and Time*; Stiegler, "Proletarianization."

43. Nunes, "Power of Repetition."

44. Mackenzie, "Codecs."

45. Maimon, "Precarious Marks," 177.

46. Ruff in "Thomas Ruff in Conversation with Hans Ulrich Obrist," 6; Hoelzl and Marie, "CODEC," 82.

47. Aside from a few exceptions, like *jpeg ny02* (2004), which cannot escape reference to 9/11, or *jpeg msh01* (2004), a mushroom cloud resulting from a massive bomb explosion.

48. Dean, "Communicative Capitalism," 56.

49. Boltanski and Chiapello, *Spirit of Capitalism*. One of the key values of their work, in the context of this chapter, is their illustration of the precariousness that underlines life and labor in the present; see Maimon, "Precarious Marks," 191.

5. CHROMA GLITCH: DATA AS STYLE

1. Chapter epigraph: Belton, "Psychology of the Photographic," 245.

2. Similar definitions can be found in Cascone, "Aesthetics of Failure," 17; Goriunova and Shulgin, "Glitch," 114; and Goodman "Contagious Noise," 132.

3. Frank, "Meet Yung Jake."

4. Pfeiffer, "At Last." See too Spieser, "Glitch Art" (I thank Christiane Paul for providing me with this reference).

5. Frank, "Meet Yung Jake."

6. See "Printer Tragedies."

7. This discussion of analog and digital colorism draws on the work of David Batchelor.

8. Sterne, *MP3*, 90. See also my brief discussion of Galloway's notion of "compression" in chapter 4.

9. See the work of Jonathan Sterne on "perceptual technics" or Lisa Gitelman on data, among others.

10. Cubitt, "Codecs," 45–46.

11. Small, *Analogue Alternative*, 8.

12. For more on this, see Batchelor, *Chromophobia*, 94–105, and Temkin et al., *Color Chart*

13. Batchelor, *Chromophobia*, 105.

14. Ibid., 94.

15. Heraclitus, fragment 50.

16. Batchelor, *Chromophobia*, 94.

17. Newton, *Opticks*, 23; Batchelor, *Chromophobia*, 86.

18. Newton, *Opticks* 21.

19. Furthermore, Newton somewhat arbitrarily chose seven colors based on perceived correlations between them and discrete musical notes and the division of days in a week.

20. For more on this distinction, see Kane, *Chromatic Algorithms,* chap 1.

21. Batchelor, *Chromophobia,* 94; Deleuze, *Nietzsche and Philosophy,* 105.

22. And here we arrive at a new point of inquiry: long after digital software became easy to use and accessible to the majority of artists and designers, a coterie of digital artists continued to work in this rigid and decisive style of digital colorism. Examples include Angela Bulloch's *Pixel Corner Piece* (2015); Cory Arcangel's *Colors* (2006); Raw Color's "Blanket Index Collection" (2013); and Fanette Mellier's "Poster Specimen" (2013).

23. Deleuze, *Cinema 2* and *Francis Bacon: The Logic of Sensation.*

24. Goethe, *Theory of Colours.*

25. Deleuze, *Sensation,* 61.

26. Ibid., 42, 94.

27. Deleuze, "Postscript on the Societies of Control," 4.

28. Deleuze, *Sensation,*104.

29. Ibid., 88–89; 104.

30. Ibid., *Sensation,* 88.

31. Deleuze, cited in Bogue, *Deleuze on Music, Painting and the Arts,* 134.

32. Bogue, *Deleuze on Music, Painting and the Arts,* 88.

33. Small, *Analogue Alternative,* 30.

34. Mackenzie, "Codecs," 53.

35. Brown and Kutty, "Datamoshing," 168.

36. Mackenzie, "Codecs," 53–55; Cubitt, "Current Screens," 31.

37. Cubitt, "Current Screens," 31.

38. See also current research on "perceptual technics" (Sterne, Stiegler). Ibid., 31.

39. Mackenzie, "Codecs," 53.

40. Namely, the historical rational organization of horizon lines, focal points, and depth perspective. Brown and Kutty, "Datamoshing," 168.

41. Smith in Deleuze, *Sensation,* xix.

42. Deleuze, *Negotiations,* 6.

43. Kant writes in *Critique of Pure Reason,* "precisely in these latter cognitions, which go beyond the world of the senses, where experience can give neither guidance nor correction, lie the investigations of our reason that we hold to be far more preeminent in their importance and sublime in their final aim," 128 (I thank Abigail Zitin and Paul Geyer for stressing this point).

44. Immanuel Kant, *Critique of Judgment,* "VII. The Aesthetic Representation."

45. Where Freud argued that "protection against stimuli [was a] . . . more important function than the reception of stimuli [because] the protective shield . . . must above all strive to preserve . . . against the effects . . . of the external world" (Benjamin, *Illuminations,* 163).

46. Deleuze, *Sensation,* 111; 54.

47. In synthesizing the new, Deleuze is in no way subscribing to Hegelian dialectics. On the contrary, his synthesis is rooted in a series of affirmations and immanent affects (qua Spinoza), whereas Hegel rigorously separates matter and idea from his dialectical structure.

48. Wölfflin, *Principles of Art History,* 14.

49. Mass periodizations easily run alongside stylistic developments, versus Batchelor's historical demarcations.

50. Wölfflin, *Principles of Art History,* 11–12

51. Ibid.

52. See Poirier, "Disegno-Colore" or Riley, *Codes,* 6.

53. Buci-Glucksmann, *Baroque Reason* 27.

54. Belton, "Psychology of the Photographic."

55. Davis, "Define Your Term."

56. Cascone, "The Aesthetics of Failure," 17–18.

6. THE X-RAY SUBLIME

1. Chapter epigraph: Burtynsky et al., *No Man's Land,* 8.

2. Peeples, "Toxic Sublime," 377. Burtynsky has won the International Center of Photography's Infinity Award and the Canadian National Media Awards Foundation's Silver medal. His work has appeared in *National Geographic, Art in America, Smithsonian, Newsweek,* the *Christian Science Monitor, the Washington Post, Harper's, Playboy, Time, Life, GQ* and the *New York Times.*

3. Peeples, "Toxic Sublime," 378. Moreover, Peeples argues his work is positively embraced by many environmental organizations as exposing industrial crimes against the environment, even in lieu of his void of an explicit environmental position. For example, see online reviews of his work in *Mother Jones, Earthisland,* and *Treehugger.*

4. I do not mean to suggest that by using the term "X-ray," Burtynsky has some sort of superpower; rather, like many artists, he thinks and feels beyond the (visually) obvious.

5. Morton, *Ecological Thought,* 2.

6. Ibid., 2.

7. Cohen, ed., *Prismatic Ecology.*

8. "The world-as-object does not occur to the human mind until it is radically divorced from it," Pettman, *Human Error,* 130, asserts.

9. Heidegger, *Being and Time,* §42. Note: female Cura is also taken as an inversion of the traditional Judeo-Christian myth, where woman is created last, as an "atomized" individual. Here, woman is first and phenomenologically connected to the world she lives in and through.

10. Pasulka, "Running the Numbers" (interview with Jordan).

11. Burtynsky, *Water,* 9.

12. Pauli, "Seeing the Big Picture," in id., *Manufactured Landscapes,* 10; Burtynsky, *Residual Landscapes,* 40.

13. Burtynsky, *Residual Landscapes,* 40–41.

14. Hoving, "Digging Deep,"; Burtynsky in Broucke, "Introduction," 1.

15. Burtynsky in Broucke, "Introduction," to *Nature Transformed,* ed. Bianco and Broucke, 1.

16. Ibid.

17. Hoving, "Digging Deep," 9; Broucke, "Introduction" to *Nature Transformed,* ed. Bianco and Broucke, 1.

18. E-waste is "electrical and electronic equipment (EEE) and the parts that have been discarded by its owner as waste without the intent of re-use" (Baldé et al., *Global E-waste Monitor*).

19. Plato, *Ion* 543a.

20. Madness and reason are entirely distinct in the *Ion*, but not so in other Platonic texts, like the *Symposium,* where they merge, creating a confusing but fascinating aberrancy.

21. Later in the *Ion,* the sublime is affiliated with the disharmonious, non-rhythmic Dionysian force, contrasted with the harmony and rhythm of bacchic possession (*Ion* 543a).

22. For more on this, see Habash, "Lack of *Technē*." Leo Marx traces the emergence of the "technological sublime" in American culture. Marx, "Does Improved."

23. Longinus, *On the Sublime,* 100.

24. According to David Nye, Longinus defines the sublime as "something which can stand up to repeated exposure and still produce the same effect"(*American Technological Sublime,* 3).

25. Longinus, *On the Sublime,* 100, 107, 136.

26. Boetzkes, "Waste and the Sublime Landscape," 24. Friedrich Schiller's theory of aesthetics also deserves mention in this respect, however, as do Horace, Hegel, Goethe, and Walter Benjamin's.

27. Burke, *Philosophical Enquiry,* 24.

28. Boetzkes, "Waste and the Sublime Landscape," 24.

29. Burke, *Philosophical Enquiry,* 132, cited in Boetzkes, "Waste and the Sublime Landscape," 24.

30. Boetzkes, "Waste and the Sublime Landscape," 24.

31. Burke, *Philosophical Enquiry,* 24. In Burke, we can also identify a clear link between the sublime and the more vernacular concept of the subliminal experience that lies below consciousness and is adept at triggering gut-level, primal survival instincts.

32. Boetzkes further clarifies Burke's conception of the sublime as follows: it is not a pleasure found *in* the corporeal experience of pain but instead, a satisfaction brought about through intellectual striving, even though such striving fails (Burke, *Philosophical Enquiry,* 24; Boetzkes, "Waste and the Sublime Landscape," 22). This is also what Friedrich von Schiller had in mind in 1795 when, in the wake of Kant, he theorized the pedagogical merit underpinning the concept (Schiller, *On the Aesthetic Education*).

33. Burke, *On Taste,* §XII; ¶191; Burke, *Philosophical Enquiry,* 36, 52, 96, 102, Peeples, "Toxic Sublime," 379.

34. Kant, *Critique of Judgment,* §26. And earlier, "for the sublime, in the strict sense of the word, cannot be contained in any sensuous form, but rather concerns *ideas* of reason [for] which . . . no adequate presentation . . . is possible" (Kant, "Transition from the faculty of estimating the beautiful," ibid.).

35. Kant also writes that "the object lends itself to the presentation of a sublimity discoverable in the mind" (*Critique of Judgment,* §23). In other words, the event occurs in the mind, not objective reality.

36. Kant, "Transition from the faculty of estimating the beautiful," ibid.

37. Kant, *Critique of Judgment,* §14.

38. Kant, "Transition from the faculty of estimating the beautiful" in *Critique of Judgment,* §23.

39. Kant also determined the mathematical sublime, discussed in the next chapter (Kant, *Critique of Judgment*, § 25)

40. Kant, "Transition from the faculty of estimating the beautiful" in *Critique of Judgment*, §23, 26.

41. Ibid., §26.

42. Also see Gatlin's discussion in "Toxic Sublimity," 722.

43. Kant *Critique of Judgment*, §30.

44. On whether or not a work of art can be considered sublime at all, see Kant, *Critique of Judgment*, §23–26.

45. Smith in Deleuze, *Francis Bacon: The Logic of Sensation*, xix.

46. Tiedemann, "Dialectics."

47. Hodgson, "Edward Burtynsky," 6.

48. International Law and Policy Institute, *Shipbreaking Practices*, 7.

49. Choudhury, "Pros and Cons."

50. International Law and Policy Institute, *Shipbreaking Practices*, 7.

51. CBS News, "Shipbreakers"; Mitchell, "On the Beach," 193.

52. Sarraf et al., "Ship Breaking," 3.

53. Choudhury, "Pros and Cons."

54. Global Marketing Systems (GMS), "Bangladesh."

55. Global Marketing Systems (GMS), "India."

56. Ship-recycling employed 300,000 people in India and 200,000 in Pakistan, according to Global Marketing Systems (GMS), "India" and "Pakistan."

57. Taylor, "Remembering the Exxon Valdez Oil Spill."

58. International Maritime Organization, "IMO Reaches Agreement," 22.

59. Pauli, *Manufactured Landscapes*, and Mitchell, "On the Beach," 193.

60. Global Marketing Systems (GMS), "GMS Leadership."

61. Ibid.; Mitchell, "On the Beach," 193.

62. International Law and Policy Institute (ILPI), *Shipbreaking Practices*, 4.

63. See also Mitchell, "On the Beach," 63.

64. National Labor Committee, "Where Ships and Workers Go to Die," 18.

65. Ibid., 19. Lead is widely used in electronic goods. It is a major component of solders (an alloy with tin) and in the lead oxide of cathode ray tubes (televisions and monitors), as well as in lead-acid batteries. Its compounds have also been used as stabilizers in some PVC cables and other products.

66. Yates, "The Human-as-Waste," 1680–81.

67. National Labor Committee, "Where Ships and Workers Go to Die,"; Mitchell, "On the Beach," 193.

68. National Labor Committee, "Where Ships and Workers Go to Die," 35.

69. Ibid., 45.

70. The ILPI reports that "in Bangladesh, the life expectancy for men in the shipbreaking industry is 20 years lower than for Bangladeshi men in the general population" (International Law and Policy Institute, "Investor," 5).

71. Kernaghan in National Labor Committee, "Where Ships and Workers Go to Die," 6. The Institute for Global Labour and Human Rights, formerly known as the National Labor

Committee in Support of Human and Worker Rights (NLC), is an NGO that investigates human and labor rights abuses by multinational corporations in the developing world.

72. Ibid., 45.

73. Burtynsky, *Oil.*

74. Boetzkes, "Waste and the Sublime Landscape," 27.

75. Bissonnette, "Toxic Sublime." Bissonnette identifies this as "ruin lust, or the pleasure taken in images of ruins." For her, this is a cultural phenomenon dating back to Piranesi's eighteenth-century prints of classical Roman ruins.

76. Segal, "Beauty in the Beast."

77. Cammaer, "Edward Burtynsky's Manufactured Landscapes," 125–26, 129.

78. Loke, "Art in Review: Edward Burtynsky."

79. See n. 75, Bissonnette applies the term "ruin porn" to art nostalgically fascinated with the destruction of the landscape, deriving from an older tradition of "ruin lust." Bissonnette, "Toxic Sublime."

80. Peeples, "Toxic Sublime," 381.

81. Pauli, *Manufactured Landscapes,* 24.

82. Burtynsky cited in Allen, "Burtynsky's Fuel for Thought."

83. "I don't want to be didactic," Burtynsky says. "I'm not trying to editorialize and say this is right or this is wrong" (Torosian, "Essential Element," 48).

84. Peeples, "Toxic Sublime" 377–78.

85. Schwartz, "Photographic Reflections."

86. The Qili port shipyard employs over twelve thousand workers, responsible for handling over half a million tons of steel.

87. This includes cathode ray tube (CRT) televisions.

88. Statista, "Forecast of Electronic Waste." Also see Greenpeace India, *Recycling of Electronic Wastes in China and India.*

89. National Safety Council, *Electronic Product Recovery and Recycling;* Royte, "E-Gad!" Greenpeace India, *Recycling of Electronic Wastes in China and India.*

90. Royte, "E-Gad!"

91. Greenpeace India, *Recycling of Electronic Wastes in China and India;* National Labor Committee, "Where Ships and Workers Go to Die."

92. The accumulating chemicals have contributed to high rates of birth defects, infant mortality, blood diseases, and severe respiratory problems, according to Chinese media. Royte, "E-Gad!"

93. Ibid.

94. Silicon Valley Toxics Coalition and Basel Action Network, "Exporting Harm," 1.

95. Sometimes referred to as "ruin porn" (see n. 79 above).

96. Nietzsche, *Genealogy of Morals.*

97. Zuromskis, "Petroaesthetics" 306. In his preface to David Hanson's 1997 book *Waste Land,* Wendell Berry observes, it is "supposable that some people will account for these photographic images [by Burtynsky] as 'abstract art,' and will see them as 'beautiful shapes'" (Peeples, "Toxic Sublime," 376).

98. Gatlin, "Toxic Sublimity," 718.

99. Peeples, "Toxic Sublime," 373.

100. Turnage, "Ansel Adams"; Lippard, *Undermining*, 9.

101. Hoving, "Digging Deep," 9–10.

102. Burtynsky, *Residual Landscapes*, 38.

103. Burtynsky, *Water.*

104. Virilio, *Politics*, and "Primal Accident"; Lotringer and Virilio, *Accident*, 86–87.

7. LANDSCAPE AS DATA: FROM THE CLASSICAL TO THE CONSUMER-MATHEMATICAL

1. Rathje and Murphy, *Rubbish!* 45–46.

2. See, e.g., Peeples, "Toxic Sublime," 373; Gatlin, "Toxic Sublimity."

3. "The toxic sublime . . . disturbs viewers' aesthetic sensibilities, not their identities as consumers, polluters, or political agents" (Gatlin, "Toxic Sublimity," 718, 720, cited in chapter 6 above).

4. See Oravec, "John Muir," 219, 248. Over a century later, does the faculty of reason still remain intact? Put differently, is a rational and well-measured response to mass waste and toxic destination even possible let alone appropriate?

5. Kant, *Critique of Judgment*, §25. In the aesthetic sublime, the initial state of destabilization and indeterminacy is relieved once the transcendent powers of analytic reason rescue the imagination from reaching beyond its limits (cf. discussion in chapter 6 above).

6. Ibid., §24–25

7. Ibid., §26. Great masses of quantities are contrasted with "absolute greatness," which is not inhibited with "limitations," insofar as a number cannot be attributed to it. Kant writes, "to assert without qualification that something is great is quite a different thing from saying that it is absolutely great. . . . The latter is what is beyond all comparison" (ibid., §25).

8. Ibid., §26, "VIII. The Logical Representation of the Finality of Nature"

9. Ibid.

10. Ibid., §24.

11. Ibid., §26.

12. The photographers Germaine Krull and Albert Renger-Patzsch and the Neue Sachlichkeit (New Objectivity) movement of the interwar years also fall into to the German tradition of landscape imaging.

13. See Sloan, *No Man's Land*, 5.

14. Unlike Burtynsky, Watkins "carefully crafted [his images] to exclude any evidence of human activity in the pristine landscape" (Peeples, "Toxic Sublime," 384; see also Gatlin, "Toxic Sublimity," 736, and DeLuca and Demo, "Imaging Nature," 243).

15. The portrait photography equivalent would be the role of Lewis Hine's work in legislation banning child labor in America. Grande, Burtynsky interview, *Perspecta*, 156.

16. Schama, "Landscape," in Kastner, ed. *Land and Environmental Art*, 14.

17. Bruce, "Chris Jordan," 9–10.

18. Also see his *Blast Furnace, Dust Catcher*, and *Ford Plant* (1927).

19. The project involved inserting massive pipes into the river to divert part of its water flow.

20. Peeples, "Toxic Sublime," 380.

21. Nye, *American Technological Sublime*, 9. He is citing Burke here.

22. Peeples, "Toxic Sublime," 380.

23. Even decades after the exhibition, photo historians continue to annotate this single body of work as earmarking a definitive shift in the history of the medium, ironically, a noteworthy pivot to seemingly prosaic subject matter. Bannon and Salvesen, *New Topographics.*

24. Ibid., 71.

25. Goldberg, "How the East Was Won"; Peeples, "Toxic Sublime," 376; see also Baillargeon, "Imaging a Shattered Earth."

26. Jenkins, *New Topographics.* Lauren Higbee argues that the "characteristics Jenkins identified in new landscape photography were first brought to the public's attention by Nathan Lyons' 1966 exhibition *Toward a Social Landscape* at Eastman House and John Szarkowski's 1967 exhibition *New Documents at the Museum of Modern Art* (Higbee, "New Topographies").

27. Mid-twentieth-century portrait photographers adopted an aloof, almost automated distance from their "human subjects." Key works include Walker Evans's photographs of *Joe's Auto Graveyard,* taken in Pennsylvania in 1935, Diane Arbus's portraits of deviant and marginal subjects, Shelby Lee Adams's documentation of impoverished life in the Appalachian Mountains, Joel Sternfeld's work, and Eugène Atget's documentation of "lowlifes" in Parisian streets and alleys. While these examples stray from the landscape genre, they are worth noting as precursors to a growing tendency towards cool and analytic imaging techniques, in contrast to the emotionally driven portraits and landscapes of the past.

28. Zuromskis, "Petroaesthetics," 289.

29. Bannon and Salvesen, *New Topographics,* 11.

30. For more on German landscape photography, see Belcove, "Ruff Cut"; Herzog, "Subjective Propaganda"; Gronert, "Photographic Emancipation"; Grosenick and Seelig, eds., *Photo Art.*

31. On related German artists like Thomas Struth and other contemporary European photographers like Rineke Dijkstra, Patrick Faigenbaum, Luc Delahaye, and Roland Fischer, see Fried, *Why Photography Matters.*

32. For more on this, see chapter 3 of Kane, *Chromatic Algorithms.*

33. Gefter, "Great Big Beautiful Pile of Junk."

34. See Canales, "Living Color."

35. Fried, *Why Photography Matters,* 156–57, 173.

36. Ibid., 156–57.

37. Galassi, *Andreas Gursky,* 29–30; Fried, *Why Photography Matters,* 174.

38. Fried, *Why Photography Matters,* 161.

39. Fried, *Why Photography Matters,* 179.

40. Gursky's depiction of the homogenizing forces of global capital in maddening color is akin to Ryan Trecartin's in *K-Corea,* discussed in chapter 3, albeit executed through radically different means; the former is chock full of affect, while the latter is totally void of it.

41. Morton, *Ecological Thought,* 38; Jordan, "Running the Numbers."

42. Schwartz, "New Optimism of Al Gore."

43. "Mobile Economy 2019."

44. For further commentary on parallels between Burtynsky and Jordan, see Fugami, "Dichotomies Coalesce."

45. Jordan does most of his research on the internet. A few searches are sufficient to locate specific government databases, such as the enormous Centers for Disease Control and Prevention website, or websites that point to other references. When he finds a few different sources that all agree on a particular number (such as, say, a *New York Times* article, "a politically neutral website" he claims), he is comfortable that he has found a defensible, verifiable number to use (Bruce, "Chris Jordan," 13).

46. Ibid., 9. "I felt I could no longer reconcile representing some of the [corporate] companies, based on what they were doing," Jordan explains (*American Environmental Leaders*).

47. Jordan, "Running the Numbers."

48. See Jordan et al., *In Katrina's Wake*.

49. Jordan, "Running the Numbers" and "Intolerable Beauty," 3.

50. Jordan's use of the word "retired" is intended to show that what we "throw away" does not just disappear but goes on to live a kind of zombie life somewhere else.

51. Jordan, "Running the Numbers."

52. Jordan, *Running the Numbers*, 7.

53. Jordan, *Running the Numbers*, 10.

54. Jordan, *Running the Numbers*, 14.

55. Jordan, "Running the Numbers."

56. *The Colbert Report*, "Interview with Chris Jordan," October 11, 2007.

57. Sue Peters, "Q&A with Chris Jordan."

58. Notable exceptions include the Midway project, discussed in the Postscript.

59. Bruce, "Chris Jordan," 7.

60. Gefter, "Great Big Beautiful Pile of Junk."

61. Kant, *Critique of Judgment*, §27; Bruce, "Chris Jordan," 12.

62. Ibid., §26.

63. Pasulka, "Running the Numbers" (2007 interview with Jordan), emphasis added.

64. Kant, Critique of *Judgment*, §27.

65. In many ways, this is the same problem of abstracted data in information systems outlined in chapter 1's discussion of Shannon's work.

66. Dunaway, *Seeing Green* 258–59; Schwartz, "New Optimism of Al Gore." Gore is the only person to win a Nobel Peace Prize based largely on his role in a movie.

67. All cited in Dunaway, *Seeing Green*, 258.

68. Ibid., 259, 262.

69. Ibid.

70. Scott, "Warning," also cited in Dunaway, *Seeing Green*, 265.

71. Dunaway, *Seeing Green*, 260.

72. Ibid., 268.

73. Dunaway, *Seeing Green*, 260.

74. Greenberg, *Heatwave*.

75. Dunaway, *Seeing Green*, 260.

76. Stephanie Smith refers to the tactic as "green porn," by which she means a "sexy but superficial environmentalism that might help popularize issues like climate change" and may lead to some meaningful action but ultimately also offers a hit of instant gratification. Smith, "Weather Systems," 13–14.

77. Ngai, "Cuteness of the Avant-Garde," 812.

78. Ngai, *Our Aesthetic Categories*, 18–19.

79. Ngai, "Cuteness of the Avant-Garde," 812–13.

80. While these last few examples have moved away from numerical abstraction per se, they shed an interesting light on issues of environmental breakdown and the problems of depicting waste in global culture.

81. Deleuze and Guattari, *Thousand Plateaus,* 10.

82. Edwards, "Vast Machine," 828; Latour, "Waiting for Gaia," 2.

POSTSCRIPT

1. Brodesser-Akner, "Marie Kondo." In pursuit of this dream, Kondo offers books, reality television shows, lectures, and contracted services, ostensibly to minimize the superfluous things bulking up one's home and life.

2. Sax, "Take It to the Max."

3. Gaulon, "Hardware Hacking Workshops"; Barbon, "Discourse."

4. Gaulon, "Hardware Hacking Workshops"; Barbon, "Discourse."

5. Barbon, "Discourse."

6. London, *Ending the Depression through Planned Obsolescence*; Veblen, *Theory of the Leisure Class,* 33.

7. Cited in Industrial Designers Society of America, "Brooks Stevens, FIDSA."

8. Lebow, "Price Competition," 7.

9. Deleuze, "Postscript," 6.

10. White, "Origin of Planned Obsolescence (1932 Pamphlet)."

11. Barbara Kruger, *Untitled (I shop therefore I am)* and 1990 MoMA exhibition. For more on this, see Packard, *Waste Makers*; Frank, *Conquest of Cool*; Slade, *Made to Break*; Fitzpatrick, *Planned Obsolescence*; Gabrys, *Digital Rubbish*.

12. Baldé et al., *Global E-waste Monitor.*

13. Ibid.

14. United Nations University, "E-waste Rises."

15. Ibid.

16. The company builds portable devices and computers for companies like Hewlett Packard. Spencer, "Companies Slash Warranties."

17. See Garnet and Parikka, "Zombie Media."

18. Section epigraph: "This Year Rediscover Plastics," 141; Barthes, *Mythologies,* 98.

19. Ibid.

20. Newman, *Plastics as an Art Form,* 30.

21. Of course, plastics were also developed in Europe and elsewhere. My focus here is on the development of plastics in the United States in the early and mid twentieth century. See Freinkel, "Our 'Toxic' Love-Hate Relationship."

22. Newman, *Plastics as an Art Form,* 1.

23. Brown, *Glamour in Six Dimensions.*

24. Freinkel, "Our 'Toxic' Love-Hate Relationship."

25. See Meikle, *American Plastic.*

26. Freinkel, "Our 'Toxic' Love-Hate Relationship."

27. Leading, e.g., Leo Amino's modernist objects, Naum Gabo's *Linear Construction in Space No. 1* (ca. 1945–46), and the Canadian artist Peggy Specht's use of Forbon, a vulcanized,

foldable paper-like plastic fiber created in the early 1900s by the NVF Company and later used in things like guitar strings.

28. Newman, *Plastics as an Art Form,* 196. Bridget Riley's *Current* (1964), as featured on the cover of the Museum of Modern Art's 1965 *Responsive Eye* exhibition catalogue. The image captures the clean precision of plastic acrylics in two-dimensional form. Key, pioneering three-dimensional plastic art from this era includes William Riemann's translucent Lucite *White Study* (1961), Fred Dreher's Plexiglas *Nightwings* (1960) and *Cathedral* (1958), Michael Chilton's *Offshore,* the work of Ed McGowan, Bruce Beasley's cast acrylic from the 1950s, and Craig Kauffman's colorful plastic sculptures.

29. This machine aesthetic is also reflected in certain titles, like Dick Artschwager's *Dresser F45* (ca. 1960), emulating the serial logic of the assembly line.

30. It is remarkable how closely these works resemble the current fashion for "3-D printing." Newman, *Plastics as an Art Form,* 89, 20.

31. Kramer, "Plastic Toys and Ersatz Monuments."

32. The Museum of Contemporary Crafts is now called the Museum of Arts and Design (MAD) and located in Columbus Circle in Manhattan.

33. But again, this has always been the case. Even with the pencil or pen, we share creativity with the technology of writing. Hilton Kramer, "Plastic as Plastic."

34. Freinkel, "Our 'Toxic' Love-Hate Relationship."

35. Meikle, "Material Doubts," 291.

36. Freinkel, "Our 'Toxic' Love-Hate Relationship."

37. The scene (not found in Charles Webb's novel on which the film was based) was inspired by the scriptwriter Buck Henry's recollection of hearing a philosophy professor, Eugen Rosenstock-Huessy, refer to plastic in a lecture at Dartmouth College in the 1950s as a product of "a civilization that abandons its values." Boyar, "When 'Plastics' Became a Bad Word."

38. When it was first administered in 1976, the TSCA grandfathered in all existing chemicals as "safe for use."

39. Brigden et al., *Recycling of Electronic Waste in China and India,* 20.

40. Wright, Thompson, and Galloway, "Physical Impacts."

41. Gamerman, "Inconvenient Bag."

42. *National Geographic,* "fast facts."

43. Gregory, "Environmental Implications"; Wagner, Engwall and Hollert, "(Micro) Plastics," 16.

44. Jordan, *Midway Project.*

45. Gabrys, *Digital Rubbish,* 80.

46. Corcoran, Moore, and Jazvac, "Anthropogenic Marker Horizon." I thank Dave Kemp for pointing me to this work.

47. Moholy-Nagy, *Vision in Motion.*

48. Galloway, "Poverty of Philosophy," 347.

49. Malabou, *What Should We Do,* 13.

BIBLIOGRAPHY

Adams, Ansel. *Ansel Adams in Color.* New York: Little, Brown, 1993.
Agre, Philip E. "Surveillance and Capture: Two Models of Privacy." In *The New Media Reader,* ed. Noah Wardrip-Fruin and Nick Montfort, 737–60. Cambridge, MA: MIT Press, 2003.
Al, Stefan Johannes. "The Strip: Las Vegas and the Symbolic Destruction of Spectacle." PhD diss., University of California, Berkeley, 2010.
Albers, Josef. *Interaction of Color.* New Haven, CT: Yale University Press, 2013.
Alberti, Leon Battista. *De Pictura.* 1435. Translated by John R. Spencer as *On Painting.* London: Routledge & Paul, 1956.
Allen, Henry. "Burtynsky's Fuel for Thought: What Are We Thinking?" *Washington Post,* October 4, 2009, E1.
American Institute of Architects (AIA) and New York's Center for Architecture. "Designing Waste: Strategies for a Zero Waste Opening." Exhibition program. New York, La Guardia Place, June 14, 2018. https://calendar.aiany.org/2018/05/08/designing-waste-strategies-for-a-zero-waste-city-opening.
Aristotle. *Poetics.* Translated by S. Halliwell. London: Duckworth, 1986.
Asghar, Rob. "Why Silicon Valley's 'Fail Fast' Mantra Is Just Hype." *Forbes Magazine,* July 14, 2014. www.forbes.com/sites/robasghar/2014/07/14/why-silicon-valleys-fail-fast-mantra-is-just-hype/#7d263f4d24bc. Accessed July 18, 2019.
Attali, Jacques. *Noise: The Political Economy of Music.* Translated by Brian Masumi. Foreword by Fredric Jameson. Minneapolis: University of Minnesota Press, 2006.
Augustine, Saint. *The Teacher; The Free Choice of the Will; Grace and Free Will.* Washington, DC: Catholic University of America Press, 1968.
Badiou, Alain. *Being and Event.* Translated by Oliver Feltham. London: Continuum, 2005.
Baichwal, Jennifer, dir. *Manufactured Landscapes.* Documentary film. National Film Board of Canada, 2006.

Baig-Clifford, Yasmeen. *Vasulka Lab, 1969–2005*. Exhibition. New York: Archives of the Electronic Arts Intermix, April 2006.

Baillargeon, Claude. "Imaging a Shattered Earth." In id., et al., *Imaging a Shattered Earth: Contemporary Photography and the Environmental Debate*. Rochester, MI: Meadow Brook Art Gallery, 2005.

Baldé, C. P., et al. *The Global E-waste Monitor 2017*. Vienna: United Nations University, 2017. www.itu.int/en/ITU-D/Climate-Change/Pages/Global-E-waste-Monitor-2017.aspx. Accessed June 27, 2019.

Ballard, Susan. "Information, Noise, et al." In *Error: Glitch, Noise, and Jam in New Media Cultures*, ed. Mark Nunes, 59–79. New York: Continuum, 2011.

———. "Out of Order: Explorations in Digital Materiality." PhD diss., University of New South Wales, Sydney, Australia, 2008.

Bannon, Anthony, and Britt Salvesen. *New Topographics*. Tucson, AZ: Center for Creative Photography, University of Arizona, 2009.

Barbon, Nicholas. *A Discourse of Trade*. 1690. Baltimore: John Hopkins Press, 1905.

———. "A Discourse of Trade (1690)." www.marxists.org/reference/subject/economics/barbon/trade.htm. Accessed June 27, 2019.

Barthes, Roland. "The Grain of the Voice." In id., *Image, Music, Text: Essays*, 179–89. New York: Hill & Wang, 1977. Originally published as "Le grain de la voix," *Musique en jeu*, no. 9 (1972), *Psychanalyse musique*.

———. *Mythologies*. Translated by Annette Lavers. New York: Hill & Wang, 1972.

———. *The Responsibilities of Forms: Critical Essays on Music, Art and Representation*. New York: Hill & Wang, 1985.

Basilico, Stefano, and Valeria Liebermann. *Paul Pfeiffer*. Essays and an interview with Pfeiffer by Thomas Ruff. K21 Kunstsammlung Nordrhein-Westfalen (Düsseldorf). Ostfildern-Ruit: Hatje Cantz, 2004.

Batchelor, David. *Chromophobia*. London: Reaktion Books, 2000.

Bates, David W. *Enlightenment Aberrations: Error and Revolution in France*. Ithaca, NY: Cornell University Press, 2002.

Battles, Matthew. "But It Moves: The New Aesthetic & Emergent Virtual Taste." *metaLAB*. www.wired.com/2012/04/matthew-battles-but-it-moves-the-new-aesthetic-emergent-virtual-taste. Accessed August 2, 2019.

Beckett, Samuel. *Worstward Ho*. New York: Grove Press, 1984.

Belcove, Julie. "Ruff Cut." *W* 30, no. 7 (July 2001): 78–85.

Bell, Daniel. *The Coming of Post-Industrial Society: A Venture in Social Forecasting*. New York: Basic Books, 1973.

Belton, John. "Psychology of the Photographic, Cinematic, Televisual, and Digital Image." *New Review of Film and Television Studies* 12, no. 3 (2014): 234–46.

Beniger, James R. *The Control Revolution*. Cambridge, MA: Harvard University Press, 1986.

Benjamin, Walter. *The Arcades Project*. Translated by H. Eiland and K. McLaughlin. Cambridge, MA: Belknap Press, 2002.

———. *Illuminations*. Edited by Hannah Arendt. Translated by H. Zohn. New York: Schocken Books, 1968.

———. "The Work of Art in the Age of Technical Reproducibility." In Benjamin, *Selected Writings*, vol. 3: *1935–1938*, ed. Howard Eiland and Michael W. Jennings . Cambridge, MA: Belknap Press of Harvard University Press, 2002.

Berlant, Lauren. *Cruel Optimism.* Durham, NC: Duke University Press, 2011.

Birnbaum, Daniel. "Thomas Ruff." *Artforum International* 35, no. 3 (November 1996): 93.

Bissonnette, Meghan. "Toxic Sublime and the Dilemma of the Documentary." *Seismopolite,* June 1, 2016. www.seismopolite.com/toxic-sublime-the-dilemma-of-the-documentary. Accessed July 12, 2019.

Bluestone, Barry, and Bennett Harrison. *The Deindustrialization of America.* New York: Basic Books, 1982.

Boehmer, Konrad. *Schönberg and Kandinsky: An Historic Encounter.* New York: Routledge, 2013.

Boetzkes, Amanda. "Waste and the Sublime Landscape." *Canadian Art Review* 35, no. 1 (2001): 22–31.

Bogue, R. *Deleuze on Music, Painting and the Arts.* London: Routledge, 2003.

Boltanski, Luc, and Eve Chiapello. *The New Spirit of Capitalism.* London: Verso, 2007.

Bosma, Josephine. "JODI and the Cargo Cult." In *Install.exe/JODI,* ed. B. Tilman. Basel: Christoph Merian, 2002.

Boyar, Jay. "When 'Plastics' Became a Bad Word." *Washington Post,* August 30, 1992.

Brassier, Ray. "Against an Aesthetics of Noise [interview with Bram Ieven]." *nY,* May 10, 2009. www.ny-web.be/transitzone/against-aesthetics-noise.html. Accessed June 27, 2019.

Breton, André. *Nadja.* Translated by Richard Howard. New York: Grove Press, 1960.

Bridle, James. *New Dark Age: Technology and the End of the Future.* London: Verso, 2018.

———. "Something Is Wrong on the Internet." *Medium,* November 6, 2017. https://medium.com/@jamesbridle/something-is-wrong-on-the-internet-c39c471271d2. Accessed June 25, 2019.

Brigden, K., I. Labunska, D. Santillo, and M. Allsopp. *Recycling of Electronic Waste in China and India: Workplace and Environmental Contamination.* University of Exeter, UK: Greenpeace Research Laboratories, 2005..

Briz, Nick. "A New Ecology for the Citizen of a Digital Age." From *Refresh,* curated by Yuri Stone at the Axiom Center for New and Experimental Media. Video installation, July 2010. https://vimeo.com/7617527. Accessed June 27, 2019.

Brodesser-Akner, Taffy. "Marie Kondo and the Ruthless War on Stuff." *New York Times Magazine,* July 6, 2016. www.nytimes.com/2016/07/10/magazine/marie-kondo-and-the-ruthless-war-on-stuff.htm.

Brown, Judith. *Glamour in Six Dimensions: Modernism and the Radiance of Form.* Ithaca, NY: Cornell University Press, 2009.

Broucke, Pieter. "Introduction" to *Nature Transformed: Edward Burtynsky's Vermont Quarry Photographs in Context,* ed. Juliet Bianco and Broucke. Hanover, NH: Hood Museum of Art, Dartmouth College and University Press of New England, 2012.

Brown, William, and Meetali Kutty. "Datamoshing and the Emergence of Digital Complexity from Digital Chaos." *Convergence* 18, no. 2 (2012): 165–76.

Bruce, Chris. "Chris Jordan: The Effective Image." In Chris Jordan, *Running the Numbers: An American Self-Portrait,* 7–14. Pullman, WA: Museum of Art/Washington State University, 2009.

Buci-Glucksmann, Christine. *Baroque Reason: The Aesthetics of Modernity.* Thousand Oaks, CA: Sage, 1994.

Burke, Edmund. *On Taste; On the Sublime and Beautiful; Reflections on the French Revolution.* New York: P. F. Collier & Son, 1909.

———. *Philosophical Enquiry into the Origin of Our Ideas of the Sublime and the Beautiful.* 1757. Edited by J. T. Boulton. New York: Columbia University Press, 1958.

Burtynsky, Edward. *China.* Photographs, 2002–5. www.edwardburtynsky.com/projects/photographs/china. Accessed July 12, 2019.

———. *Edward Burtynsky: Quarries.* Göttingen: Steidl, 2007.

———. *Oil.* Photographs, 1999–2007.www.edwardburtynsky.com/projects/photographs/oil. Accessed July 12, 2019.

———. *Residual Landscapes: Studies of Industrial Transfiguration.* Toronto: Lumiere, 2001.

———. *Water.* Gottingen: Stiedl; New Orleans Museum of Art, 2013.

Burtynsky, Edward, Emmet Gowin, and David Maisel. *No Man's Land: Contemporary Photographers and Fragile Ecologies.* Charleston, SC: Halsey Gallery and Institute of Contemporary Art at the College of Charleston School of the Arts, 2004.

Burtynsky, Edward, M. Mitchell, P. Roth, and W. Rees. *Burtynsky: Oil.* Göttingen: Steidl, 2009.

Burtynsky, Edward, W. Davis, and R. Lord. *Burtynsky: Water.* Göttingen: Steidl, 2013.

Butler, Judith. *Parting Ways: Jewishness and the Critique of Zionism.* New York: Columbia University Press, 2012.

Cammaer, Gerda. "Edward Burtynsky's Manufactured Landscapes: The Ethics and Aesthetics of Creating Moving Still Images and Stilling Moving Images of Ecological Disasters." *Environmental Communication: A Journal of Nature and Culture* 3, no. 1 (2009): 121–30.

Canales, Jimena. "Living Color: Jimena Canales on the Art of Eliot Porter." *Artforum International* 54, no.1 (2014): 334–41.

Cascone, Kim. "The Aesthetics of Failure: 'Post-digital' Tendencies in Contemporary Computer Music." *Computer Music Journal* 24, no. 4 (2000): 12–18.

Cates, Jon. "ḅRОК3 ᴡR3XXXОRĐZ (AKA: Broken Records: Hystories i Of Noise && Dirty New Media)." http://glitch.us/BrokenRecords.html. Accessed June 27, 2019.

Cheetham, Mark. *The Rhetoric of Purity: Essentialist Theory and the Advent of Abstract Painting.* Cambridge, MA: Cambridge University Press, 1991.

Chevrier, Jean-François. "The Adventures of the Tableau Form in the History of Photography." In *The Last Picture Show: Artists Using Photography, 1960–1982,* ed. Douglas Fogle. Minneapolis: Walker Art Center, 2003.

Christov-Bakargiev, Carolyn. "Thomas Ruff at the End of the Photographic Dream." In *Thomas Ruff,* ed. Carolyn Christov-Bakargiev. Milan: Skira, 2009.

Choudhury, Tanzina. "Pros and Cons of the Ship Breaking Industry in Bangladesh." www.worldpulse.com/fr/node/14390. Posted January 11, 2011. Accessed June 27, 2019.

Cohen, Jeffrey Jerome, ed. *Prismatic Ecology: Ecotheory beyond Green.* Minneapolis: University of Minnesota Press, 2014.

Colberg, Jorg. "Intolerable Beauty [interview with Chris Jordan]." *Orion Magazine,* March–April 2007. www.orionmagazine.org/index.php/articles/article/70. Accessed June 27, 2019.

Colbert Report. "Interview with Chris Jordan." Aired October 11, 2007, on *Comedy Central.* Video, 6:07. www.cc.com/video-clips/zv1p01/the-colbert-report-chris-jordan. Accessed June 27, 2019.

Colour: The Spectrum of Science. Hosted by Helen Czerski. BBC 4, July 2017.

Corcoran, Patricia L., Charles J. Moore, and Kelly Jazvac. "An Anthropogenic Marker Horizon in the Future Rock Record." *GSA Today* 24, no. 6 (June 2014): 4–8. www.geosociety.org/gsatoday/archive/24/6/article/i1052-5173-24-6-4.htm. Accessed July 17, 2019.

Condorcet, Marie-Jean-Antoine-Nicolas de Caritat, Marquis de. *Esquisse d'un tableau historique des progrès de l'esprit humain*1795. Edited by Alain Pons. Paris: Flammarion, 1986. Translated by June Barraclough as *Sketch for a Historical Picture of the Progress of the Human Mind* (New York: Noonday Press 1955).

Connor, Michael J. *JODI: Computing 101B.* Liverpool: Foundation for Art and Creative Technology, 2004.

Cooper, Dennis. "A Family Finds Entertainment." www.eai.org/titles/a-family-finds-entertainment. Accessed June 29, 2019.

Cotter, Holland. "Video Art Thinks Big: That's Showbiz." *New York Times,* January 6, 2008.

Cox, Christopher, and D. Warner. *Audio Culture: Readings in Modern Music.* New York: Continuum, 2004.

Cox, Lindsay George. "The Birth and Rebirth of the Glitch." MA thesis, RMIT University, Melbourne, Australia, 2009.

Crary, Jonathan. *24/7: Late Capitalism and the Ends of Sleep.* New York: Verso, 2013.

Crimp, Douglas, and Andy Warhol. *"Our Kind of Movie": The Films of Andy Warhol.* Cambridge, MA: MIT Press, 2012.

Cubitt, S. "Codecs and Capability." In *The Video Vortex Reader 4: Responses to YouTube,* ed. Geert Lovink and Sabine Niederer, 45–50. Amsterdam: Institute for Networked Cultures, 2009.

———."Current Screens." In *Imagery in the 21st Century,* ed. O. Grau and T. Veigl, 21–36. Cambridge, MA: MIT Press, 2011.

Cwelich, Lorraine. "Ryan Trecartin: Art for the Age of YouTube." *Wall Street Journal,* July 20, 2010. http://blogs.wsj.com/speakeasy/2010/07/20/ryan-trecartin-art-for-the-age-of-youtube. Accessed June 29, 2019.

Daston, Lorraine, and Peter Galison. *Objectivity.* New York: Zone Books, 2010.

Davidson, Adam. "Welcome to the Failure Age!" *New York Times Magazine,* November 12, 2014.

Davis, Paul B. "The Creator's Project." www.vice.com/en_us/article/ypnxnw/digital-artist-paul-b-davis-hacks-his-way-to-institutional-critique. Accessed August 2, 2019.

———. "Define Your Terms (or Kanye West Fucked Up My Solo Show)." www.beigerecords.com/paul/defineyourterms. Accessed August 15, 2019.

Davis, Paul B., and Jacob Ciocci. "Compression Study #1 (Untitled Data Mashup)." www.youtube.com/watch?v=CWG5jqzYsEI. Accessed June 30, 2019.

Dean, Jodi. "Communicative Capitalism: Circulation and Foreclosure of Politics." *Cultural Politics* 1, no. 1 (2005): 51–74.

———. *Democracy and Other Neoliberal Fantasies: Communicative Capitalism and Left Politics.* Durham, NC: Duke University Press, 2009.

Deleuze, Gilles. *Cinema 2: The Time-Image.* Translated by R. Galeta and H. Tomlinson. Minneapolis: University of Minnesota Press, 1989.

———. *Difference and Repetition.* 1968. Translated by Paul Patton. New York: Columbia University Press, 1994.

———. *Francis Bacon: The Logic of Sensation.* Translated and with an introduction by Daniel W. Smith. London: Continuum, 2003.

———. *Logique du sens.* Paris: Minuit, 1966. Translated by Mark Lester with Charles Stivale as *The Logic of Sense,* ed. Constantin V. Boundas (New York: Columbia University Press, 1989).

———. *Negotiations.* Translated by Martin Joughin. New York: Columbia University Press, 1990.

———. *Nietzsche and Philosophy.* Translated by H. Tomlinson. New York: Columbia University Press, 2006.

———. "Postscript on the Societies of Control." *October* 59 (Winter 1992): 3–7. Originally published in *L'Autre journal,* no. 1 (May 1990).

Deleuze, Gilles, and Félix Guattari. *A Thousand Plateaus: Capitalism and Schizophrenia.* Translated by Brian Massumi. Minneapolis: University of Minnesota Press, 1987.

DeLuca, K.M., and A.T. Demo. "Imagining Nature: Watkins, Yosemite, and the Birth of Environmentalism." *Critical Studies in Media Communication* 17, no. 3 (2000): 241–60.

Derrida, Jacques. "A Certain Impossible Possibility of Saying the Event." *Critical Inquiry* 33, no. 2, (2007): 441–61.

———. *Dissemination.* Translated by Barbara Johnson. Chicago: University of Chicago Press, 1981.

———. "Typewriter Ribbon." In *Without Alibi,* trans. Peggy Kamuf, 72–74. Stanford, CA: Stanford University Press, 2002.

Descartes, René. *Discourse on Method and Meditations on First Philosophy.* 4th ed. Translated by Donald Cress. Indianapolis, IN: Hackett, 1999.

———. "Discourse on Method." In *Descartes: Meditations on First Philosophy: With Selections from the Objections and Replies: A Latin-English Edition,* ed. John Cottingham, 37–38. Cambridge, MA: Cambridge University Press, 1996.

Detienne, Marcel, and Jean-Pierre Vernant. *Les ruses de l'intelligence: La mètis des Grecs.* Paris Flammarion, 1974.

Doane, M.A. "Information, Crisis, Catastrophe." In *New Media, Old Media: A History and Theory Reader,* ed. Wendy Chung and Thomas Keenan, 251–64. London: Routledge, 2005.

Donohue, John. "Fail Fast, Fail Often, Fail Everywhere." *New Yorker,* May 31, 2015. www.newyorker.com/business/currency/fail-fast-fail-often-fail-everywhere. Accessed July 22, 2019.

Dunaway, Finis. *Seeing Green: The Use and Abuse of American Environmental Images.* Chicago: University of Chicago Press, 2015.

Durkheim, Émile. *The Division of Labor in Society.* Translated by George Simpson. New York: Free Press, 1933.

Dyson, Frances. 2014. *The Tone of Our Times: Sound, Sense, Economy, and Ecology.* Cambridge, MA: MIT Press.

Edwards, Paul. "'A Vast Machine': Standards as Social Technology." *Science New Series* 304, no. 5672 (2004): 827–28.

"E-Waste to Exceed 93.5 Million Tons Annually." www.environmentalleader.com/2014/02/e-waste-to-exceed-93-5-million-tons-annually. Accessed July 8, 2019.

Falconer, Bruce. "What Is the Perfect Color Worth? Inside the Mysterious Art—and Big Business—of Color Forecasting." *New York Tines Magazine,* February 28, 2018. www.nytimes.com/2018/02/28/magazine/what-is-the-perfect-color-worth.html?searchResultPosition=1. Accessed July 6, 2019.

Famighetti, Michael. "Thomas Ruff: Photograms for the New Age. Conversation with Michael Famighetti." *Aperture,* Summer 2013, 82–89.

Fidler, Mailyn. "Anarchy or Regulation: Controlling the Global Trade in Zero Day Vulnerabilities." PhD diss., Freeman Spogli Institute for International Studies, Stanford University, 2014.

Fineberg, Jonathan. *Art since 1940.* 2nd ed. New York: Prentice Hall, 2003.

Fitzpatrick, Kathleen. *Planned Obsolescence: Publishing, Technology, and the Future of the Academy* New York: New York University Press, 2011.

Fisher, Anne. "Why Most Innovations Are Great Big Failures," *Fortune,* October 7, 2014. http://fortune.com/2014/10/07/innovation-failure. Accessed July 8, 2019.

Foucault, Michel. *The Archaeology of Knowledge.* Translated by A. M. Sheridan Smith. New York: Pantheon Books, 1972.

———. Introduction to *The Normal and the Pathological,* by Georges Canguilhem. Translated by Carolyn R. Fawcett. New York: Zone Books, 1991.

———. "What Is Critique?" In *The Politics of Truth,* ed. Sylvère Lotringer, trans. Lysa Hochroth and Catherine Porter. Cambridge, MA: Semiotext(e)/MIT Press, 1997.

Frank, Priscilla. "Meet Yung Jake, the Art World's Favorite Rapper." *Huffington Post,* May 27, 2014. www.huffingtonpost.com/2014/05/27/yung-jake_n_5376062.html. Accessed July 8, 2019.

Frank, Thomas. *The Conquest of Cool: Business Culture, Counterculture, and the Rise of Hip Consumerism.* Chicago: University of Chicago Press, 1997.

Freinkel, Susan "Our 'Toxic' Love-Hate Relationship with Plastics." *NPR,* April 19, 2011. www.npr.org/2011/04/19/135245835/our-toxic-love-hate-relationship-with-plastics. Accessed July 8, 2019.

Freud, Sigmund. "Errors." In *The Psychopathology of Everyday Life.* New York: Macmillan, 1914.

Fried, Michael. *Why Photography Matters as Never Before.* New Haven, CT: Yale University Press, 2008.

Fuller, Glen. "Simondon and Techno-Aesthetics." 2012. http://eventmechanics.net.au/2012/08/simondon-technoaesthetics. Accessed July 8, 2019.

Fugami, Tracey. "Dichotomies Coalesce." *Afterimage* 33, no. 4 (2006): 38–39.

Gabrys, Jennifer. *Digital Rubbish: A Natural History of Electronics.* Ann Arbor: University of Michigan Press, 2011.

Gagosian Gallery. "Thomas Ruff." Press release. February 13, 2012. https://gagosian.com/media/exhibitions/2012/thomas-ruff-mars/Gagosian_Thomas_Ruff_Mars_2012_Press_Release.pdf. Accessed July 8, 2019.

Galassi, Peter. *Andreas Gursky.* New York: Museum of Modern Art, 2002.

Galloway, Alexander R. *Laruelle: Against the Digital.* Minneapolis: University of Minnesota Press, 2014.

———. "The Poverty of Philosophy: Realism and Post-Fordism." *Critical Inquiry* 39, no. 2 (2013): 347–66.

———. "The Black Box of Philosophy: Compression and Obfuscation." Talk given at Incredible Machines conference, Vancouver, BC, March 7, 2014.

Galloway, Alexander R., and Jason R. LaRivière. "Compression in Philosophy." *boundary 2* 44, no. 1 (2017): 125–47.

Gamerman, Ellen. "An Inconvenient Bag." *Wall Street Journal,* September 26, 2008. www.wsj.com/articles/SB122238422541876879. Accessed July 8, 2019.

Gamson, Joshua. *Claims to Fame: Celebrity in Contemporary America.* Berkeley: University of California Press, 1994.

Gatlin, Jill. "Toxic Sublimity and the Crisis of Human Perception: Rethinking Aesthetic, Documentary, and Political Appeals in Contemporary Wasteland Photography." *Interdisciplinary Studies in Literature and Environment* 22, no. 4 (2015): 717–41.

Gaulon, Benjamin. "Hardware Hacking Workshops." www.recyclism.com/hardwarehck.php. Accessed July 8, 2019.

Gawthrop, Rob. "Thunder and Lightning: Noise, Aesthetics and Audio-Visual Avant-Garde Practice." In *Reverberations: The Philosophy, Aesthetics and Politics of Noise,* ed. Michael Goddard, Benjamin Halligan and Paul Hegarty, 164–78. New York: Continuum, 2012.

Gefter, Philip. "A Great Big Beautiful Pile of Junk." *New York Times,* July 24, 2005. www.nytimes.com/2005/07/24/arts/design/a-great-big-beautiful-pile-of-junk.html. Accessed July 8, 2019.

Gilmore, J., I. Moradi, C. Murphy, and A. Scott, eds. *Glitch: Designing Imperfection.* New York: Mark Batty, 2009.

Gjære, Erlend Andreas, "Human Errors in Cyber Security—A Swiss Cheese of Failures." *Security and People* (July 2017). https://securityandpeople.com/2017/07/human-errors-in-cyber-security-a-swiss-cheese-of-failures. Accessed August 12, 2019.

Global Marketing Systems (GMS). "Bangladesh." www.gmsinc.net/gms_new/index.php/bangladesh. Accessed July 8, 2019.

———. "GMS Leadership." http://gmsinc.net/gms/aboutus.php. Accessed July 8, 2019.

———. "India." gmsinc.net/gms_new/index.php/india. Accessed July 8, 2019.

———. "Pakistan." www.gmsinc.net/gms_new/index.php/pakistan. Accessed July 8, 2019.

Goddard, Michael, Benjamin Halligan, and Paul Hegarty, eds. 2012. *Reverberations: The Philosophy, Aesthetics and Politics of Noise.* New York: Continuum.

Goethe, Johann Wolfgang von. *Theory of Colours.* Translated by C. L. Eastlake. Cambridge, MA: MIT Press, 1970.

Goldberg, Vicki. "How the East Was Won: A Photographic Portrait." *New York Times,* July 6, 2017.

Goodman, Steve. "Contagious Noise: From Digital Glitches to Audio Viruses." In *The Spam Book: On Viruses, Porn and Other Anomalies from the Dark Side of Digital Culture,* ed. Jussi Parikka and Tony D. Sampson. Cresskill, NJ: Hampton Press, 2009.

Goriunova, Olga, and Alexei Shulgin. "Glitch." In *Software Studies,* ed. Matthew Fuller, 110–19. Cambridge, MA: MIT Press, 2008.

Graiwer, Sarah Lehrer. "In the Studio: Ryan Trecartin." *Art in America,* June–July 2013.

Grande, John K. "Interview with Edward Burtynsky." *Perspecta* 41 (2008): 153–58.

Greenberg, Grant, dir. *Heatwave.* Collaboration between V Magazine and Oliver Peoples, March 18, 2019. Accessed July 27, 2019.

Greenpeace India. *Recycling of Electronic Wastes in China and India: Workplace and Environmental Contamination.* August 17, 2005. www.greenpeace.org/austria/Global/austria/marktcheck/uploads/media/report_recycling_electronic_waste_2005.pdf.   Accessed August 15, 2019.

Gregory, M. R. "Environmental Implications of Plastic Debris in Marine Settings—Entanglement, Ingestion, Smothering, Hangers-on, Hitch-hiking, and Alien Invasions." *Philosophical Transactions of the Royal Society B Biological Sciences* 364, no. 1526 (2009): 2013–25. https://doi.org/10.1098/rstb.2008.0265. Accessed July 8, 2019.

Gronert, Stefan. "Photographic Emancipation." In *The Düsseldorf School of Photography,* ed. Stefan Gronert, 13–71. New York: Aperture, 2009.

Grosenick, Ute, and Thomas Seelig, eds. *Photo Art: The New World of Photography.* London: Thames & Hudson, 2008.

Grunenberg, Christoph, ed. *Summer of Love: Art of the Psychedelic Era.* Exhibition catalogue. Liverpool: Tate Liverpool, 2005.

Habash, Nicolas Lema. "Lack of *Technē* and the Instability of Poetry in Plato's *Ion.*" *Classical World* 110, no. 4 (2017): 491–521. doi:10.1353/clw.2017.0040. Accessed July 10, 2019.

Hainge, Greg. *Noise Matters: Towards an Ontology of Noise.* London: Bloomsbury Academic, 2013.

Halberstam, Jack. *The Queer Art of Failure.* Durham, NC: Duke University Press, 2011.

Halter, Ed. "The Matter of Electronics." http://heavysideindustries.com/wp-content/uploads/2010/11/THE-MATTER-OF-ELECTRONICS-by-Ed-Halter.pdf. Accessed July 1, 2019.

Hanson, David, *Waste Land: Meditations on a Ravaged Landscape.* New York: Aperture, 1997.

Harrison, Thomas. *1910: The Emancipation of Dissonance.* Berkeley: University of California Press, 1996.

Harvey, David. *The Condition of Postmodernity: An Enquiry into the Origins of Cultural Change.* 1st ed. Cambridge, MA: Blackwell, 1989.

Hayles, Katherine N. *Chaos Bound: Orderly Disorder in Contemporary Literature and Science.* Ithaca, NY: Cornell University Press, 1990.

———. *How We Became Posthuman: Virtual Bodies in Cybernetics, Literature, and Informatics.* Chicago: University of Chicago Press, 1999.

Hegarty, Paul. *Noise/Music: A History.* New York: Continuum, 2007.

Hegel, G. W. F. *Phenomenology of the Spirit.* Translated by A. Miller. Oxford: Oxford University Press, 1976.

Heidegger, Martin. *Being and Time.* Edited by John Macquarrie and Edward Robinson. New York: Harper & Row, 1962.

———. "On the Essence of Truth." In id., *Basic Writings: From "Being and Time" (1927) to "The Task of Thinking" (1964),* ed. David Farrell Krell, 133. New York: Harper & Row, 1977.

———. *Platons Lehre von der Wahrheit.* Berlin: Küpper, 1942. 4th rev. ed. Frankfurt am Main: Klostermann, 1997.

———. *The Question Concerning Technology, and Other Essays.* Translated by W. Lovitt. New York: Harper & Row, 1977.

Hertz, Garnet, and Jussi Parikka. "Zombie Media: Circuit Bending Media Archaeology into an Art Method." *Leonardo* 45, no. 5 (2012): 424–30.

Herzog, Catherine Hurzeler. "Subjective Propaganda: Thomas Ruff." *Parachute* 95 (July–September 1999): 28–35.

Higbee, Lauren G. "New Topographies and Generic Transformation in Landscape Photography of the 1970s." MA thesis., Department of Art History, Florida State University, 2013.

Hobbes, Thomas. *Leviathan; or, The Matter, Forme and Power of a Commonwealth, Ecclesiasticall and Civil.* Oxford: Blackwell, 1960.

Hodgson, Francis. "Edward Burtynsky." In *Edward Burtynsky.* Exhibition catalogue. New York: Sundaram Tagore Gallery, 2010.

Hoelzl, Ingrid, and Remi Marie. "CODEC: On Thomas Ruff's JPEGs." *Digital Creativity* 25, no. 1 (January 2014): 79–96.

Hoffmann, Christoph, and Jutta Schickore, "Secondary Matters: On Disturbances, Contamination, and Waste as Objects of Research." *Perspectives on Science* 9, no. 2 (Summer 2001): 123–25.

Hoving, Kristin. "Digging Deep: Edward Burtynsky's Vermont Quarry Photographs." In *Nature Transformed: Edward Burtynsky's Vermont Quarry Photographs in Context,* ed. Juliet Bianco and Pieter Broucke. Hanover, NH: Hood Museum of Art, Dartmouth College and University Press of New England, 2012.

Industrial Designers Society of America. "Brooks Stevens, FIDSA." Madison: Wisconsin Historical Society. www.idsa.org/content/brooks-stevens-fidsa. Accessed July 8, 2019.

International Law and Policy Institute (ILPI). *Shipbreaking Practices in Bangladesh, India and Pakistan: An Investor Perspective on the Human Rights and Environmental Impacts of Beaching.* Oslo, 2016. www.shipbreakingplatform.org/wp-content/uploads/2019/01/Shipbreaking-report-mai-2016.pdf. Accessed July 26, 2019.

International Maritime Organization. Marine Environment Protection Committee, 45th session. "IMO Reaches Agreement on Single-Hull Tanker Phase-Out." *IMO News* (London), October 2–6, 2000. www/imo/org/en/MediaCentre/MaritimeNewsMagazine/Documents/2000/imonews4.pdf. Accessed July 11, 2019.

Institute for Networked Cultures, "MoneyLab #3 Failing Better." http://networkcultures.org/moneylab/program-3/conference-sessions. Accessed August 11, 2019.

Inwood, M. J. *A Heidegger Dictionary.* Oxford: Blackwell, 1999.

iSixSigma-Editorial. "What Is Six Sigma?" www.isixsigma.com/new-to-six-sigma/what-six-sigma. Accessed July 8, 2019.

Jackson, Rebecca. "The Glitch Aesthetic." MA thesis., Georgia State University, Atlanta, 2011.

Jackson, S. J. "Rethinking Repair." In *Media Technologies: Essays on Communication, Materiality, and Society,* ed. Gillespie Tarleton, Pablo J. Boczkowski, and Kristen A. Foot, 221–40. Cambridge, MA: MIT Press, 2014.

Jameson, Frederic. "Cognitive Mapping." In *Marxism and the Interpretation of Culture,* ed. Cary Nelson and Lawrence Grossberg, 347–60. Urbana: University of Illinois Press, 1988.

———. "The 60's without Apology." *Social Text,* nos. 9–10 (Spring–Summer, 1984): 178–209.

Jenkins, William. *New Topographics: Photographs of a Man-Altered Landscape.* Exhibition. Rochester, NY: George Eastman House, 1975.

Jonas, Joan. *Organic Honey's Vertical Roll.* 1973–99. Electronic Arts Intermix. http://www.eai.org/title.htm?id=531. Accessed July 1, 2019.

Jordan, Chris. *American Environmental Leaders: From Colonial Times to the Present.* Toronto: Gray House, 2008.

———. "Intolerable Beauty: Portraits of American Mass Consumption (2003–2005)." www.chrisjordan.com/gallery/intolerable/#cellphones2. Accessed July 1, 2019.

———. *Running the Numbers: An American Self-Portrait.* New York: Prestel, 2009.

———. "Running the Numbers." https://orionmagazine.org/article/running-the-numbers. January 2007. Accessed July 1, 2019.

———. *The Midway Project.* Six-minute color video produced by Riley Morton. March 2011. www.youtube.com/watch?v=-M9t2fm__Ko. Accessed July 25, 2019.

Jordan, Chris, Bill McKibben, Susan Zakin, and Victoria Sloan Jordan. *In Katrina's Wake: Portraits of Loss from an Unnatural Disaster.* Princeton, NJ: Princeton Architectural Press, 2006.

Kahn, Douglas. *Noise, Water, Meat.* Cambridge, MA: MIT Press, 1999.

Kandinsky, Wassily. "On the Question of Form." In Kandinsky, *Concerning the Spiritual in Art,* trans. Michael Sadleir. New York: Dover Publications: 1977.

———. "On the Spiritual in Art." In *Complete Writings on Art,* ed. Kenneth C. Lindsay and Peter Vergo, 161–95. New York: Da Capo, 1994.

Kane, Carolyn L. "Broken Color in a Modern World: Chromatic Failures in Purist Art and Architecture." *Journal of the International Colour Association* 14 (2015): 1–13.

———. *Chromatic Algorithms: Synthetic Color, Computer Art, and Aesthetics after Code.* Chicago: University of Chicago Press, 2014.

———. "Designing with Digital Color." *Design Journal* (Cooper Hewitt, Smithsonian Design Museum, New York), May 2018, 15–19.

———. "The Electric 'Now Indigo Blue': Synthetic Color and Video Synthesis circa 1969." *Leonardo* 46, no. 4 (2013): 360–66.

———. "The Synthetic Color Sense of Pipilotti Rist, or, Deleuzian Color Theory for Electronic Media Art." *Visual Communication* 10, no. 4 (November 2011): 475–97.

Kant, Immanuel. *Critique of Judgment.* 1790. Translated by James Creed Meredith. New York: Dover Publications, 2005.

———. *Critique of Pure Reason.* Translated by Paul Geyer and Allen Wood. Cambridge: Cambridge University Press, 1998.

———. "Of Transcendental Illusory Appearance." In Kant, *Critique of Pure Reason.* Translated by Max Müller. New York: Doubleday, 1961.

Kastner, Jeffrey, ed., and Brian Wallis, survey. *Land and Environmental Art.* New York: Phaidon Press, 2015.

Kelly, Kevin. "The Best Technology in the Future Is Invisible." https://kk.org/wp-content/uploads/2010/06/Kevin-Kelly_-the-best-technology-in-the-future-is-invisible-Xinhua-_-English.news_.pdf. Accessed July 26, 2019.

Kemp, Martin. *The Science of Art: Optical themes in Western Art from Brunelleschi to Seurat.* New Haven: Yale University Press, 1990.

Kennedy, George, and D. A. Russell. "'Longinus,' on Sublimity." *Classical World* 59, no. 9 (1966): 316.

Kennedy, Randy. "His Nonlinear Reality, and Welcome to It." *New York Times,* January 28, 2009.

Kinder, Marsha. "The Conceptual Power of Online Video." In *Video Vortex Reader 4: Responses to YouTube,* ed. Geert Lovink and Sabine Niederer, 53–60. Amsterdam: Institute of Network Cultures, 2008.

Kissinger, Henry. *The White House Years.* Boston: Little, Brown, 1979.

Kittler, Friedrich. *Gramophone, Film, Typewriter.* Translated by Geoffrey Winthrop-Young and Michael Wutz. Stanford, CA: Stanford University Press, 1999.

Koestenbaum, Wayne. "Situation Hacker: Wayne Koestenbaum on the Art of Ryan Trecartin." *Artforum International* 47, no. 10 (Summer 2009): 272–76, 279.

Kostelanetz, Richard. *Conversing with John Cage.* New York: Limelight, 1988.

Kracauer, Siegfried. *The Mass Ornament: Weimar Essays.* Edited and translated by Thomas Y. Levin. Cambridge, MA: Harvard University Press, 1995.

Kramer, Hilton. "Plastic as Plastic: Divided Loyalties, Paradoxical Ambitions." *New York Times,* December 1, 1968.

———. "Plastic Toys and Ersatz Monuments." *New York Times,* December 25, 1966.

Krapp, Peter. *Noise Channels: Glitch and Error in Digital Culture.* Minneapolis: University of Minnesota Press, 2011.

Krauss, Rosalind E. "Close-up: Frame by Frame." *Artforum International* 50 (September 2012): 416–19.

Kwastek, Katja, Niamh Warde, and Dieter Daniels. *Aesthetics of Interaction in Digital Art.* Cambridge, MA: MIT Press, 2015.

LaBelle, Brandon. 2006. *Background Noise: A History of Sound Art.* London: Continuum

Lagadec, Patrick. *States of Emergency: Technological Failures and Social Destabilization.* Translated by Joselyn Phelps. Boston: Butterworth-Heinemann, 1990.

Lane, G. "Thomas Ruff: Space Explorer." *Art World* 12 (2009): 136–43.

Larkin, Brian. "Degraded Images, Distorted Sounds: Nigerian Video and the Infrastructure of Piracy." *Public Culture* 16, no. 2 (2004): 289–314.

Latour, Bruno. "Waiting for Gaia: Composing the Common World Through Arts and Politics." Lecture at the French Institute, London, November 2011.

Lebow, Victor. "Price Competition in 1955." *Journal of Retailing,* Spring 1955. http://ablemesh.co.uk/PDFs/journal-of-retailing1955.pdf. Accessed July 8, 2019.

Le Feuvre, Lisa, ed. *Failure.* Cambridge, MA: MIT Press, 2010.

Léger, Fernand. *Functions of Painting.* Translated by Alexandra Anderson. Edited and with an introduction by Edward F. Fry. New York: Viking, 1973.

———. "The Machine Aesthetic: The Manufactured Object, the Artisan and the Artist, Part I." Translated by C. Green. First published in *Bulletin de L'Effort moderne* 1 (1924).

Lehrer-Graiwer, Sarah. "In the Studio: Ryan Trecartin." *Art in America,* June 2013.

Lichtenstein, Jacqueline. *The Eloquence of Color: Rhetoric and Painting in the French Classical Age.* Translated by Emily McVarish. Berkeley: University of California Press, 1993.

Linger, Michael. "From Being to Seeing: Michael Linger on Franz Erhard Walther." *FORUM International* 4 (1990): 50–55.

Lippard, Lucy. *Undermining: A Wild Ride through Land Use, Politics, and Art in the Changing West.* New York: New Press, 2014.

Locke, John. *An Essay Concerning Human Understanding.* 12th ed. London: C. and J. Rivington, 1824.

Loke, Margarett. "Art in Review: Edward Burtynsky." *New York Times,* February 22, 2002.

London, Bernard. *Ending the Depression through Planned Obsolescence.* New York: Bernard London, 1932. https://babel.hathitrust.org/cgi/pt?id=wu.89097035273&view=1up&seq=7. Accessed July 8, 2019.

Longinus. *On the Sublime.* In *Classical Literary Criticism,* trans. Penelope Murray and T. S. Dorsch. London: Penguin Books, 2001.

Lotringer, Sylvère, and Paul Virilio. *The Accident of Art.* Translated by Michael Taormina. Cambridge, MA: MIT Press, 2005.

Lynch, Kevin. *Wasting Away: An Exploration of Waste—What It Is, How It Happens, Why We Fear It, How to Do It Well.* San Francisco: Sierra Club, 1991.

Mackenzie, Adrian. "Codecs." In *Software Studies,* ed. M. Fuller, 48–55. Cambridge, MA: MIT Press, 2006.

———. *Cutting Code: Software and Sociality.* New York: Peter Lang, 2006.

———. "Every Thing Thinks: Sub-representative Differences in Digital Video Codecs." In *Deleuzian Intersections: Science, Technology, Anthropology,* ed. C. Brunn Jensen and K. Rödje, 139–54. New York: Berghahn, 2010.

Maimon, Vered. "Precarious Marks: Thomas Ruff's *jpegs.*" *Oxford Art Journal* 37, no. 2 (2014), 173– 92.

Malabou, Catherine. *What Should We Do with Our Brain?* Translated by Sebastian Rand New York: Fordham University Press, 2009.

Manon, Hugh S., and Daniel Temkin. "Notes on Glitch." *World Picture* 6 (Winter 2011). www.worldpicturejournal.com/WP_6/Manon.html.

Manovich, Lev. *The Language of New Media.* Cambridge, MA: MIT Press, 2001.

Maritain, Jacques. *Art et scolastique.* Paris: Librairie de l'art catholique, 1920. Translated by J. F. Scanlan as *Art and Scholasticism with Other Essays* (London: Sheed & Ward, 1946).

Markets and Markets. "Electronic Waste Market." www.marketsandmarkets.com/Market-Reports/electronic-waste-management-market- 373.html. Accessed August 22, 2018.

Marx, Leo. "Does Improved Technology Mean Progress?" *Technology Review,* January 1987, 33–41. http://w3.salemstate.edu/~cmauriello/Course%20Development/IDS271%20Readings/Marx-Does%20Improved%20Technology%20Mean%20Progress.pdf. Accessed June 29, 2019.

Masheck, Joseph. "Alberti's 'Window': Art-Historiographic Notes on an Antimodernist Misprision," *Art Journal* 50, no. 1 (Spring 1991): 34–41.

McGarry, Kevin. "Lizzie Fitch / Ryan Trecartin." www.galleriesnow.net/shows/lizzie-fitch-ryan-trecartin. Accessed July 26, 2019.

———. "Ryan Trecartin." Hammer Projects Catalogue. Los Angeles: Hammer Museum, 2008.

Meikle, Jeffrey L. *American Plastic: A Cultural History.* New Brunswick, NJ:: Rutgers University Press, 1995.

———. "Material Doubts: The Consequences of Plastic." *Environmental History* 2, no. 3 (1997): 278–300.

Melville, Herman. *Moby Dick: or the Whale.* New York: Modern Library, 1992.

Menkman, Rosa. *The Glitch Moment(um).* Institute of Network Cultures, 2011. https://networkcultures.org/_uploads/NN%234_RosaMenkman.pdf. Accessed August 15, 2019.

Metzger, Gustav. *Liquid Crystal Environment.* Installation 1965, remade 2005.www.tate.org.uk/art/artworks/metzger-liquid-crystal-environment-t12160. Accessed July 8, 2019.

Mitchell, Michael. "On the Beach." In *Edward Burtynsky: Oil.* Washington, DC: Corcoran Gallery of Art, 2009.

"The Mobile Economy 2019." GSM Association/GSMA Intelligence, 2019. www.gsmaintelligence.com/research/?file=b9a6e6202ee1d5f787cfebb95d3639c5&download. Accessed July 22, 2019.

Moholy-Nagy, László. *Vision in Motion.* Chicago: P. Theobald, 1947.

Moles, Abraham. *Information Theory and Esthetic Perception.* 1958. Translated by Joel E. Cohen. Urbana: University of Illinois Press, 1969.

Morton, Timothy. *The Ecological Thought.* Cambridge, MA: Harvard University Press, 2010.

Munster, Anna. *An Aesthesia of Networks: Conjunctive Experience in Art and Technology.* Cambridge, MA: MIT Press, 2013.

———. *Materializing New Media: Embodiment in Information Aesthetics.* Hanover, NH: University Press of New England, 2006.

Murata, Takeshi. *Monster Movie.* Uploaded November 5, 2009. YouTube Video, 4:35.www.youtube.com/watch?v=t1f3St51S9I. Accessed July 8, 2019.

Najafi, Sina, David Serlin, and Scott A. Sandage. "The Invention of Failure: An Interview with Scott A. Sandage." *Cabinet,* no. 7 (Summer 2002), www.cabinetmagazine.org/issues/7/inventionoffailure.php. Accessed July 9, 2019).

National Labor Committee in Support of Human and Worker Rights (NLC; now the Institute for Global Labour and Human Rights). "Where Ships and Workers Go to Die: Shipbreaking in Bangladesh and the Failure of Global Institutions to Protect Worker Rights." Pittsburgh, PA: NLC, 2009.https://recyclingships.blogspot.com/2011/08/where-ships-and-workers-go-to-die.html. Accessed August 15, 2019.

National Safety Council. *Electronic Product Recovery and Recycling Baseline Report.* Washington, DC: National Safety Council Environmental Health Center, 1999.

Newman, Thelma, R. *Plastics as an Art Form.* Philadelphia: Chilton Book Company, 1964.

Newton, Isaac. *Opticks: Or, a Treatise of the Reflections, Refractions, Inflection and Colours of Light.* 3rd ed. London: William and John Innys, 1721.

Ngai, Sianne. *Our Aesthetic Categories: Zany, Cute, Interesting.* Cambridge, MA: Harvard University Press, 2012.

Nietzsche, Friedrich Wilhelm. *The Birth of Tragedy, and the Case of Wagner.* Translated by Walter Kaufmann. New York: Vintage Books, 1967.

———. *The Birth of Tragedy: Out of the Spirit of Music.* Translated by Shaun Whiteside. London: Penguin Books, 1993.

———. *On the Genealogy of Morals.* Translated by Walter Kaufmann. New York: Vintage Books, 1989.

———. *On Truth and Untruth: Selected Writings.* Translated by Taylor Carman. New York: Harper, 2010.

Nunes, Joseph. "The Power of Repetition—Repetitive Lyrics in a Song Increase Processing Fluency and Drives Market Success." March 2017. https://papers.ssrn.com/sol3/papers.cfm?abstract_id=2938838. Accessed July 25, 2019.

Nunes, Mark, ed. *Error: Glitch, Noise, and Jam in New Media Cultures.* New York: Continuum, 2011.

Nye, David E. *American Technological Sublime.* Cambridge, MA: MIT Press, 2007.

Nyquist, Harry. "Certain Topics in Telegraph Transmission Theory [1928]." *Proceedings of the IEEE* 90, no. 20 (February 2002): 280–305.

Oravec, Christine. "John Muir, Yosemite, and the Sublime Response: A Study in the Rhetoric of Preservationism." *Quarterly Journal of Speech* 67 (1981): 245–58.

Packard, Vance. *The Waste Makers.* New York: Pocket Books, 1963.

Parikka, Jussi, and Tony D. Sampson, eds. *The Spam Book: On Viruses, Porn and Other Anomalies from the Dark Side of Digital Culture.* Cresskill, NJ: Hampton Press, 2009.

Parker, Laura. "Fast Facts about Plastic Pollution," *National Geographic,* December 20, 2018. https://news.nationalgeographic.com/2018/05/plastics-facts-infographics-ocean-pollution. Accessed July 23, 2019.

Pasulka, Nicole. "Running the Numbers." An interview with Chris Jordan. *Morning News,* July 23, 2007. https://themorningnews.org/gallery/running-the-numbers. Accessed July 8, 2019.

Paul, Christiane. *Digital Art.* London: Thames & Hudson, 2015.

Pauli, Lori. *Manufactured Landscapes: The Photographs of Edward Burtynsky.* New Haven, CT: Yale University Press, 2003.

Paulson, William. *The Noise of Culture: Literary Texts in a World of Information.* Ithaca, NY: Cornell University Press, 1988.

Peeples, Jennifer. "Toxic Sublime: Imaging Contaminated Landscapes." *Environmental Communication* 5, no. 4 (2011): 373–92.

Peters, John Durham. *Speaking into the Air: A History of the Idea of Communications.* Chicago: University of Chicago Press, 1999.

Peters, Sue. "Q&A with Chris Jordan." *Seattle Weekly,* September 20, 2006.

Pettman, Dominic. *Human Error: Species-Being and Media Machines.* Minneapolis: University of Minnesota Press, 2011.

Pfeiffer, Alice. "At Last, Artists Harness the Internet." *New York Times,* September 11, 2009.

Pfeiffer, Paul. *Paul Pfeiffer.* Düsseldorf: Hatje Cantz, 2005.

Phelan, Peggy, Hans-Ulrich Obrist, Elisabeth Bronfen, and Pipilotti Ris. *Pipilotti Rist.* New York: Phaidon, 2001.

Planet Money. "Will Your Job Be Done by a Machine?" (May 21, 2015). www.npr.org/sections/money/2015/05/21/408234543/will-your-job-be-done-by-a-machine. Accessed August 12, 2019.

Plato. *The Republic.* Translated by Allan Bloom. New York: Basic Books, 1968.

Poirier, M. "The Disegno-Colore Controversy Reconsidered." *Explorations in Renaissance Culture* 13, no. 1 (1987): 52–86.

Porte, Rebecca Ariel. "The Zany, the Cute, and the Interesting: On Ngai's 'Our Aesthetic Categories.'" *Los Angeles Review of Books,* October 14, 2012. https://lareviewofbooks.org/article/the-zany-the-cute-and-the-interesting-on-ngais-our-aesthetic-categories/#!

"Printer Tragedies: What Happens When a Docucolor 240 Stops Being Polite, and Starts Being Real." Bloomberg Businessweek www.flickr.com/photos/bizweekdesign/sets/72157628902987075/detail. Accessed June 27, 2019.

Rancière, Jacques. *The Politics of Aesthetics: The Distribution of the Sensible.* Translated and with an introduction by Gabriel Rockhill. New York: Continuum, 2004.

Rathje, William L., and Cullen Murphy. *Rubbish! The Archaeology of Garbage.* Tucson: University of Arizona Press, 2001.

Reason, James. "Human Error: Models and Management." *British Medical Journal* 320, no. 7237 (March 18, 2000): 768–70.

Rescher, Nicholas. *Error: On Our Predicament When Things Go Wrong.* Pittsburgh, PA: University of Pittsburgh Press, 2007.

Richter, Gerhard, Dietmar Elger, and Hans-Ulrich Obrist. *Gerhard Richter: Text: Writings, Interviews and Letters, 1961–2007.* London: Thames & Hudson, 2009.

Riley, Charles A. *Color Codes: Modern Theories of Color in Philosophy, Painting and Architecture, Literature, Music, and Psychology.* Hanover, NH: University Press of New England, 1995

Roberts, John. *The Necessity of Errors.* New York: Verso, 2011.

Royte, Elizabeth. "E-Gad!" *Smithsonian Magazine,* August 2005.

Ruff, Thomas. "Thomas Ruff in Conversation with Hans Ulrich Obrist." In *Thomas Ruff: Nudes,* 5–6. London: Gagosian Gallery, 2012.

———. *Thomas Ruff: Nudes.* London: Gagosian Gallery, 2012.

Russolo, Luigi. *The Art of Noises* [*Arte dei rumori*]. Translated by Barclay Brown. New York: Pendragon Press, 1986.

———. *New Topographics: Photographs of a Man-Altered Landscape.* Exhibition catalogue. New York: International Museum of Photography, 1975.

Sandage, Scott A. *Born Losers: A History of Failure in America.* Cambridge, MA: Harvard University Press, 2005.

Sangild, Torben. "The Aesthetics of Noise." www.ubu.com/papers/noise.html. Accessed July 1, 2019.

Sarraf, Maria, Frank Stuer-Lauridsen, Milen Dyoulgerov, Robin Bloch, Susan Wingfield, and Roy Watkinson. "The Ship Breaking and Recycling Industry in Bangladesh and Pakistan." *World Bank,* December 2010. http://documents.worldbank.org/curated/en/872281468114238957/The-ship-breaking-and-recycling-industry-in-Bangladesh-and-Pakistan. Accessed July 25, 2019.

Satrom, Jon. "Glitch: Investigations into the New Ecology of the Digital Age." https://jonsatrom.wordpress.com/2009/11/09/glitch-investigations-into-the-new-ecology-of-the-digital-age. Accessed August 22, 2018.

Sax, David. "Take It to the Max." *Esquire,* December 2016–January 2017.

Schiller, Friedrich. *On the Aesthetic Education of Man: In a Series of Letters.* Translated by Reginald Snell. New York: F. Ungar, 1965.

Schoenberg, Arnold. *Style and Idea: Selected Writings of Arnold Schoenberg.* Edited by Leonard Stein. Translated by Leo Black. New York: St. Martins Press, 1975.

———. *Theory of Harmony.* Translated by Roy E. Carter. 100th anniversary ed. Berkeley: University of California Press, 2010.

Schumpeter, Joseph. *Capitalism, Socialism and Democracy.* New York: Harper & Brothers, 1942.

Schwartz, Joan M. "Photographic Reflections: Nature, Landscape, and Environment." *Environmental History* 12, no. 4 (October 2007): 966–93.

Schwartz, John. "The New Optimism of Al Gore." *New York Times,* March 17, 2015.

Scott, A. O. "Warning of Calamities and Hoping for Change in 'An Inconvenient Truth.'" *New York Times,* May 24, 2006. www.nytimes.com/2006/05/24/movies/24trut.html. Accessed Thursday, August 15, 2019.

Segal, David. "Beauty in the Beast." *Washington Post,* October 31, 2005, C1. www.washington post.com/wp-dyn/content/article/2005/10/30/AR2005103001161.html. Accessed July 12, 2019.

Serres, Michel. *Genesis.* Translated by G. James and J. Nielson. Ann Arbor: University of Michigan Press, 1995.

———. *The Parasite.* Translated by L. R. Schehr. Minneapolis: University of Minnesota Press, 2007.

Shannon, Claude. "Information Theory." In *Claude Elwood Shannon: Collected Papers,* ed. N. J. A. Sloane and Aaron D. Wyner. Piscataway, NJ: IEEE Press, 1993.

———. "A Mathematical Theory of Communication." *Bell System Technical Journal* 27 (July–October 1948): 379–423, 623–56.

Shannon, Claude, and Warren Weaver. *The Mathematical Theory of Communication.* Urbana: University of Illinois Press, 1949.

"The Shipbreakers of Bangladesh." www.cbsnews.com/news/the-ship-breakers-of-bangladesh. Accessed June 27, 2019.

Silicon Valley Toxics Coalition [SVTC] and Basel Action Network [BAN]. "Exporting Harm: The High-Tech Trashing of Asia." February 25, 2002. www.ban.org/E-waste/techno trashfinalcomp.pdf. Accessed July 9, 2019.

———. "On Techno-Aesthetics." Translated by Arne De Boever. *Parrhesia* 14 (2012): 2.

Simondon, Gilbert. "On Techno-Aesthetics," Translated by Arne De Boever. *Parrhesia* 14 (2012): 1–8.

Slade, Giles. *Made to Break: Technology and Obsolescence in America.* Cambridge: MA: Harvard University Press, 2006.

Sloan, Mark. *No Man's Land: Contemporary Photographers and Fragile Ecologies—Edward Burtynsky, Emmet Gowin, and David Maisel.* Charleston, SC: Halsey Gallery and Institute of Contemporary Art at the College of Charleston School of the Arts, 2004.

Small, James. *The Analogue Alternative: The Electric Analogue Computer in Britain and the USA, 1930–1975.* London: Routledge, 2001.

Smith, Roberta. "Like Living, Only More So." *New York Times,* June 23, 2011. www.nytimes. com/2011/06/24/arts/design/ryan-trecartins-any-ever-at-moma-ps1-review.html. Accessed August 13, 2019.

Smith, Stephanie. "Weather Systems: Questions about Art and Climate Change." In *Weather Report: Arts and Climate Change,* curated by Lucy R. Lippard. Boulder, CO: Boulder Museum of Contemporary Art, 2007.

Solomon-Godeau, Abigail. "The Rightness of Wrong." In *John Baldessari: National City,* ed. H. M. Davies and A. Hales, 33–36. San Diego, CA: Museum of Contemporary Art, 1996.

Spencer, Jane. "Companies Slash Warranties, Rendering Gadgets Disposable." *Wall Street Journal,* July 16, 2002. www.wsj.com/articles/SB1026764790637362400.

Spieser, Alexandra, "Glitch Art: Noises as a Creative Act—Challenging the Myth of a Perfect Technology." http://mediacultures.net/xmlui/handle/10002/925?show=full. Accessed July 9, 2019.

Statista [by T. Wang]. "Forecast of Electronic Waste Generated Worldwide from 2010 to 2018 (in million metric tons)." December 14, 2018. www.statista.com/statistics/499891/projection-ewaste-generation-worldwide. Accessed July 22, 2019.

Sterne, Jonathan. *The Meaning of a Format MP3*. Durham, NC: Duke University Press, 2012.

Stewart, John, Francis McManus, Nigel Rodgers, Val Weedon, and Arline Bronzaft. 2016. *Why Noise Matters: A Worldwide Perspective on the Problems, Policies and Solutions*. London: Taylor & Francis.

Steyerl, Hito. 2013. *The Wretched of the Screen*. Berlin: Sternberg.

Stiegler, Bernard. "The Proletarianization of Sensibility." Lecture. Reprinted in *boundary 2* 44, no. 1 (2017).

———. *Technics and Time 1: The Fault of Epimetheus*. Translated by R. Beardsworth and G. Collins. Stanford, CA: Stanford University Press, 1998.

———. *Technics and Time 2: Disorientation*. Translated by Stephen Barker. Stanford, CA: Stanford University Press, 2009.

Stokel-Walker, Chris. "Algorithms Won't Fix What's Wrong With YouTube." *New York Times*, June 14, 2019. www.nytimes.com/2019/06/14/opinion/youtube-algorithm.html. Accessed July 27, 2019).

"Sweden's Museum of Failure Highlights Products That Flopped." Associated Press. *Washington Post*, June 12, 2017. www.washingtonpost.com/lifestyle/kidspost/swedens-museum-of-failure-highlights-products-that-flopped/2017/06/12/3f24cd48-4ba7-11e7-9669-250d0b15f83b_story.html?utm_term=.a46b371f6514. Accessed June 25, 2019.

Taylor, Alan. "Remembering the Exxon Valdez Oil Spill." *The Atlantic*, March 24, 2014. Thirty-nine photographs. www.theatlantic.com/photo/2014/03/the-exxon-valdez-oil-spill-25-years-ago-today/100703. Accessed July 9, 2019.

Taylor, Frederick Winslow. *Scientific Management: Comprising Shop Management; The Principles of Scientific Management; [and] Testimony before the Special House Committee*. New York: Harper, 1947.

Temkin, Ann. *Color Chart: Reinventing Color, 1950 to Today*. New York: Museum of Modern Art, 2008.

Tiedemann, Rolf. "Dialectics at a Standstill." In *The Arcades Project*, trans. Howard Eiland and Kevin McLaughlin, 929–45. Cambridge, MA: Harvard University Press, 2002.

Tilman, B., ed. *Install.exe/JODI*. Exhibition. Basel: Christoph Merian, 2002.

"This Year Rediscover Plastics." *House Beautiful* 97 (1995): 56.

Thompson, Emily. *The Soundscape of Modernity: Architectural Acoustics and the Culture of Listening in America, 1900–1933*. Cambridge, MA: MIT Press, 2004.

Toh, Michelle, Ben Geier, and Ivana Kottasová. "Global Backlash Spreads over Apple Slowing Down iPhones." CNN Business, February 1, 2018. https://money.cnn.com/2018/01/12/technology/apple-iphone-slow-battery-lawsuit/index.html. Accessed July 10, 2019.

Tolman, Edward C. "Cognitive Maps in Rats and Men." *Psychological Review* 55, no. 4 (1948): 189–208.

Torosian, Michael. "The Essential Element: An Interview with Edward Burtynsky." In *Manufactured Landscapes: The Photographs of Edward Burtynsky*, ed. Lori Pauli, 46–55. Ottawa, ON: National Gallery of Canada; New Haven, CT: Yale University Press, 2006.

Trecartin, Ryan. *Center Jenny*. 2013. HD Video, 53:15. Electronic Arts Intermix. www.eai.org/titles/center-jenny. Accessed July 6, 2019.

———. *K-CoreaINC. K (section a)*. 2009. Electronic Arts Intermix.www.eai.org/titles/k-coreainc-k-section-a. Accessed July 6, 2019.

———. *(Tommy Chat Just E-mailed Me.)* 2006. Electronic Arts Intermix. www.eai.org/titles/tommy-chat-just-e-mailed-me. Accessed July 6, 2019.

Trecartin, Ryan, and Hans-Ulrich Obrist. "Ryan Trecartin in Conversation with Hans-Ulrich Obrist." Serpentine Gallery, January 2014. www.youtube.com/watch?v=3EDEONmuPHw. Accessed July 25, 2019.

Trecartin, Ryan, and Kristina Lee Podesva. "When the Time Comes You Won't Understand the Battlefield." *Fillip* 13 (Spring 2011): 101–5.

Trecartin, Ryan, Kevin McGarry, Lauren Cornell, Lizzie Fitch, Linda Norden, Cindy Sherman, and Jeffrey Deitch. *Any Ever: Ryan Trecartin.* New York: Skira Rizzoli Publications in association with Elizabeth Dee, 2011.

Turnage, Robert. "Ansel Adams: The Role of the Artist in the Environmental Movement." Ansel Adams Gallery, March 1980. Reprinted courtesy of the Wilderness Society from *The Living Wilderness.* http://anseladams.com/ansel-adams-the-role-of-the-artist-in-the-environmental-movement. Accessed July 10, 2019.

Turner, Fred. "The Arts at Facebook: An Aesthetic Infrastructure for Surveillance Capitalism." *Poetics* 67 (2018): 53–62.

United Nations University. "E-Waste Rises 8% by Weight in 2 Years as Incomes Rise, Prices Fall." 2017. https://unu.edu/media-relations/releases/ewaste-rises-8-percent-by-weight-in-2-years.html. Accessed July 24, 2019.

Van Tomme, Niels. "From Readymade to Readybought: An Ongoing History of Computer Art—JODI in Conversation with Niels Van Tomme." *Art Papers Magazine* 35, no. 1 (2011): 30.

Veblen, Thorstein. *The Theory of the Leisure Class.* New York: Macmillan, 1899.

Vernant, Jean-Pierre. "Pratiques culinaires et esprit de sacrifice." In *La cuisine du sacrifice en pays grec,* ed. Marcel Detienne and Vernant. Paris: Gallimard, 1979.

Virilio, Paul. *Politics of the Very Worst: An Interview with Philippe Petit.* Translated by Michael Cavaliere. Cambridge, MA: Semiotext(e)/MIT, 1999.

———. "The Primal Accident." In *The Politics of Everyday Fear,* ed. Brian Massumi, 211–20. Minneapolis: University of Minnesota Press, 1993.

Von Kaenel, Camille Diane. "Failure Has Never Been More Successful." *Fast Company,* November 14, 2014.www.fastcompany.com/3038446/failure-has-never-been-more-successful. Accessed July 10, 2019.

Wagner, Martin, Magnus Engwall, and Henner Hollert. "(Micro)Plastics and the Environment." *Environmental Sciences Europe* 26, no. 16 (2014). https://doi.org/10.1186/s12302-014-0016-3. Accessed July 10, 2019.

Waite, Geoffrey C. W. "Worringer's Abstraction and Empathy: Remarks on Its Reception and on the Rhetoric of Criticism." In *The Turn of the Century: German Literature and Art, 1890–1915,* ed. Gérald Chapple and Hans H. Schulte, 197–224. Bonn: Bouvier, 1981.

Wall, Jeff. "'Marks of Indifference': Aspects of Photography in, or as, Conceptual Art." In *Reconsidering the Object of Art: 1965–1975,* ed. Ann Goldstein and Anne Rorimer, 247–67. Los Angeles: Museum of Contemporary Art, 1995.

Watson, Stephen. "On the Errancy of Dasein." *Diacritics* 19, nos. 3–4 (Autumn–Winter 1989): 49–61.

White, Micah. "Origin of Planned Obsolescence (1932 Pamphlet)." www.micahmwhite. com/adbusters-articles/ending-the-depression-through-planned-obsolescence. Accessed July 10, 2019.

Wiener, Norbert. *Cybernetics: Or Control and Communication in the Animal and the Machine.* Cambridge, MA: MIT Press, 1948.

Williams, Raymond. *Marxism and Literature.* Oxford: Oxford University Press, 1977.

———. *The Sociology of Culture.* Chicago: University of Chicago Press, 1995.

Winzen, Matthias. "A Credible Invention of Reality: Thomas Ruff's Precise Reproductions of Our Fantasies of Reality." In *Thomas Ruff: 1979 to the Present,* ed. Matthias Winzen. New York: Distributed Art Publishers, 2003.

Wölfflin, Heinrich. *Principles of Art History: The Problem of the Development of Style in Later Art.* 1915. Translated by M. D. Hottinger. New York: Dover Publications, 1950.

Wollen, Peter. "Godard and Counter Cinema: *Vent d'Est.*" *Afterimage* 4 (Autumn 1972): 6–17.

Worringer, Wilhelm. *Abstraction and Empathy: A Contribution to the Psychology of Style.* Translated by Michael Bullock. New York: International Universities Press, 1953.

Wright, S. L., R. C. Thompson, and T. S. Galloway. "The Physical Impacts of Microplastics on Marine Organisms: A Review." *Environmental Pollution* 178 (2013): 483–92. 1 0.1016/j. envpol.2013.02.031. Accessed July 10, 2019.

Yates, Michelle. "The Human-as-Waste: The Labor Theory of Value and Disposability in Contemporary Capitalism." *Antipode* 43, no. 5 (2011): 1679–95.

Zielinski, Siegfried. *Deep Time of the Media: Toward an Archaeology of Hearing and Seeing by Technical Means.* Translated by Gloria Custance. Cambridge, MA: MIT Press, 2006.

Zulueta, Ricardo E. *Queer Art Camp Superstar: Decoding the Cinematic Cyberworld of Ryan Trecartin.* New York: State University of New York, 2018.

———. "Queer Art Camp Superstar: Decoding the Video Cyberworld of Ryan Trecartin." PhD thesis., University of Miami, 2014.

Zuromskis, Catherine. "Petroaesthetics and Landscape Photography: New Topographics, Edward Burtynsky, and the Culture of Peak Oil." In *Oil Culture,* ed. Ross Barrett and Daniel Worden, 289–308. Minneapolis: University of Minnesota Press, 2014.

Founded in 1893,
UNIVERSITY OF CALIFORNIA PRESS
publishes bold, progressive books and journals
on topics in the arts, humanities, social sciences,
and natural sciences—with a focus on social
justice issues—that inspire thought and action
among readers worldwide.

The UC PRESS FOUNDATION
raises funds to uphold the press's vital role
as an independent, nonprofit publisher, and
receives philanthropic support from a wide
range of individuals and institutions—and from
committed readers like you. To learn more, visit
ucpress.edu/supportus.